CW00409729

'KHAKI SHORTS'

Major Bob Smith

OLD BAKEHOUSE PUBLICATIONS

© Major Bob Smith

First published in June 1995

All rights reserved

ISBN 1 874538 45 X

Published in the U.K. by
Old Bakehouse Publications
Church Street
Abertillery, Gwent NP3 1EA
Telephone: 01495 212600   Fax: 01495 216222

Made and printed in the U.K.
by J.R. Davies (Printers) Ltd.

This book is sold subject to the condition that it shall
not, by any way of trade or otherwise be lent, resold,
hired out, or otherwise circulated without the
publisher's prior consent in any form of binding or
cover other than that in which it is published and
without a similar condition, including this condition,
being imposed upon the subsequent purchaser.
No part of this publication may be reproduced, stored
in a retrieval system, or transmitted in any form or
by any means electronic, mechanical, photographic,
recording or otherwise, without prior permission of
the author and/or publishers.

2

Foreword

by

Major General L.A.H. Napier C.B., O.B.E., M.C., D.L.
(Late of The South Wales Borderers and The Royal Regiment of Wales)

From the moment any reader starts this book he or she will begin to smile and, at times laugh uproariously. Bob Smith is an outstandingly skilled and entertaining raconteur of stories. Although the amusing and extraordinary accounts are based around his long and varied military experiences in Welsh regiments, King's African Rifles and Malaysia Rangers anyone, with or without Service experience, will be well entertained by the humorous style as well as the remarkable events he has encountered over a long career.

Bob Smith has an extremely good eye and a keen memory for the ridiculous and frivolous and sometimes for unfortunate events. They are told so entertainingly in this collection of delightful stories. He has clearly enjoyed his military service, though I doubt if many of us can recall so many amusing incidents, often where the author himself seems accident prone or downright unlucky! Read this book for a good laugh, as well as for an insight into the sort of life in the British Army which no longer exists.

To:

Des & Eileen with grateful thanks for looking after us

Bob & Vesta

Crickhowell 26 may 2001.

3

This book is dedicated to Welsh, African and Asian soldiers with whom I have served during the last half century. Behind the humorous situations I have portrayed runs the way of life of a soldier; the finest profession in the world.

I am indebted to my wife, Nesta, for the many hours she has spent helping me edit the book.

I am grateful to the many characters, some of whom I have given pseudonyms, who are the source of my material.

I give special thanks to Mr George Robinson for providing cartoons and giving me encouragement.

Major Bob Smith spent 49 years of his life in the service of his regiment and the British Army. He was commissioned into The Welch Regiment in 1944 and also served with The South Wales Borderers, The King's African Rifles, Malaysia Rangers and The Royal Regiment of Wales. Too young to see action in World War Two, he redressed the balance by taking part in a number of 'brush fire' campaigns in Eritrea, Malaya, Kenya, Cyprus and Borneo. He spent three and a half years with Rhine Army Public Relations before spending the last nine years of his service on the active list as publicity officer for the infantry regiments of Wales. On retirement in 1980 he was appointed assistant regimental secretary of his regiment, curator of The Royal Regiment of Wales Museum (South Wales Borderers and Monmouthshire Regiment) in Brecon and editor of the regimental magazine, 'Men of Harlech'. He finally retired in 1993 and is now a freelance writer and photographer.

Contents

CHAPTER ONE

'Sign here, Sir'

I was travelling from Paddington to Newport, South Wales on an Inter City 125 when a disembodied voice with a Pakistani accent informed me and my fellow passengers that there had been a fatal accident in the Severn Tunnel. The unsympathetic voice went on to say that we would continue our journey via Gloucester and that it regretted any delay this would cause.

British Rail do not believe in giving away anything more than the briefest details about their disasters, and we were shunted off in a north westerly direction at Swindon, not knowing if there was a dead cow on the line or if there had been a complete collapse of the tunnel.

My son was with me and he expressed surprise that the train could reach Newport by another route. Being Clifton educated and brought up in the tradition of that great engineer, Isambard Kingdom Brunel, he had never heard about the 'romantic route' that wound its way through the Cotswolds.

For me it was a journey I had not travelled for well over forty years and my mind flipped back through the decades to the time when I was a young subaltern serving at The Welch Regiment depot in Cardiff in 1947.

One day I received a call from the adjutant saying that he wanted to see me. Such a command usually meant that something had gone wrong, so I moved with leaden steps from my office on the 30 yards range to his office in the main block.

'Enter', he thundered, as I knocked on his door. 'I've got a job for you'. I had already learnt to be cynical about any of the adjutant's jobs, so I waited with some anxiety for the punch line.

'I want you to go to London on Saturday, stay the night and on the Sunday morning collect three German generals and deliver them to the prisoner of war cage at Bridgend.' I had spent a total of ten months in various Army units being trained to be an officer. During that time I had been subjected to every sort of challenge and situation that an officer might be expected to meet, but this order took my breath away.

'The orderly room quartermaster sergeant has booked you into a hotel adjacent to the cage for senior German officers in Cromwell Road. Report there at 09.00hrs on Sunday morning, collect the generals and take them to Paddington rail station. From there you will proceed to Island Farm prisoner of war camp, Bridgend where you will hand them over. Any questions?' I knew that the question 'Any questions?' did not mean that you should actually ask a question, so I replied, 'No thank you Sir,' saluted, and marched out.

I had only been to London once in my life and that was when I was a boy just before the start of the second world war. During the war the capital was a city to be avoided as it took a considerable pasting from the Luftwaffe and was the last place to go for a week end. When I arrived at Paddington, I took a taxi to my hotel in Cromwell Road and during the evening I went out to see the bright lights of the west end.

The following morning I had breakfast, paid my bill and then walked about 200 yards up the road to the prisoner of war cage. It was just another hotel and one of many in that area that bore the look of a place that had been requisitioned. A young corporal in the Military Police was sitting behind a six foot table in front of what, in pre war days, had been the reception desk. 'I've come to collect three German generals,' I said. He nodded and pushed towards me a familiar little pad of Army forms 108 on which was written, 'General Heinricci - General Schmidt - General Von Dittmar.' He then turned his head and bellowed, 'OK you guys, over here.'

From the deep leather sides of some elegant armchairs appeared three dignified figures wearing strange uniforms which looked as if they had been made out of blankets. They approached me, clicked their heels and gave me a 'British' salute. 'Sign here, Sir', said the corporal.

10

The driver of a 15 cwt truck helped me with my suitcase, while the three generals picked up their kit and climbed into the back of the vehicle. We then set off for Paddington. The train was at the platform when we got there and my generals followed me like a trio of spaniels as I led the way into a first class carriage. As soon as we had placed our luggage on the rack, steam gushed from the engine and we were on our way to South Wales.

I had been fairly accurate in my guess that their uniforms had been made from blanket material, but somehow or other these high ranking German aristocrats wore them with such panache that I, in my new service dress and Sam Browne belt, felt in awe of them. They all spoke fluent English and with me, their reluctant gaoler, they struck up a friendly rapport.

Up until the time we boarded the train I had no idea where they had come from, and I was amazed therefore when they told me that they were returning from leave with their families in Germany. Knowing now what the conditions were like for Germans in that bitter winter of 1947, the generals were indeed fortunate to spend those freezing months in warm huts in Island Farm Camp, Bridgend.

As we travelled through the Berkshire and Wiltshire countryside my three prisoners talked about the war. They talked about Hitler and Rommel, about the campaign in Libya and the allied invasion of Normandy. Each had played an important part in the German war effort and their conversation, in English for my benefit, was fascinating.

When we arrived at Swindon, because it was a Sunday and the day of the week when maintenance work is carried out in the Severn Tunnel, we headed north west towards Gloucester. This did not mean much to me, but when I felt the pangs of hunger at about midday I realised that I had not brought any haversack rations with me, and there was no buffet car on the train. The generals realising my plight, most generously shared their rations with me. The kitchen staff of the prisoner of war cage must have been kept on since pre war days as I had never seen such delicious packed meals, complete with two bottles of wine, in all my service.

The train, after a long journey via Gloucester, eventually arrived at Cardiff, where we had to change before going on to Bridgend. My parents lived in Barry, about ten miles away, and I usually went home at weekends if, for no other reason, to get my laundry exchanged. I therefore gave General Heinricci a shilling and an order to go to Platform 2 and get four cups of tea while I went to telephone my mother.

I had to go down to the main entrance of Cardiff General (now called 'Central') station and wait in a queue until a telephone became free. When I managed to get through I said, 'Hello Mother, I'm sorry that I will not be able to get down to see you today, I'm taking three German generals to Bridgend.' I had to hold the earpiece of the telephone at arms length as my mother hurled questions at me about the 'enemy'. 'Where are they now?' she yelled. 'On platform 2 having a cup of tea', I replied. 'What !!! ---?' she screamed, 'get back there at once before they escape, you'll be court martialled.' I tried to explain to her that 'escape' was the last thing they had in mind, but it was no good, she had lived through two world wars and the only place for Germans, as far as she was concerned was their own country or behind bars in ours. 'I'll bring my washing home tomorrow,' I cried. When I arrived at platform 2, General Heinricci handed me a cup of tea and fourpence change.

The Bridgend train came in about ten minutes later and we all climbed aboard for the last stage of our journey. A truck was waiting for us when we arrived and within a few minutes we pulled up at the reception centre at Island Farm Camp.

It was like a return to school after the 'hols' as scores of high ranking officers turned out to greet their friends and hear news from home. I wished that I had had an autograph book with me and asked them all to sign it! The driver of the truck was waiting to take me back to Bridgend railway station, so I bade farewell to the three generals. Once again there were smart clicks of their heels and a British salute before we shook hands.

For the next eighteen months I used to pass Island Farm Camp once a week when I took national servicemen, under training at Maindy Barracks, Cardiff, to the shooting ranges at Porthcawl. I often used to see German officers taking exercise as they walked unescorted along the side of the road. Field Marshall Von Runstedt was easily recognised by the two walking sticks he used. I kept looking for 'my generals', but I never saw them again.

CHAPTER TWO

Beware - Bouncing Bullets

Things were getting back to normal again when I was stationed at the depot of my regiment in Cardiff in 1947. The place had been occupied by American forces during the war, but two years after the hostilities ended a basic recruit training centre for national servicemen was set up.

I remember feeling very honoured when asked if I would like to be one of the training team in the new '41st Primary Training Centre'. I had recently attended a small arms course at Hythe and I felt confident I could handle the job of weapons training officer.

I might have come away from Hythe with a reasonable grading but I soon learnt that I knew very little about musketry when I matched myself with the two sergeants who were with the weapons training team.

Sergeant 'Dai' George of The Welch Regiment was the senior NCO and he patiently listened to the new theories I propounded about marksmanship. But when it came to shooting, it was 'Dai' George who could group consistently to four inches over 100 yards.

Sergeant 'Nick' Rees of The Royal Welch Fusiliers was my other NCO. He used to travel from Brecon every day on a motor bike with a side car. At least once a week, during the winter months, he would bring me a pheasant which he said he had been unable

to avoid as he was travelling over the Beacons. During the summer months he would occasionally remove a salmon from the inner depths of his side car. Each story he told of their procurement was more implausible than the last.

When he left my team in 1947 I lost contact with him. The next time I saw him was 14 years later when I bumped into him on the banks of the River Usk in Brecon. Like so many of his kind he had crossed the divide and had become a water bailiff. Knowing all the tricks of the trade, he was always one step ahead of the poachers.

Maindy Barracks in 1947 was not as well equipped with training aids as it is today, but at least we had a 30 yards range. I can well remember standing on the firing point and giving the first post war order to fire. 'Load with seven rounds. Two rounds in the bank (to warm the barrels) and five rounds grouping. Carry on.'

We had been shooting in this fashion for half an hour when a head appeared around the wall of the stop butts. 'Stop!' I yelled. 'Open your breech and stand by your weapons.' When it was safe to proceed I went forward to speak to the fellow who still had his head sticking around the corner of the wall. 'Do you realise you could have been killed if I had not seen you? We are firing live ammunition on this range.' 'I know,' he replied, 'they're landing on my bowling green, and if you don't stop it there's going to be trouble.' It sounded preposterous that rounds should ricochet out of the butts and I replied, 'I'll need some proof of that.' Without wasting any time the groundsman pulled out of his pocket half a dozen 'sharp ends' of .303 rounds. 'There you are,' he said, 'there's plenty more where they came from.'

Someone at officer training school told me never to admit anything to a civilian if it looked as if the Army might have to pay, so I just reminded him never to stick his head around the side of a stop butt again, and left it at that.

We had come to the end of the afternoon's training, which was just as well, so I gave the orders to 'boil out' rifles and 'fall out'.

Over tea in the officers' mess I had a word with my company commander who was horrified to hear that bullets had landed on the bowling green. He was all for putting the range out of bounds until I explained my plan for making it safe.

The following day Sergeants Dai George and Nick Rees accompanied me to Curran's engineering works in Cardiff docks where we collected a pile of railway sleepers. We took them back to Maindy Barracks and spent the rest of the day making them into a box which, being strongly constructed of sleepers and sand bags, would catch any ricochet rounds. I felt confident that my contraption of sand and wood would be the answer to the problem, so I decided to try it out at once; and at what better time than when the local bowling team were playing a league game at home.

We fired about a hundred rounds into the 'box' before I peeped around the corner of the stop butts to see if there had been any reaction. Woods were rolling gently down the green towards the jack with nothing but the occasional butterfly to disturb their progress.

The company commander and the commanding officer were delighted with my simple solution of the problem, but a few weeks later we received a visit from the Small Arms School touring team. When they arrived at the 30 yards range they nearly had a fit when they saw my 'box' in the stop butts. I explained to them the reason why it was there, but it had no effect upon the boffins from Hythe and I was ordered to remove it at once. They gave me some advice about raking the sand, sieving it for lead and making sure that the sand was at a certain angle to the trajectory of the bullets.

A considerable number of national servicemen were diverted from potato peeling fatigues to the 30 yards range where an immense amount of sand was given the full cleansing treatment. By the end of the week I was quite satisfied that every piece of lead had been removed and that the angle of sand conformed to the regulations of The Small Arms School.

On the following Monday afternoon another batch of national servicemen were lined up to shoot on the range. I gave the usual orders and the crackle of rifle fire disturbed what was otherwise a quiet summer afternoon. Suddenly a familiar voice boomed out from the stop butts, 'Eh - mister - your bullets are landing on my bowling green again'. 'Cease fire!' I yelled, shattered to find that all our hard work had been to no avail. I went forward to impress on him once again that his regard for the bowling green, although commendable, was highly dangerous.

It was obvious to me that my solution worked, while the one from Hythe did not. I stalked off to the company office, rang up the chief instructor at the school and told him so. Within a few days one of the warrant officers of the touring team came to Cardiff to see for himself what was wrong. Without firing a shot he pronounced that we were using the wrong sort of sand.

The range was out of action for a few weeks while fleets of vehicles removed the old sand and others brought in pure 'Severn' sand. Once again tape measures were brought out to ensure that the angle of the surface was correct to the last degree.

I stood on the firing point as half a dozen national servicemen were brought forward to shoot for the first time, an experience they would never forget - but for a reason quite unconnected with their introduction to gunfire.

'Eh - mister - now you've really gone and done it!' The familiar voice once again rang from the area of the stop butts. 'Cease fire!' I shouted, and then went forward to find out what had gone wrong this time.

The groundsman had with him a young lady who was holding a spent .303 round. 'That's him,' he said. 'He's the one who's been shooting all the bullets on the bowling green.' The young lady was not concerned about the bowling green, but she let me know in positive terms that she was going to sue me for every penny I possessed. I gathered from her invective that her small daughter, who had been gurgling contentedly in her pram alongside the bowling green, had suddenly let out a yell. When her mother investigated the cause of the baby's discomfort she found a hot spent round in the child's nappy. The thing had become trapped in a fold of the towelling and had branded the little girl as effectively as a cowboy would brand a steer.

I was posted overseas in 1948 and I never heard any more about it, but I have often wondered if the mother of the child took the matter further.

If officialdom had only allowed me to use my box of rail

sleepers there would have been no trouble, but the so called experts knew best and I had to conform to their instructions. Nevertheless, I still have a guilty feeling and that is why I pay attention during the summer months to the bare midriffs of 42 year old ladies wearing bikinis and speaking with a Cardiff accent. Perhaps one day I will see the brand mark of a .303 round and then, maybe, I will introduce myself.

CHAPTER THREE

Mediterranean Merry-go-Round

I arrived in Liverpool on a bright sunny day in August 1948 to begin my journey to Cyprus. Although I had been commissioned for two years, this was to be my first experience of travelling aboard a troopship. 'That'll be two and sixpence Guv,' said the taxi driver as he drew up alongside the gangway of the Canadian Pacific Line's 'Empress of Australia' moored at Prince's Quay. As he unloaded my kit I looked up at the ship which was to be my home for the next two weeks. Troopships in those days were painted white with a blue line just above the anchor all way round. This one, which displaced 21,830 tons, had three funnels and two masts from which were draped signal flags of many colours. She made a fine sight which became etched in my memory for all time.

The Troopship 'Empress of Australia' (21,833 tons)

The taxi driver handed me over to a porter who told me that he would attend to my baggage. 'I see you've got it well labelled, Sir,' he said. 'Don't you worry, your cabin baggage will be delivered to the Purser's square, the 'wanted on voyage' will be put in the baggage room and the rest will go down the hold.' He seemed to know what he was doing so I picked up a Gladstone bag which contained my travel documents and a few other odds and ends and went aboard.

I shared a cabin with another officer who soon had all his cabin baggage stowed beneath his bunk, but despite a number of trips

17

to the Purser's square, there was no sign of the rest of my cabin baggage. I looked over the ship's side to the place where I had left it on the quayside, but there was nothing there. The baggage room and the hold were out of bounds and no one was able to help me find my kit. At 6 p.m. the restraining hawsers of the ship splashed into the water and we moved out into the River Mersey. Tugs fussed about like terriers, nosing here and pulling there until we were in midstream and able to look after ourselves. We then left Liverpool behind and headed down the river to the open sea.

The loss of my kit did not worry me for the first few days, but when we reached Gibraltar everyone else was able to change into lightweight clothes. I was the exception and had to put up with my heavy winter uniform for the rest of the voyage. It was not too bad during the day time but I missed the white 'drill' mess jackets and blue trousers which I had had specially made for tropical use.

Our arrival in Malta was an unforgettable experience. I awoke to hear the sound of church bells and when I looked out of the port hole I saw tiers of buildings rising from the green sea. We were entering Grand Harbour, Valetta. My cabin companion and I soon got dressed and were up on deck to see more of the island which, only six years before, had been battered by the German and Italian air forces. There was still plenty of evidence of the damage they had caused.

Our next landfall was Haifa in what was then called Palestine, soon to be re-named Israel when the avalanche of Jewish emigrants from Europe forced the hands of the United Nations. Many soldiers disembarked at this point and then, in the late afternoon, we drew anchor and sailed for Port Said in Egypt, only twelve hours away.

Up to this time I was a free agent, but as we left Haifa I was called to the adjutant's office and told I would be responsible for exchanging English money for Egyptian piastres for about 50 soldiers who would be disembarking at Port Said. The process started that evening when I assembled the soldiers and relieved them of all their spare cash, which I handed to the adjutant for safe keeping. As I was leaving the adjutant's office one of his clerks was putting a list of names on the notice board. This gave details of all those who would be disembarking at Port Said the following day. To my amazement I saw that my name was entered. This was an obvious mistake as the next port of call for the ship after Port Said was Limassol in Cyprus, the island where the South Wales Borderers were stationed. I went back and told the adjutant about the mistake on the list, but all I got was a rude reply and an order to prepare myself for disembarkation the following day.

We arrived at Port Said early the next morning and most people were up on deck to see the grand waterway that joined the Mediterranean to the Red Sea. History came to life when I saw the huge statue of Ferdinand de Lessops, the French engineer who master minded the project, at the entrance to the canal. The 'Empress of Australia' moved majestically down the canal, parallel to the waterfront where shops were already open and ready for business. I could see the well known store of SIMON ARTZ which claimed to stock everything required by the discerning traveller whether going east, west or deep into Africa. We tied up close to the Canal Building.

'Bum-boats' were the first to make contact and it was not long before rope lines were thrown aboard and trading commenced. Baskets containing merchandise ranging from rugs to sculpted wooden figures passed up and down until a purchase price was agreed. Soon to follow were the 'gilli-gilli' men who squatted on the deck and drew a crowd of soldiers by shouting their 'trade sound' 'Gilli-gilli-gilli-gilli -'. At the same time they juggled with their props which consisted of chickens' eggs, dice and small brass pots. They had a quick fire routine which started off with the apparent disappearance of an egg which had been placed beneath one of the pots, only to reappear in a soldier's pocket five or six feet away. The ship's regimental sergeant major was heard to say, 'Take care lads, if this chap 'ere can make those eggs disappear, what chance have you got keeping your wallet in this thieving town?'

As soon as I had finished my breakfast, I went to the adjutant's office to get the bag of money and the form which I was to present to the field cashier of The Royal Army Pay Corps when he came aboard. I was not the only one who had to change English money into Egyptian piastres. There must have been five or six of us who had been detailed to act for various groups of soldiers and there were officers, warrant officers and families who were being dealt with individually. The cashiers, about half a dozen of them, sat in a row behind tables on the purser's square and we formed queues in front of them. Eventually my turn came to be served, but when the cashier took my bag of money and inspected the form he said, 'You haven't completed this bit.' Cursing under my breath, I took the form to a spare table and spent a few minutes completing the extra detail. The queue had filled up again and when my turn came, for the second time, I looked into the face of an officer I had not seen before. I glanced right and left at the other cashiers but none of them looked like the one to whom I had given my bag of cash. The chap in front of me held out his hand but all I could say was that I had given my money to someone in this exact spot only a few minutes ago, and now he seemed to have gone. 'What was his name and what did he look like?' the cashier asked. When I tried to answer the question I only had a vision of the 'gilli-gilli' man on the promenade deck. The impatient field cashier was anxious to get on with his business. 'You had better go along to the pay office in Port Said,' he said, 'someone might have taken your bag there.' For the second time on the voyage I was the unwitting victim of loss of chattels. The first and, as yet, unresolved disappearance of my kit was, at least, a personal problem. But this loss of soldiers' money was in a different category. I went to see the adjutant to get a pass to go ashore. When he heard what had happened he said, 'Do you make a habit of this sort of thing?' Covered with embarrassment, I took the pass and made a hasty retreat.

I had only a sketchy idea of the location of the Army pay office. On my way there I was accosted by a number of small boys who showed me photographs of their sisters, all of whom were available that morning. Thanking them for their offers, and nearly falling over another three small boys who were trying to clean my shoes, I headed in the direction I had been given. More by luck than judgement I found the building, identifiable by a Union Jack flying from a pole on the roof. I explained my presence and once again

experienced a lack of sympathy for my misfortune. The Royal Army Pay Corps are activated by signatures and, as I did not have one, they were not interested. Just as I was about to give up, return to the ship and surrender myself to the mercy of the soldiers whose money I had lost, a door opened to reveal a fellow whom I immediately recognised. I grabbed him and demanded that he return my money. He looked at me for a second or two and said, 'Ah - now the penny's dropped, I wondered why I was £500 up.' Within a few minutes he gave me the equivalent amount in piastres. Having never seen a piastre before, which comes in coins or exceedingly grubby notes, I spent a considerable time counting them. When I had finished, the cashier arranged for me to be taken back to the ship in a staff car. 'You wouldn't last more than five minutes in this area with that bag of cash,' he said. I have never experienced such a feeling relief in all my life as I felt that day as I was being driven back to the waterfront. As soon as I got aboard the ship, I called my soldiers together and paid them out to the last piastre.

Not all the soldiers on the ship had changed their money because many of them were going to join units in Cyprus, including The South Wales Borderers. I went to the adjutant's office again and remonstrated with him, but it was no use. 'I don't give a damn about where you say you are going. I have orders to put you off here and that's what I'm going to do,' he said. 'What about my kit which I haven't seen since Liverpool,' I asked. 'It will catch up with you sooner or later,' he replied.

When the time came to disembark we descended into lighters which took us across to the east side of the canal. From there we marched to Port Fuad transit camp, which was only a few hundred yards away. We passed through pleasant tree lined avenues where opulent houses were set back from the road in well tended gardens. This was obviously the wealthy residential area for the metropolis of Port Said which at the time was one of the great ports of the world. I began to buck up at the prospect of spending some time in this cheerful place. The 'cheer' faded however as we entered the transit camp and saw the rows of khaki '160' pounder tents which we were allocated.

If you have never experienced the heat of the Mediterranean countries in August, a tent in Port Fuad is not the best place to start. Even with both ends open and lying on my bed in a state of near nudity, the stifling heat numbed my senses. It was not until about 5 p.m., when a slight breeze brought some relief, that I started to take an interest in things again. I placed my canvas backed camp chair at the entrance to the tent and picked up one of the novels I had brought. Before I had read one page I heard the sound of squeaky wheels. Looking up I saw an Arab coming towards me pulling a barrow. When he stopped alongside my tent, he took out a small book from within his long white nightshirt. He looked at the number on my tent pole and then moved around to the other side of his barrow. A few seconds later he re-appeared carrying two suitcases which I immediately recognised as mine. He made a few more trips and eventually all my kit, which I had not seen since I got out of the taxi in Liverpool, was deposited outside my tent. I had never kissed an Arab, but on second thoughts I emptied my pockets and gave

him all my loose change. I knew exactly where I could find a pair of white shorts and a shirt and I could hardly wait to get them on. What a joy it was, to be properly dressed again.

No sooner had I got dressed than an announcement was made over the PA system that anyone wanting an advance of pay should report to the camp office. My pay was then about £25 a month so, as I had about £20 in credit in my bank at home, I cashed a cheque for the lot. That was a considerable amount of money in those days and, as life was sweet and the morrow could take care of itself, I and a few other friends went out for a night on the town in Port Said.

I must have been in that transit camp for three or four days, thoroughly enjoying the routine of swimming at the French Club and spending the evenings in Port Said. Cyprus seemed a long way away and if the British Army could not make up its mind where it wanted me, I was prepared to soak up the good life - providing the field cashier would continue to sustain me. The Army had not lost contact with me though and I was told that I would be transferred to Base Transit Depot, Suez the following day and that I would be responsible for a draft of 40 men who were going there as well. At this stage I began to wonder if these people had any idea of sending me to join my regiment at all. Perhaps it was East Africa or India they had in mind! I had learnt that it was useless to argue.

After an early breakfast I reported to camp office, collected the documents and met the draft that was formed up ready to move. Our kit was put aboard a truck and we marched to the canal, which we crossed by ferry - then another short march to the railway station.

Before we boarded the train I told the men not to stick their heads out of the windows when the train was moving along the platform. It seemed that there were thieves about who would be only too pleased to relieve passengers of their watches and rings as they moved past. I had heard some particularly nasty stories about these people who were not averse to cutting off leather watch straps with cut-throat razors to get what they wanted. As we moved away from Port Said and out into the delta area of Egypt we saw the moving pattern of life in this fertile region irrigated by the mighty River Nile. On one side was a pastoral scene, while on the other, huge ships seemed to be floating through the desert but were, in fact, on passage through the Suez Canal.

The journey from one end of the canal to the other is about 110 miles, with a stop at Ismailiya at the half way stage, where we had to change trains. I had to attend to the documentation of the draft and I told the sergeant to look after the men and get them to the right platform. I was immediately involved in an argument with the station master who objected to the amount of personal kit I wanted to take aboard the train. There was no way I was going to let any of it out of my sight in the guard's van, so I had to come to an understanding with him. When he was satisfied with the grubby pile of piastres I put in his hand, I was allowed to proceed. The station master himself summoned a porter and led the way to the platform for the train to Suez. There was nobody there but

23

eventually the sergeant and a corporal arrived. They looked mystified when I asked them what had happened to the draft. We looked everywhere but they could not be found. We eventually came to the conclusion that they had boarded the train for Cairo which had recently departed from the other side of the platform. Half an hour later the train for Suez was shunted alongside the platform and we, the remaining three of the draft, climbed aboard and set off on the second part of the journey. This latest loss of mine had the potential for being the biggest one so far and I saw very little of the Bitter Lakes, which is a natural deep water section of the canal - I was far too busy rehearsing my plea of mitigation.

I had always imagined Suez to be a romantic outpost of the Middle East, but the reality of the place dispelled my illusions. The town was set in an uninspiring stretch of flat desert which provided the location for some of the ugliest blocks of flats I have ever seen. The rest of the sprawling township consisted of mud and corrugated iron huts. We went on for a few more miles to a place called Port Tewfik, where the southern part of the Suez Canal flows into the Red Sea - or vice versa.

I stuck my head out of the window and saw some soldiers with red arm bands on their khaki shirts. I recognised them as Army Movements staff and realised that the time had come for me to report the loss of my draft. I went up to one of them and handed him the documents I had been given and said, 'I'm sorry to tell you I have only got two left. I think the others have gone to Cairo.' The movements officer opened the envelope and scanned the contents as if it were an unwelcome bill. 'We were not expecting a draft today,' he said. 'Where did you say they've gone?' I told him I could not be sure they had gone to Cairo, as I was not conversant with the Egyptian railway system. 'It could be Alexandria,' I suggested, as this was the only other place I could think of. The officer to whom I had given the documents put them in his briefcase and went off to attend to some military personnel who were going to Port Said. I found it difficult to understand why no one seemed the slightest bit interested in 38 men going adrift, but I had done everything I could, so the sergeant, the corporal and I climbed into a truck which took us to the transit camp. Base Transit Depot (Suez), at Port Tewfik, was much the same as the one at the north end of the canal, and the inside of a '160' pounder tent looks the same anywhere in the world. The township was within walking distance and it reminded me of its northern counterpart with spacious houses and wide boulevards. The Europeans who lived there were mainly French and there was an even better club there than in Port Fuad. British officers were most welcome. For the next six days I reported to the camp office each morning to see if there was any news about the missing draft, but the answer was always negative. I would then wander down to the French Club and spend the day by the pool. During the evening there would be a film show and I learnt more of the French language in that week than I ever did at school. On my seventh day in Port Tewfik I was told that I would be going back to Port Said the following day and that I should make myself ready to embark on a train leaving at 8 a.m.

Even though there were a number of British soldiers travelling on the same train, I was not made responsible for them. I do not think they believed in 'drafts' in Port Tewfik and even if they did, I was surely the last person they would have chosen to be the one in charge. When I boarded the train I noticed that some of the soldiers were putting their heads out of the windows, so I told them what I had heard about the 'cut-throat razor' thieves. Most of them took my advice, but when we arrived at Suez railway station one soldier continued to lean out of the window. As the train stopped a native spat in his face. The soldier immediately retaliated by punching the fellow on his nose. That was the signal for all hell to be let loose. I could see that the natives were eager to get to grips with the unarmed soldiers, so I gave orders for the windows to be closed. This made the Egyptians try another line of attack, and I watched them as they went further up the train to make their entry. Before I left home in Wales, a friend of my father had given me a Colt .45 revolver which he had used during the second world war. I thought it was a kind gesture at the time, but later I realised that I was an easy means of getting rid of a weapon that had become an embarrassment to him. The Egyptians were now racing down the carriage towards me, so, with their leader only about ten yards away, I pulled my enormous revolver out of its leather holster and stuck the muzzle into the fellow's stomach. This had the desired effect and I herded the Egyptians, with their hands in the air, to the nearest door where they fell out onto the platform. The guard had realised something was wrong and he acted promptly when I told him to

get his train moving. The enraged natives ran alongside the carriage for the whole length of the platform letting us know, what they would do to us if we ever came to Suez again.

When we arrived in Port Said we had the problem of getting ourselves and our kit to the waterfront. A sergeant mustered the soldiers into three ranks and then contracted a porter with a large barrow to carry the kit. When all was ready we moved off with the soldiers up front followed by the porter and finally me, bringing up the rear and looking after the kit. When we were half way to the waterfront the porter stopped and put the shafts of his barrow on the ground. I shouted to the sergeant to halt the men while I dealt with the porter who had gone on strike for more money, most probably because of the enormous weight of my luggage. The sergeant, who wore a kilt and was made of stern Highland stuff, was not prepared to renegotiate the contract and gave orders to three of the soldiers to take over the barrow and proceed. The porter was outraged and shouted so loud that he soon collected a hostile crowd around us. Our little force closed ranks and, like a Roman phalanx - with the barrow in the middle, we progressed slowly to the canal. Reinforcements in the shape of half a dozen military policemen came to our assistance when we arrived at the waterfront. The sergeant, with magnanimity typical of his race, handed the purple faced porter a handful of piastres and advised him, in a broad Highland dialect, 'Dinnae try yurr tricks wi me agin laddie.'

When I reported to the officer in the transit camp at Port Fuad, I asked him if there were any more interesting places I could visit. A trip along the North African coast as far as Tobruk would, I suggested, be most acceptable. He looked sourly at me and told me that I would be sailing in three days time for Cyprus in the 'Empire Comfort'.

The 'Empire Comfort' turned out to be an ex Royal Navy

corvette which carried about 50 soldiers in extreme discomfort and a dozen or so officers in medium discomfort. She had a sister ship called the 'Empire Peacemaker' aptly called the 'Empire Sickmaker'. We sailed out of Port Said harbour into a rough sea and found that our sea legs from 'The Empress of Australia' were inadequate for this vessel which bobbed around like a cork. I consoled myself with the thought that I would only have to spend one night on board.

Famagusta came into view the next morning and we were soon alongside the jetty. Familiar Welsh voices greeted me as I stepped ashore, and one of my friends from Brecon days whisked me away in a jeep to Karaolas Camp, the home of the 1st Battalion, The South Wales Borderers, a few miles out of town. I was allocated half a Nissen hut in the officers' compound and given the rest of the day to get settled. The adjutant told me that the commanding officer would like to see me first thing the following day.

At the appointed hour I appeared before the commanding officer. He was interested to hear what I had done since commissioning and we talked generally about world affairs. He explained to me the role of the battalion which was guarding 20,000 illegal Jewish immigrants and then he dropped the bombshell! 'How would you like to be my signals officer?' Anyone less technical about wireless sets than me would have been hard to find, and I told him so. 'We'll soon fix that,' he said. 'If you think you can do the job, I propose to send you home to do a signals course in Yorkshire in six weeks time.' Naturally, I accepted the offer but I was beginning to believe I was destined to be a human 'albatross', forever travelling over the oceans of the world with only temporary visits to dry land. When I had time to reflect on the offer, I realised how lucky I was to be given, what many people believed to be, the best job for a young officer.

I travelled home from Port Said on the 'Asturias', a huge and luxurious ship, returning to Southampton after carrying British emigrants to Australia. I successfully completed an 11 week course in Richmond, Yorkshire, spent Christmas 1948 with my parents and returned to Cyprus in the good old 'Empress of Australia'. This time I had no trouble with my kit - after all, I was now a seasoned traveller.

CHAPTER FOUR

He went that way

The first time I saw Jenkins 17 he was flying through the air having been ejected from the driving seat of a twin horse power gharry near the old city of Famagusta in Cyprus.

I was on my way back to camp near the old Roman town of Salamis, after spending a pleasant weekend in Nicosia. I had rounded a corner in a taxi when I saw coming towards me, a Cypriot gharry travelling at speed and drawn by two wild eyed horses. Ahead of me was another taxi and it was obvious that the

two converging parties would collide. This they did with dramatic effect. The two horses were killed instantly, while the driver was catapulted over the mangled remains of the horses and the other vehicle, to end up within a few feet of the front bumper of my taxi.

At this stage I did not know the identity of the person who did the flying act, but I got out of the taxi quickly to see if I could help. He lay quite still for a moment and I thought he was dead. He then opened one eye, rose to his feet, dusted himself down and uttered a few expletives which clearly identified him as a Welshman. A trio of military policemen and the owner of the gharry hurried breathlessly to the scene.

The poor old Cypriot driver was not at all pleased with what he saw. His livelihood had come to an abrupt end and what was left of his horses was not likely to bring him much change from the knacker's yard. He quivered with rage at the sight of the person who was responsible for his ill fortune and would have hurled himself at his wrong doer if the two military policemen had not held him in a firm grip.

'He went that way,' said the young man without batting an eyelid. 'Who did?', I asked. 'The bloke who was driving the gharry,' he replied. For an example of coolness in the face of damning evidence, this was surely a masterpiece. The military policemen then took over and one of them asked me if I had seen the crash and if I knew the person who was the focus of the gharry owner's outrage. To the first question I answered 'Yes', and to the second I replied 'No, and furthermore this is the man who was in the driving seat.' The young man gaped at me with a look of innocence and said, 'It wasn't me, Sir. I can't drive a gharry. To drive a gharry you have to make clucking sounds to the horses, and I can't do that.' He then proceeded to demonstrate how he could not make a clucking noise. His face wrinkled into a variety of shapes as he gurgled, sucked and squelched. 'There you are, Sir, I can't make a clucking noise,' he said. The two military policemen, who had watched the demonstration with inscrutable faces, decided that enough was enough. The young man's feet left the ground as the burly cops marched off to their van.

That was my introduction to 'Jenks', or Jenkins 17 as he was known, by the use of the last two digits of his Army number. After well over forty years of soldiering, during which time I have met many remarkable people, I can honestly say that I have never met anyone who approached Jenkins 17 for sheer originality in committing military offences.

I was the prime witness in the aforementioned incident and Jenkins had the book thrown at him. For his own good he was banned from going anywhere near the town of Famagusta during the remainder of the battalion's stay in Cyprus. But this did not work, as a few months later he stowed away on a cargo ship leaving Famagusta and was picked up in Malta. He was returned to Cyprus two weeks later where he took up residence in one of the cells in the guard room with which he had become familiar.

Except for the regimental sergeant major and the provost sergeant, Jenkins got on quite well with the rest of the provost staff who made life reasonably comfortable for him.

When he was finally let out of jail to enjoy what was left of the summer of 1948, Jenkins was put on guard duty in one of the watch towers surrounding the main illegal Jewish immigrant camp. The Jews inside the two high walls of barbed wire looked upon us in very much the same way as they had looked upon the Nazis under whom many of these poor people suffered in concentration camps during the war. Their one great aim was to get to Palestine and turn it into the Jewish state of Israel as soon as they could. They knew that they would have to fight for their country and during their enforced seclusion in Cyprus the young men and women of military age were kept busy with a strict programme of military training. The walls of their lecture rooms were made of unopened cans of pineapples and peaches provided in vast quantities by American Jewish organisations. They had wooden rifles, which they had fashioned themselves, parade grounds, assault courses and all the paraphernalia you would expect to find in a normal infantry battalion 'up country' station.

Our sentries used to sit in the watch towers and keep an eye on things, in particular the many young Jewesses in the briefest of swim-wear. One day the commanding officer, accompanied by the adjutant and the regimental sergeant major, was making a routine inspection. As the party approached one of the watch towers they were startled to hear the sound of British parade ground orders being shouted, while the Jews on their parade ground responded with commendable smartness. All the usual stuff like 'Saluting to the front', 'Left wheel', 'Right wheel', 'Advance in review order' etc. came thundering out from somewhere or other, but it was not until the regimental sergeant major looked upwards to the watch tower that the penny dropped. There was Jenkins 17, with his beret stuck on the back of his head, so thoroughly in command of the parade he was quite oblivious to the high powered party beneath him. With a roar the regimental sergeant major brought Jenkins's drill parade to an abrupt end. A substitute sentry was found and Jenkins was put under arrest and taken to the guard room where, once again, he occupied the familiar little cell.

Jenkins cultivated a friendship with our national service medical officer who practiced natural methods to bring relief from pain and suffering. Ailments ranging from tonsilitis and torn ligaments to athlete's foot received the same prescription; 'Let the sun get at it,' he would say. But for Jenkins, it was different and the whole range of the pill and medicine cupboard were available to him. He had the knack of being able to press the right button just before battalion drill parades and no matter how hard his company sergeant major tried, Jenkins - with the help of the medical officer, could always pip him at the post.

On one occasion Jenkins had been given some exotic mixture by the medical officer which made his hair fall out. 'Excused haircuts until further notice', was the entry on his 'sick note' which he was careful to carry in the back of his pay book. When he wore his beret his bald patch could not be seen, and even though he could not grow hair on the top of his head, it grew in profusion around the level of his ears and the back of his neck. The blonde curls and wisps of hair that hung over his collar were like red rags to a bull when the company and regimental sergeant majors were about, but there was nothing that they could do as the medical officer guarded him like a prize poodle.

When we arrived in Asmara in Eritrea in 1950, Jenkins's wanderlust was re-activated and he started off on his own to walk to South Africa. After he had trudged a few hundred miles, and the mountains of Ethiopia were getting higher and higher, he realised he had bitten off more than he could chew, so he turned around and headed back. The regimental sergeant major was waiting for him when he got back to Asmara, and once again he was back in the cell in the guard room.

A few months later he had another go. I was on my way back to Asmara from Massawa where I had been spending a couple of days fishing, when Jenkins passed me on the orderly room bicycle doing about 40 miles an hour on one of the very steep stretches of road. He was heading for the coast, about 75 miles away, where he planned to stow away on a ship. I felt that it was my duty to stop at the next police post and request them to alert another post further down the road about a British civilian on a bicycle. This they did and later that day Jenkins, and the orderly room bicycle, were tipped off the back of a police truck outside the guard room. His cell had been made ready for him and once again he took up residence.

The adjutant, who had tried everything to reform Jenkins, tried the last trick in his bag - 'absolution'. He made Jenkins the orderly room runner and gave him the bicycle he had used to get away to the Red Sea coast. This seemed to do the trick and from then on, and certainly until I left the battalion in 1951, Jenkins became a model orderly room runner.

The bicycle, which had never before seen an oily rag, was polished and burnished until it shone like a new medal. He carried a brew-can on the handle bars and this was always full of the cook sergeant's very best tea. Jenkins became a welcome visitor in the company offices. Not only did he deliver messages and letters from the orderly room, but he also knew what was inside the envelopes and would often give some good advice about their contents. I remember him coming into the signals office one day with a steaming mug of tea in his hand and giving me my annual confidential report. As I read it Jenkins observed, 'I'm sure you're pleased with that one, Sir.'

When old soldiers look back on their service they think about the good times, the not so good times and the many people who have enriched their lives. I will always remember Jenkins 17 because he was an individual who liked to do things his way. The full power of authority was often directed against him, and it hurt, but that did not stop him from doing what he wanted when he felt the urge.

I have not seen him for well over forty years, but I am still hoping to buy him a drink at the next re-union.

CHAPTER FIVE

'TIFFY' of the 24th

The first Saint David's day I spent overseas was with the 1st Battalion The South Wales Borderers in Cyprus in 1949. I was one of four officers of The Welch Regiment serving with 'The 24th' at that time and we were all made to feel completely at home. This regiment, renowned for its stand against the Zulus at Rorke's Drift in 1879, has always prided itself on offering hospitality in the good 'club' atmosphere of its officers' mess.

Charles Brewis took me aside on the eve of St. David's Day and said, 'These 24th people don't put on much of a show on 'Dai's Day' so it's up to us, of the 41st, to keep the Welsh flag flying.' (He was completely wrong as the Borderers made 1st March the most important day of the year.) So far I had no idea what was in his mind, but then he said, 'I know where we can get a goat.' He explained that he had made a reconnaissance of the old city of Famagusta and had seen a herd of goats, one of which was pure white. 'We'll go down there this evening and snatch it,' said Charles. I timidly put the question of ownership of the goat to my company commander but he dismissed my caution saying, 'There are thousands of goats on the island, they won't miss one. Besides, we'll take it back tomorrow.'

As the sun crept towards the horizon, Charles and I set off for Famagusta in his Morris Eight. There was hardly room for the two of us, especially as Charles had a wooden leg and needed all the room he could get to manipulate the pedals. We arrived at the old city and Charles pointed towards the herd. Sure enough, there was a pretty little white goat standing on a pile of rubbish.

Morris Eights are not built for cross country work in the Middle East and the squeaks and groans of the one in which we were travelling made this abundantly clear. Charles drew up as near to the goat as he could without scaring it off, then gave the command - 'get him!' I flung myself at the animal and managed to grab a leg. I soon had hold on another and began to bundle it into the back seat. While I had been struggling among the rubbish with the goat, Charles saw the goat-herd appear from behind a rock to investigate the commotion. We sped away as fast as we could and finally outdistanced the enraged Cypriot.

Our camp was about three miles away and Charles drove to the drums store where he had arranged for the goat to be accommodated. The drums storeman was sitting outside his bunk and he helped us unload. It was a pleasant little animal and had settled down quite well. This could have been due to the pile of newspapers which Charles had put on the back seat to save the upholstery. Most of it had been converted to cud.

The storeman, by virtue of his trade, was quite handy with rope and he soon made a head collar. When I went back to the drums store after tea he had also made an improvised coat for the goat from one of the leopard skin aprons. It fitted him like a glove and the whole appearance of the animal was so cute I decided to take it to the officers' mess to show it off.

'Tiffy', as the drums storeman had named him, trotted by my side as if he had been used to this sort of thing for all of his short life. A few of the officers were sitting under the cane loggia about 30 yards from the sea enjoying one of those magnificent sunsets for which Cyprus is famous. 'Tiffy' had quite an effect upon them and he was soon devouring an assortment of digestive biscuits, mint humbugs and cigarettes. On my way back to the drums store, I poked my head into the mess and saw the commanding officer reading the latest copy of 'The Field'. Here was an opportunity for me to put myself on the map and gain a few bonus points for initiative.

I led 'Tiffy' into the ante-room and approached the commanding officer without making a sound. Just as I was about to come into view around his right shoulder, the goat let out a cry for its mother, its goat-herd or another mint humbug. Whatever the reason, the effect upon the colonel was as if someone had

thrown the switch on an electric chair. In an instant he was on his feet, with rage so distorting his face that I wondered for a moment if it actually was the CO. 'Get that animal out of here,' he yelled. The good 'club' atmosphere of the 24th evaporated in a flash, and to make it worse 'Tiffy' peed on the carpet. 'Now look what the beast has done,' stormed the colonel. 'Remove it at once, and then clean up the mess,' he snapped. As I slunk away, the colonel let off a final salvo. 'This is the 24th Regiment, not the 41st. We don't worship graven images or goats.' (We had to wait another 21 years before the two regiments amalgamated and that dictum was reversed).

St. David's Day dawned and to give credit to the South Wales Borderers, they put on as good a show as I have ever experienced with my own regiment. We had cricket in the morning, a three course bumper lunch for soldiers in the cookhouse, officers and sergeants drinks in the messes and rugby sevens in the afternoon. Some of the officers asked me what had happened to the goat, but my enthusiasm for the ruminant had disappeared, especially as the regimental sergeant major told me that the Military Police had visited the camp to see if anyone knew anything about a missing goat from the Old City.

The drums storeman took over where I left off and spent the previous night getting to know 'Tiffy'. During the outdoor festivities the two of them paraded through the outer field and touch line where 'Tiffy', in his pipe clayed halter and leopard skin coat, was the centre of attraction.

When darkness fell, Charles Brewis and I loaded 'Tiffy' into the

Morris Eight and set off for Famagusta. Near Othello's Tower, beneath the walls of the old city, we opened the door and lifted him out. We gave him a mint humbug, with the paper on - the way he liked them, and then drove away slowly.

In the short time 'Tiffy' had been with us he made quite an impresssion with the soldiers. I don't suppose he was aware of the exalted position he held in the Regiment on its National Day. Neither did the goat-herd who must have have been surprised to find he had a full complement again.

CHAPTER SIX

A Dark Patch on the Surface

Just before I retired from the regular Army in 1980, I visited the 1st Battalion of my regiment which was engaged on a four month tour of duty in Northern Ireland. In the course of publicity work I was doing I required some photographs of signalling equipment in current use in an infantry battalion, so I went along to the stores with my camera. The thought went through my mind of the remarkable changes that had taken place since the days when I had been the signals officer of the 1st/24th Regiment. I claim to be the last British officer to use pigeons on active service, not that I sought to establish a record, it was only because my wireless communications were so abysmally inefficient.

I was instructed in the intricacies of the numbers 18, 19 and 22 wireless sets at the school of signals which, in 1948, was based in Gallowgate Camp, Richmond, Yorkshire. We used to spend the weekdays in or above the clouds in what must have been the most dismal army camp in the country at the time. At weekends we would descend to lower levels and enjoy the bright lights of Richmond.

The course lasted 11 weeks and at the end of it I was still just as mystified by radio waves, oscillating valves and battery charging as when I arrived. The rest of the students must have felt the same because the commandant of the school gave us some advice before we left.

'Gentlemen,' he said, 'you are about to return to your units to become regimental signals officers. We have taught you as much as we can during the last 11 weeks but it will not have escaped your notice that the wireless sets you have used are, to say the least, pretty inefficient. You will have to make the most of them though until the new range of equipment comes through. There will be times when you will have to carry the can for the short-comings of your equipment, and your commanding officers might well get angry with you. If this happens I suggest that you tell them it's the worst time of year for sunspots.' With that he turned on his heel and left the room. I remember asking the fellow next to me what sunspots were, but he did not know either. I can't remember when I added 'sunspots' to my vocabulary but I must have looked up the word in the dictionary and found that a sunspot is 'one of the dark patches sometimes observed on the sun's surface.' On further investigation I found that the dark patches were caused by enormous eruptions of nuclear energy which had a detrimental effect upon radio waves. We collected our suitcases, boarded the transport and went our separate ways.

Within a few weeks I was back with my unit in Cyprus, but only just in time to check the stores and take over from the outgoing signals officer before we packed up and set sail for the Sudan. It was not until early April 1949 when we had unpacked all our kit that I was able to see what equipment I had. The old hands in the signals platoon were soon busy erecting aerials, laying telephone lines and coaxing our reluctant charging engines to put some energy into the large secondary batteries that were used to power our wireless sets. These batteries were to cause me more trouble than anything else in the months ahead.

Khartoum is a hot place to be at any time of the year, but even before we were properly acclimatised the commanding officer announced that we were to have a two day signals exercise in the desert south of Omdurman. This was going to be my first big test and I worked hard over the weekend to ensure that all my wireless sets were in good working order and that the batteries were charged to their full capacity. We set out for the exercise area on the Monday morning with each company HQ vehicle having aboard a No.19 set on the main battalion net. We made a fine sight as we sped across the desert, each vehicle leaving a wide dust trail behind it.

Battalion headquarters was established under a solitary group of palm trees and the commanding officer, after checking that he was in wireless communication with me, roared off in his jeep. For the first hour or so the outstations managed to speak to each other but then voices grew weaker, crackles and squeaks grew louder until, by midday, nothing could be heard except me shouting to myself, 'All stations, report my signals'. In the end even I gave up when I saw that my batteries were flat.

I was munching my way through a cheese sandwich when I became aware of a dust cloud coming towards me from the south. As it came closer, I recognised the vehicle by the pennant on the bonnet. It was the commanding officer. Before the vehicle had stopped he had his feet on the ground and was yelling, 'Why can't I hear anybody?' Slipping my half eaten sandwich into the headset carrier bag I gave thought to the words of the commandant of the school of signals - this is just the sort of occasion he had in mind, I thought.

I put on what I believed to be my most studious look and said, 'You do realise, Sir, this is the very worst time of year for sunspots?' The CO looked at me for a second or two before he erupted.  'Sunspots!! - you'll have sunspots on your arse if you don't get these wireless sets working.'

With my trump card cast aside there was not much that I could do and, as there did not seem much point in carrying on with the exercise when nobody could hear each other, the CO set off once again in his jeep to tell the others to pack up and go home.

There was much mirth about the next day and I was the recipient of many uncomplimentary remarks. The commanding officer had been heard muttering 'sunspots, I'll give him - - - sunspots.' The adjutant thought that the CO had taken too much sun and had spoken to the medical officer about it, but eventually the truth came out.

I was known as 'Sunspots' for a long time after that and I had a good mind to write to the commandant of the school of signals and tell him that his advice did not work in the Sudan.

Postscript: The young signaller to whom I spoke in the signals stores looked owlishly at me when I asked him if he had any trouble with sunspots. I was just testing him to see if 'sunspots' was still an emotive word in the signals platoon. He didn't react so I suppose its forgotten now.

The mule panniers had gone as well.

CHAPTER SEVEN

Fire Call

I could never understand why I was selected to be the unit fire officer. I had no qualifications for the job, very little interest - compared with one member of the regimental police who loved fire duties so much that he used to start them and, what seemed to be the most remarkable thing of all, I missed every real fire during my first overseas tour; all four of them.

I remember sitting in my office in South Barracks, Khartoum, smarting under the injustice of being saddled with this onerous duty when, as signals officer, I had more than enough to do keeping my old wireless sets working. The quartermaster made me sign for scores of stirrup pumps and red buckets, all of which had to be kept full of sand or water. The former commodity was no problem as sand got into everything in the Sudan. I also had two smart fire engines which were always ready for action.

The commanding officer expected everyone to follow his own high standard of good order and cleanliness; fire precautions were high on his list of priorities. His eagle eye could detect a missing flake of paint on a fire bucket or a defaced copy of fire orders at 200 yards range. I soon got used to the routine of being summoned to the adjutant's office after Saturday morning barrack inspection and asked to account for my idleness.

After receiving one particular nasty reprimand for not having a length of rubber pipe on a stirrup pump I decided that I had to do something spectacular to restore my standing with the commanding officer.

The colonel was a well regulated person and I had a good idea how he would react to a given situation. One of the events in his weekly routine was to go for a sail on a Sunday morning on the Blue Nile, which ran only a hundred yards or so in front of the officers' mess. The clubhouse was one of the gunboats Kitchener used on his expedition of 1898 and was anchored close to the bank a few hundred yards down the road. A plan began to form in my mind. A more than ample supply of water was available in the river which flowed past our barracks, the fire engines had suction pumps capable of drawing water from the river and the flowers in the officers' mess garden always needed watering. The whole scenario fell into place and I only had to smooth a few edges to show the commanding officer what an imaginative fire officer I had become.

On the dot, at 08.00hrs the following Sunday, the colonel entered the dining room to have his breakfast. A bevy of white robed Sudanese waiters attended to his needs and the latest copy of The Times was propped up in front of him as he tucked into his kedgeree. He must have wondered why I kept popping up and down outside the window, but my feigned interest in the spiky plants which passed for flowers was merely a cover so that I could keep my eye on him. I was ready to run out to Kitchener Avenue at a moment's notice and give my fire engines the signal to advance. That moment arrived when I saw a couple of Sudanese waiters descend upon the CO's empty plates as he rose from the table. He picked up a few sailing items and marched smartly down the broad stone steps of the mess portico towards the huge wrought iron gates that opened onto Kitchener Avenue.

I was in position in the middle of the road, like a race starter at Le Mans, and I waved my handkerchief as a signal for the fire engines to advance. The timing could not have been  better. Both vehicles were far enough away for a good three furlong race and they made a fine sight as they charged down Kitchener Avenue towards the colonel and me. I began to explain what I was doing and I recognised the CO's approval by the nods and smiles as he listened to my plan. The fire engines seemed to be travelling much faster than I had expected and it was not supposed to be a race. What I had not taken into consideration was the rivalry that existed between the two crews who were determined to be the first to bring succour to the officers' mess flowers. I had to break off my conversation with the commanding officer to take control of the second phase of the operation which involved directing the vehicles towards the river.

During winter months the Blue Nile is swollen with flood waters that come from Lake Tana in Ethiopia. But as the hot summer months arrive so the water level gets lower and lower exposing the muddy banks which bake hard in a crazy paving design. Anyone with a grain of common sense would have appreciated that the closer one got to the river the softer the surface would become, but not the two drivers of the fire engines who continued their race, now going backwards, to the water's edge. I shouted at the top of my voice and waved my arms but it did no good as the crews were looking the other way. Slowly but inexorably the surface of the bank collapsed and both fire engines sank into thick brown mud. They were not even near enough to the river for the crews to throw the pipes, with wicker baskets on the end, into the river to suck up the water.

I looked at the colonel and his eyes had narrowed into thin black slits. 'How do you propose to get them out?' he said. The two vehicles were now wallowing in the mud like a pair of hippos and I wondered if they were going to disappear completely. Trying to sound brisk and business like, I said, 'I'll have a word with the motor transport officer, Sir. The bren carriers (tracked vehicles, like small tanks - with an open top) should be able to pull them out.' 'No you won't,' snapped the colonel, 'the annual vehicle inspection takes place tomorrow and I'm not having them messed up - you'll have to think of something else.' With that he strode off in the direction of the sailing boats.

The transport officer was not available, he had gone off to shoot duck, and the transport sergeant let me know in even stronger terms than the commanding officer that the carriers were not to be used. Instead, he gave me the telephone number of the local REME workshops who, he said, would be able to help with a Scammel breakdown vehicle.

Trying to get a Scammel in Khartoum on a Sunday in mid August turned out to be quite a problem and I spent most of the morning on the telephone and pacing up and down on the banks of the river waiting for it to arrive.

At last, at about 1 p.m., it appeared. A Scammel is a large beast and as it drew up alongside me a head popped out of the cab window high above me. I pointed to the two fire engines in the mud and the driver gave a nod of understanding. The cab door opened and three soldiers clambered down the side of their vehicle to survey the problem.

'Ok, we'll fix it in no time.' said one of them, while the others pulled a large hook from the inner depths of the vehicle. They attached the hook to one of the fire engines, took up the slack and slowly pulled the first vehicle from its muddy hole. An identical operation was carried out on the other vehicle and within a matter of minutes they were both back on the road. My morale, which had taken a nasty knock, was restored and the prospect of a cold beer in the mess began to occupy my thoughts.

The crew of the Scammel were replacing their kit and getting ready for the return journey to Gordon's Tree, on the White Nile. As they climbed up and over the huge wheels, who should come around the bend in the river but the colonel in his sailing boat. What a perfect piece of timing I thought.

As the driver of the Scammel had seen how my fire engines had got into difficulties, I did not think it necessary to warn him of the danger of the unstable bank. I gave the crew a wave as they moved off but within a few seconds I could see that they were also on a disaster course. Instead of taking the shortest route to Kitchener Avenue, the driver took a wide track which brought his huge vehicle too close to the river. With a lurch and a grunt and the sound of spinning wheels it broke through the surface of baked mud and started to sink.

Even though he was a hundred yards away and sailing fast with a following wind, I could see the colonel was not amused. It was not long before he had tied up at the moorings, come ashore and was striding purposefully towards the scene of the latest disaster. 'Are you playing some sort of game?' he said. The lack of humour in his voice gave me no reason to think he wanted to join in.

There was no other recovery vehicle in the Sudan, the nearest one was in Egypt - about a thousand miles away. It became obvious to the commanding officer that the only way to get the Scammel out of the mud was to use the bren carriers. The transport sergeant was ordered to get the carriers and tow ropes at once.

The carriers, in immaculate condition for the following day's inspection, were harnessed to the Scammel like a pack of huskies. Their engines roared under full throttle and the recovery vehicle was pulled free from its muddy embrace. The transport sergeant was almost in tears as he surveyed the carriers which were now covered with mud and dust.

I have never been so unpopular with so many people in all my life. The carrier platoon worked all night to get their vehicles back into the gleaming condition they had been before I got my hands on them. The regimental police were turned out and spent hours restoring the shine on the fire engines. The colonel was furious, and so was the adjutant - but he was always furious. The transport officer returned without shooting any duck, and he was furious as well. It was without doubt the worst day of my life and the after shocks caused me to twitch for a long time.

I have often wondered why I was not given the sack on that disastrous day. Maybe the colonel and the adjutant, under their severe expressions, really did have a sense of humour. Perhaps they anticipated some of the other remarkable things that were yet to happen. Even to this day elderly retired officers greet me with such remarks as, 'Remember the time you blew your hair off in Eritrea?' - but that's another story.

44

CHAPTER EIGHT

A Point to Remember

When I was a young officer I learnt many valuable lessons from the experience of others. One of them was never to use a bamboo shooting stick.

Shooting sticks had not really come into my orbit until I went overseas. If I had been asked to describe one I would most probably have said that it was some sort of blow pipe from the East Indies.

The first one that I saw belonged to Major 'Windy' Bennett who had been posted as second in command. I met 'Windy' on the day that he joined us in Khartoum in the middle of the 'hot season' of '49. He was standing of the steps of the officers' mess verandah in South Barracks looking down the Blue Nile. He was wearing the most enormous pair of shorts that I have ever seen. Their knife edge creases stood out fore and aft like two huge rudders. I learnt later that he wore two pairs of shorts each day, one for standing up and one for sitting down. If you were summoned to his office you could have been forgiven for thinking that you had come face to face with the 'invisible man' for standing in the corner of his office, supported by nothing but starch, would be Windy's standing up shorts ready for him to slip into when he was ready to make his round of the barracks.

'It's good to be back in the Sudan,' said Windy. 'I was here many years ago as a subaltern.' I looked at him and had a vision of a young Bennett swiping dervishes with a sabre as he battled up the Nile with Kitchener's Army. A glance at an Army List in my office shows that Windy was 38 years old when he joined us in Khartoum, but there was a presence about the man that gave him an air of majesty far beyond his years. Maybe it was his eyebrows that made him different from other men, they were about twice as long as normal. He used to twirl them until they stuck up like two wireless aerials on each side of his face. He had a thick moustache over a broad upper lip and a voice that seemed to get its resonance from a 44 gallon drum buried deep inside him.

I do not mind admitting that he frightened me at first and there were occasions when he almost stopped my flow of blood. To be at the end of one of Windy's 'rockets' was an unforgettable experience, but these outbursts were like tropical storms, they passed as quickly as they came.

Windy soon set about his duties as overseer in training matters and announced that there would be an officers' TEWT in a few days time. For the uninitiated in Army jargon a TEWT is a 'tactical exercise without troops.' In other words a simple way of keeping officers occupied by practising them in waging a campaign without doing any damage to anyone.

Windy committed his plans to paper and none of us were surprised to hear that the TEWT was going to be held in the usual area. Jebel Meriam was the only place for a hundred miles or so where the ground rose slightly above desert level. It was well known to the rest of the officers and we had already beaten off scores of imaginary attacks from all quarters on previous exercises. It was therefore with a feeling of gloom that we heard we must spend another four or five hours being baked alive on this pimple in the desert.

We set out from Khartoum at sunrise on the day of the exercise. We drove over the bridge where the White and the Blue Niles meet, turned left and headed through the maze of mud huts that was Omdurman. We went past the Mahdi's tomb and then south to Jebel Meriam. Within an hour we were standing on the summit; all 200 feet of it.

Windy outlined the tactical situation and waved his shooting stick in the direction of the 'enemy'. For those who could not remember all that he said, a hand-out was issued. A few minutes later we were given a piece of paper with 'Question 1' written on the top. The routine was always the same on these occasions, first of all trying to understand what the directing staff (ie. Windy Bennett) had said, and then trying, within one's syndicate, to write down a sensible answer. The mess sergeant at this stage would produce a splendid breakfast and, as the wind on the top of Jebel Meriam always blew at 50mph, it was a toss up which would fly off first, the corn flakes or the question paper. There was never enough time to eat breakfast and consider the problem before we were called forward to give our solution.

Windy finished his breakfast and bellowed that he was ready. We quickly assembled before him in our syndicates, hoping that one of the others would be asked to give the solution. The law of averages has never given me any free throws and on this occasion, not only was my syndicate selected - but I was nominated as spokesman.

Windy was sitting on his shooting stick and looking at me in such a way that I knew instinctively anything I said would be wrong. He allowed me to go through the rigmarole of preparing for battle before he spoke his mind, which consisted of a single word of five letters. He waved his shooting stick above his head and stabbed at various points in the desert to emphasize points which were nonsense. It was an impressive performance by someone who had real battle experience.

Like a conductor bringing a symphony to a tumultuous finale, Windy twirled his shooting stick once more around his head before driving it into the ground and depositing his voluminous shorts into the seat. Instead of a crash of cymbals there was a crack like a pistol shot and Windy travelled a further 30 inches until he was in the sitting position on the ground.

Despite his size Windy was remarkably light on his feet, so obviously there was something wrong when he just sat there and did nothing. The awful truth dawned when we went to help and

saw his broken shooting stick alongside him. A jagged spike on the ground meant that a matching piece was somewhere underneath him.

Very slowly we heaved him up and saw the rest of the shooting stick sticking out of his shorts. With commendable initiative and enormous courage the quartermaster gave the broken piece of bamboo a sharp tug and withdrew it. Windy was not capable of walking, so we carried him down the Jebel to a jeep which took him off at top speed to Khartoum military hospital. He remained remarkably cheerful throughout the journey even though he still had a nasty splinter of bamboo in a very tender part of his body.

The doctor and nurses in the hospital did a great job on Windy's bottom, so we were led to believe. It was one of those operation scars that Windy could not show his friends. By the evening of the same day he was receiving visitors in his hospital room which was full of flowers.

Windy was up and about within a few days and was soon his usual snorting, eye brow twisting, bristly but humorous self once more. As far as I know he did not carry a bamboo shooting stick again. Come to think of it, I have never seen anyone carry a bamboo shooting stick since that day in the Sudan. It's amazing how the word gets around.

CHAPTER NINE

Poles Apart

Early in 1950 the 1st Battalion The South Wales Borderers mounted its first large scale operation against shifta (bandits) of Eritrea. Banditry has been a way of life since time began in this rugged East African country sandwiched between the Red Sea, Abyssinia and the Sudan, but a few years after the end of the second world war a political flavour was introduced to their national sport. It was Mussolini's dream to have an East African empire, but things turned sour on him in 1940 and 1941 when British, Indian and South African forces defeated his army in Somaliland, Abyssinia and Eritrea.

When we arrived in Asmara nine years later there were still plenty of Italian expatriates about. In fact the whole country, radiating from its beautiful capital city, gave the impression of a pleasant part of northern Italy. Our job was to look after the interests of these poor Italians and stop shifta from wiping them out, which they would do given half a chance.

The area selected for our first anti shifta operation was an expanse of semi desert country west of Keren. On the appointed day the transport wound its way from Asmara through the spectacular scenery of the western province. Here mighty outcrops of rock, densely covered in prickly pear cactus, provided excellent observation posts for shifta who would be waiting for an opportunity to snipe at vehicles. For this reason we always travelled in convoy with everyone armed and alert.

We reached the edge of the plateau where in March 1941 British and Indian troops under General Platt fought one of the toughest battles of the war. As we descended through the gorge we marvelled at the tenacity of our soldiers who levered themselves to victory with their finger nails. Marked on a rock in white paint for all to see were the words HLI SCOTLAND FOR EVER (HLI means Highland Light Infantry). At the bottom of the gorge the road ran through undulating country sparsley covered with thorn bush. Twenty miles or so further on we turned left and headed for a place on the map marked ARRESA. This was to be the location of battalion headquarters.

I remember arriving just as the sun was going down; we were able to erect our tents before darkness enveloped us. The next morning the commanding officer held his 'O' (orders) group. The operation had already started and I, as signals officer, felt a certain amount of satisfaction, as wireless communications were working reasonably well and information was trickling in. When operational matters had been covered the CO came to the 'command and signal' part of his orders. 'I have decided I will have my Tac HQ (tactical headquarters) in the police post on the

top of the hill over there,' he said. We followed the direction of his finger and saw a small hut sitting like a pimple on a hill about three quarters of a mile away.

Tac HQ Transport and Arressa Police Post

'Signals officer - I want a wireless and a telephone to be set up. Any problems?' 'No, Sir,' I replied, 'we'll get that fixed right away.' 'Good,' said the CO as he rose from his camp chair and made ready to go off to his Tac HQ. Striding off towards his jeep, he looked over his shoulder and said, 'Just one more thing, pole the telephone cable.' 'Hang on, Sir,' I said, 'we haven't brought any poles with us.' The colonel turned around slowly and said, 'I'm not concerned whether or not you have brought any poles with you, but get that cable poled.' With that he got into his jeep and drove off.

I was fortunate to have an efficient signals sergeant called 'Duke' Dyer. I went across to the signals tent and gave him the outline of the CO's orders. 'That's the place over there,' I said, pointing to the small hut on the hill. 'Righto', Sir, no problem,' said the resourceful 'Duke'. 'There's just one more thing Sgt Dyer,' I said, 'pole the cable.' 'We haven't brought any poles with us,' he replied. I gave him my sternest look and said, 'I don't give a damn whether or not you have brought any poles, get that cable poled.' I turned on my heel and walked off.

I give credit to Sgt Dyer and the signallers for trying hard. They collected all the spare tent poles and every bit of wood they could find in the quartermaster's compound which would lift the cable off the ground, but it wasn't enough. After a short distance from the magneto (field) exchange the 'poles' came to an end and the cable had to lie on the ground.

The following day at the CO's 'O' group I had a feeling that things were not going well. When he got around to the 'command and signal' bit he looked at me and said, 'Didn't I tell you to pole the cable to my Tac HQ?' 'Yes, Sir,' I replied. He fixed me with cold eyes and said, 'then-why-have-you-not-done-it?' I remember spluttering out a lame excuse about not being able to find anything else to hold up the cable. 'Absolute nonsense,' bellowed the CO. 'The place is littered with poles. Come here and I will show you.' Outside the tent he picked up a piece of wood which turned and coiled back on itself until it resembled a surrealist's corkscrew. 'What's wrong with this then?' he said.

'A few of these tied together will be ideal. The trouble with you, my boy, is that you do not use your head.' Just to add substance to his words he  picked up a few more bent sticks he found under a bush. 'I want that cable poled by 17.00 hrs today,' he snapped.

I gathered 'Duke' Dyer and the signallers together and we set about scouring the barren landscape for anything made of wood. Nothing was rejected and we soon had a production line of signallers tying together an assortment of twisted shapes. We made slow progress getting the cable off the ground and every time we erected a 'pole' I would look at the small hut on the hill - but it seemed no closer. At last, at about 16.30 hrs, we struggled up the remaining few yards to the CO's Tac HQ and drove in the final 'pole', which resembled three badly damaged bicycle wheels.

The colonel came out of the hut and surveyed the undulating cable stretching back to battalion headquarters. I wiped the sweat off my brow and gasped, 'I never thought we would do it, Sir', He looked at me with a smile on his face and said. 'I'll let you into a secret Bob, I didn't think you would either. Well done.'

CHAPTER TEN

Watch Out! - Seagull's about

For forty years or so from the start of the second world war to 1984, the Army had a code which radio operators were obliged to use when transmitting official messages. A commanding officer, be he an army commander or a platoon commander, was known as 'sunray'; the quartermaster general down to a battalion quartermaster was known as 'molar', while adjutants, through their various levels, from top brass in Whitehall to the infantry battalions in the field, were known as 'seagull'. The whole idea was to confuse the enemy and to give them no indication of what sort of sunray, molar or seagull was sending or receiving the message. I was never convinced that the enemy could be stupid enough to think that a request for fifty pairs of socks, five hundred packets of fly papers and twenty latrine buckets would come from Whitehall and not from some poor dispirited unit camped on the edge of a swamp. The origin of these code words always puzzled me, but it wasn't until I looked up 'seagull' in a wild-life book that I found a clue.

A seagull (code name for adjutant) is a bird that likes the company of others of its kind, but is quite likely to attack them with its beak or flail them with its wings. It is always in immaculate condition despite the grotty areas it may inhabit. Its rasping cries are heard early in the morning, throughout the day and well into the night. Its eyesight and hearing are sharp and clear, and it is aware of everything that happens around it. Possessed of an ability to propel its waste matter with unerring accuracy at a recipient of its choice, the code name 'seagull' was, without doubt, most appropriate for adjutants the world over.

When I was a young officer I could never understand why adjutants changed their personalities when they were appointed to that particular office. Before their apppointment they were nice ordinary fellows, and they reverted to their natural state when they moved on or sideways. It was the bit in the middle, when they became so bloodthirsty, that intrigued me.

As an officer cadet I was led to believe that on being commissioned into an infantry regiment I would be joining a good club. What a rude awakening I received when as a newly pipped second lieutenant I was gripped hard not only by the adjutant of my unit, but by the senior subaltern and the regimental sergeant major as well.

The first time I felt the sharp prick of the adjutant's fangs was when he came into the local hostelry one evening and saw me sitting in the corner of the bar with one button of my service dress undone. He said nothing to me at the time, but I had to take his word for it when I appeared before him the following morning. Civilians must think that we soldiers are a strange lot when an unfastened button can cause such a head of steam! For that offence I was awarded three extra orderly officer duties.

The award of 'three extras' was the cue for some hearty back slapping from one's contempories who would be delighted to hear that someone else would be doing their duties. I have known some officers, totally lacking in charm, suddenly become the most popular officers in the mess after an award of 'fourteen extras.'

Eighteen months of pounding barrack squares as a private soldier and an officer cadet had obviously not brought me and the young subalterns up to the standard required by the adjutant in Dering Lines in Brecon 1946. We were therefore ordered to parade before that particular 'seagull' and the RSM twice a week at 07.30 hrs, until further notice. We had already received instruction at OCTU (officer cadet training unit) in the difficult movements associated with carrying a cane on parade, but we did not measure up to seagull's requirement. We were told to bring our canes with us on the next parade.

One of our number was a young subaltern called Rex Farrow. Rex found it hard to get out of bed in the morning and was never properly effective until his mid morning break. Someone always had to make sure that he was on his feet with a towel in one hand and a bar of soap and a razor in the other.

Rex had been seen in the dining room but when the time came for us to assemble on the side of the square there was no sign of him. It was too far for one of us to run back to the mess to find out what had happened, and anyway time was up as the adjutant and the RSM were nodding their heads as they checked their watches. With only seconds to spare 2/lieut Farrow came panting around the corner and joined us. 'Got held up in the bog', he said, relieved that he had made it in time. His jaw dropped open though when I asked him what had happened to his cane. He

53

was almost on the point of volunteering for 'seven extras' when one of the subalterns spied a length of hollow copper pipe which some workmen had been using, and thrust it into Rex's hand, saying, 'Use this, it's about the same length as your cane, but for God's sake don't drop it.'

Almost immediately we were called forward and the complicated business of twiddling our canes commenced. It was only a matter of time before someone dropped a cane and that person turned out to be Rex Farrow. It was during that particularly difficult manoeuvre when the cane, in the perpendicular position, is brought to the horizontal when you step off. The piece of copper pipe shot out of his hand like a spear and then clattered and clanged about twenty feet across the barrack square. The adjutant

screamed a command to halt and both he and the RSM marched across to the strange object that lay in the middle of the square. The RSM prodded it with his pace stick and it clanged again. It was not hard for the adjutant to find out where it had come from. Rex Farrow was nervously twitching both thumbs as the adjutant asked him for an explanation. He tried to explain that he had left his cane in the 'bog', but this did him no good and he was thereupon awarded seven 'extra orderly officer' duties for showing disrespect.

The parade ground adjacent to South Barracks in Khartoum must be the largest in the world. With your back to the perimeter wall it extends from the Blue Nile north and east for hundreds of miles. The surface is natural crunchy gravel and all that is required to give the desert a 'Horse Guards' appearance is the application of some straight whitewash lines and some spots for the markers. Twice a month Joe Friend would hold a regimental sergeant major's parade for everyone of and under the rank of warrant officer class two. There would also be an adjutant's parade for everyone junior to the adjutant and, to complete the trio, the commanding officer would hold his parade when everyone would have to turn out. These parades started just after first light and one of my enduring memories of Khartoum is the sight of a blood red sun reflected on hundreds of bayonets of Welsh soldiers formed up in open order of companies. These parades were held at such an early hour because the heat was prohibitive once the sun had risen. One other advantage, which I am sure was not considered by the commanding officer, adjutant or regimental sergeant major, was 'FLIES'. These obnoxious insects, not to be confused with the comparatively friendly British branch of the family, were late risers, rather like Rex Farrow. Even so, anyone unfortunate enough to cut himself shaving before going on parade, and then forced to stand immobile during the inspection, would be subjected to a mind cracking form of torture as scores of these little monsters would pile in like a rugby scrum on the area of bare flesh.

An enormous amount of effort was expended by soldiers the night before a parade to make sure that their turn-out was perfect. Fortunately for the officers, most of the work was carried out by their batmen and all that they had to do was to ensure they put their puttees on properly.

Half an hour after we had fallen out from the first adjutant's parade to be held in Khartoum, the orderly room runner came to my office and told me that the adjutant wanted to see me. This sounded ominous and I wondered what could have gone wrong as I trudged across to battalion headquarters. I knocked on the adjutant's door and heard his call to enter. Four full paces, halt and a smart salute brought me face to face with him. 'Why were you improperly dressed on my parade this morning?' he barked. I did a mental check of everything I wore and could find nothing wrong. 'I am sorry, Sir,' I replied, 'but I do not understand.' 'You were not wearing your medal,' said seagull. I looked at him incredulously and spluttered, 'but I've only got one.' 'That's correct,' he replied, 'and you were not wearing it.' I was one of those young national servicemen who joined the Army in December 1944 - five months before the end of the war in Europe; the victory medal which I was awarded occupied a fluffy corner of my kit bag. Many members of the battalion had been in the thick of action during the war, and this was evident on occasions such as adjutant's parades when the desert groaned under the weight of medals honourably won in service to King and country. 'I can't wear just one, Sir,' I protested, but it was no good. 'If you appear improperly dressed again you will receive seven extra orderly officer duties,' snapped the adjutant. 'This time you are awarded three 'extras'. Now get out.'

The seven 'extras' were not long in coming, but I received them for a quite unrelated incident. The second in command was a major who had spent the last two years of the war as a brigadier. He was the most be-medalled person in the battalion and the junior officers had the impression he had won the war single handed. He was a very fiery gentleman indeed and we all treated him with great respect. It was therefore with dismay that I received a note from the adjutant ordering me, as a member of an audit board, to report to the second in command at the sergeants' mess the following Monday morning at 0800hrs to check the bar stock. One advantage about being signals officer was that I had my own transport in the form of two motor cycles. I therefore did not make my move to the sergeants' mess until 0750hrs, which allowed me ample time to cover the quarter mile distance. I straddled the machine, slipped the gears into neutral, primed the carburettor and lunged at the kick start. There was no reponse from the engine at the first attempt, nor was there from the next half dozen. Fortunately the other machine was nearby so I quickly went through the same procedure, but to no avail. Both machines made it quite clear that they had no intention of carrying me to the sergeants' mess. I looked at my watch and saw that I had about six minutes to get to the far end of the barracks. Deliverance came in the form of one of my signallers on a bicycle. Without bothering to explain, I requisitioned his machine and pedalled for my life. I skidded into some spiky bushes outside the entrance to the mess and hurled myself through the doors. Standing beneath the clock above the bar was the second in command. 'Where the hell have you been?' he thundered, 'you are five minutes late.' Sure enough the clock above the bar registered five minutes past eight o'clock, but I sneaked a look at my own watch and saw that the time was exactly 0800hrs. I was not brave enough to point out the discrepancy between the two timepieces, even though I was the officer responsible for keeping accurate time in the battalion. I merely muttered 'I'm sorry, Sir,' before I started to count the bottles and cans which had been put out for me to check.

An hour later I picked up the bicycle, straightened the handle bars and rode back to my office. Just to be on the safe side, I checked the correct time with the main signals exchange in Khartoum. There was no doubt about it, my watch showed the correct time.

I was pretty sure that the second in command would put in a report about my 'late arrival' and I was not surprised when I received a call from the orderly room to report to the adjutant. This time I walked with a spring in my step to battalion headquarters and confidently saluted the adjutant when I appeared before him. 'Why were you five minutes late reporting to the second in command this morning?' he said. 'I wish to say I was not late when I reported to him, Sir. If you would care to check with the telephone exchange you will find that the mess clock is five minutes fast,' I replied. This was my trump card and I thought that it would not be long before an apology would be forthcoming. Perhaps the second in command would buy me a drink in the mess and say, 'Really old chap, no hard feelings.' The adjutant continued to stare at me and I began to feel uneasy. Suddenly he exploded, 'I know that the clock in the sergeants' mess is five minutes fast', he snapped, 'You should have been there five minutes early, at 0755hrs. I ask you once again, why were you late?' There was no answer to that question, so I said nothing. 'Seven extra orderly officer duties,' said the predatory bird.

This episode did not seem to have any long term effect upon my popularity among the higher echelons of command in the battalion because a few weeks later the commanding officer asked me if I would like to go on attachment to the Equatoria Corps of the Sudan Defence Force. It seemed that an officer of the regiment commanded the corps in the Southern Sudan and that he had made the kind offer to host four young officers. Mike Hughes-Morgan was to be my companion and we were given a warning order to prepare ourselves for a flight to Juba in seven days time.

The day before we departed, I went for a drink in the Grand Hotel in Khartoum and there met a fellow with whom I shared a few cold beers. The Grand Hotel was always an interesting place as it was one of the great meeting places in Africa. Empire flying boats of British Overseas Airways Corporation would land conveniently at 'sundowner' time on the White Nile, and the picturesque stern paddle wheel steamers from Atbara would off-load their passengers just a few yards away from the entrance to the hotel. The ghosts of General Gordon and the Mahdi seemed to stalk the tree lined avenues and one could almost hear the sounds of distant battle. Looking over the water where the White and Blue Niles meet, I told my companion about my trip to the south. 'What's it all about then, why are they sending you all the way down there?' he asked. 'It's a 'swan' really,' I replied 'and a good opportunity to get away from the heat of this place.' We chatted for a short while and then I joined another group of people with whom I had a few more drinks before hailing a taxi and driving back to South Barracks.

Mike and I made an early start the following morning and before the sun was high in in the sky we were winging our way south in a De Havilland Dove of Sudan Airways.

This is not the time to describe all the fascinating experiences we had in that beautiful part of Africa which lies between the upper reaches of the White Nile, Lake Rudolph in Northern Kenya and the southern foothills of the Ethiopian highlands. It was a big milestone in my life which eventually led me to join The King's African Rifles.

Time passed all too quickly and soon we were on our way back to Khartoum. Arriving at the airport we were met by the duty officer who gleefully told me that the adjutant wanted to see me as soon as I arrived in barracks. 'What's gone wrong?' I asked. 'I don't know,' he said, 'but he looked angrier than usual.' I went to my quarters, put on some clean khaki drill and reported to the adjutant. The pleasantries about the trip were soon despatched and then he opened his desk drawer and pulled out a newspaper. 'What have you got to say about this?' he said. He held up the newspaper for me to read and I could see that it was a copy of the Sudan's only English language newspaper, 'The Sudan Star'. Emblazoned across

the front page was the headline, 'South Wales Borderers Officer goes on a 'SWAN' to the Southern Sudan'. The article described, with emphasis on 'relaxation', how I viewed the prospect of a safari around Equatoria. We were not paid to relax in those days and it seems that the Kaid (commander in chief) nearly had a fit when he read the story.

The commanding officer had also seen the story and he was none too pleased either. All this displeasure with me for giving 'off the cuff' interviews with the press filtered through to the adjutant's office. I was given three extra orderly officer duties 'for giving military information to a person not authorised to receive it'. This was a chastening experience which stayed with me for a very long time. It was not until sixteen years later, when I became a member of the staff of Army Public Relations, that I found courage to speak freely with the press again.

Khartoum was an extremely hot place to be during the summer months and most British government officials and their families would go home on leave. In early November they began to return and the run up to Christmas was a very sociable time.

Most of us found girl friends and we were soon engaged in a hectic round of parties and dances which were held in the clubs and sumptuous houses of their parents. We were getting into our stride and looking forward to many more months of this pleasant routine when orders came for the battalion to move to Asmara, the capital of the adjacent ex Italian colony of Eritrea. We spent Christmas 1949 in Khartoum, but a few days later Mike Hughes-Morgan and I took the advance party of the battalion by train and vehicle to Asmara.

Mike was one of those officers who exuded charm and was without doubt the most popular young officer in the battalion. The young ladies of Khartoum loved him and he managed to keep three of them in a state of complete adoration while being friends with each other. They, along with the one that I was friendly with, came along to Khartoum railway station to see us off. Despite the jokes and the smiles it was a sad occasion because an extremely happy period was coming to an end. We promised each other, in the case of Mike - all three of them, that we would write and see each other again. The green flag was waved, steam gushed from the engine and the train started to move. It was then that I cupped my girl friend's face in my hands and gave her a farewell kiss. She stood on the platform, with the others, waving good bye as we gathered speed and headed north along the Blue Nile. I never saw her again, but cursed my luck six years later when I noticed her name in the register of the New Stanley Hotel in Nairobi. Unfortunately she had left the day before.

Meanwhile the adjutant, in a rare misappreciation of time, had arrived on the platform just in time to see me kiss my girl friend. I heard that his legs left the ground as he vented his fury at seeing me 'behaving in a manner unbecoming an officer'. It was obvious that the real reason for his anger was his failure to get to the station on time. In an ugly mood he returned to his vehicle, drove back to barracks and summoned all the young officers to his office. When they were all assembled he told them about the lascivious behaviour he just witnessed and warned them that if there was any more of it the person concerned would not see the light of day for three months.

A week or so after we arrived in Asmara we were joined by the motor transport officer who brought some trucks up from Khartoum. He could hardly wait to get out of his vehicle to tell me about the adjutant's fury. I knew this particular 'seagull' well enough to know that the passage of time would not mellow his attitude, and I was therefore prepared for the rocket I received three weeks later when he arrived in Asmara. The other subalterns were very pleased to have a free week from doing orderly officer duties when they arrived in that pleasant city 8,000 feet up on the Hamasien plateau above the Red Sea.

Bandits, known as shifta, abounded in Eritrea and there was nothing that they liked better than shooting up Italian vehicles. The battalion was responsible for organising convoys and supplying armed escorts to travel with them. Most of these convoy duties lost their appeal after the soldiers had travelled the route a few times, but one route was always popular and that was the Littorina trip to Massawa on the Red Sea coast about 80 miles from Asmara.

Italians excelled in the construction of mountain railways, and this one in the Red Sea hills was certainly a fine example of their skill. The subaltern whose duty it was to control the Asmara - Massawa convoys would supervise the despatch of the road convoy and then the steam train convoy. When these were on their way he would embark in the Littorina diesel train and 'roller coast' down to Massawa where he would relax for two days in the Ciao Hotel. The Ciao Hotel, as far as I know, never earned a mention in the Good Food book of Africa, but the beds were comfortable, the fans worked and, best of all, there was a swimming pool which contained fresh water, not the salty stuff that made swimming in the Red Sea distasteful. The following morning the same routine of seeing the convoys off on the return trip to Asmara would take place. After a final swim in the pool and a drink in the bar, the officer would board the afternoon Littorina and climb back up the mountains to Asmara.

Rifle company subalterns were the ones who usually did these duties while I, as signals officer, rarely had the opportunity to be involved. Either there was a shortage of subalterns, or perhaps the adjutant considered that I needed some fresh air, because one day I found I was detailed to be the convoy/escort commander on the Asmara - Massawa run. I went through the whole routine and had a thoroughly enjoyable two days in Massawa. I arrived back in Asmara feeling quite refreshed and after I had put my kit in my room I went along to the signals office to see if there was anything which needed my attention. 'Duke' Dyer, my signals sergeant was there and he told me the only problem had been the signals despatch service which had run late for two days. This was the 'mail run' for which my organisation was responsible, and it seemed that those infernal motor cycles had broken down again. As I was walking back to the mess I saw through the open door of the orderly room the adjutant sitting at his desk. He called out to me and asked me how I had enjoyed myself. I replied in effusive terms and told him that I would be delighted to do that job again any time he liked. I mentioned that I had been to the signals office and I was aware that the 'mail' had been late on the two days I had been away. 'Yes', said seagull, 'it was most annoying.' We walked out to the verandah of battalion headquarters and he said, 'Stand properly at ease.' Thinking that a senior officer was about to appear I did what I was told, expecting to be called up for the salute. The next command was, 'Subaltern right turn, quick march.' Upon his further directions I found myself marking time in front of the second in command, who was sitting at his desk. 'I have a complaint to make against

61

the signals officer, Sir', said the adjutant. 'Twice in the last two days the signals despatch service has been late.' The 2 I/C narrowed his lids and said, 'What have you got to say?' I could hardly believe what had happened and I tried to explain to him that I had been 80 miles away for the last two days and I could not possibly be held to blame for the inadequacy of the battalion mail service. The florid cheeks of the second in command became redder than usual. 'Not to blame!', he thundered, 'don't try and shovel off your responsibilities just because you were not here, I won't have it. Now listen to me young man,' he went on, 'you make sure that the mail service runs properly whether you are here or not. You will be in serious trouble if it happens again.' With that stern rebuke I was ordered to 'dismiss'. I did not collect any extra orderly officer duties for that incident. Instead, an hour later in the officers' mess, seagull, accompanied by his wife, asked me to have supper with them the following night. I learned a valuable lesson that day which I have always remembered - the 'buck' stops with the officer in charge. It just goes to show that you do not always have to be punished to be taught a lesson.

In April 1951 I completed my two and a half year tour of duty with The South Wales Borderers and travelled further south in Africa to join the 3rd (Kenya) Battalion The King's African Rifles. The battalion was stationed in Nanyuki where, in common with the island of Waigeo in the Pacific Ocean, Padang in Sumatra and Quito in Ecuador one could, in a local hotel, order one's drink in the northern hemisphere and drink it in the southern, or vice versa. The Equator ran through the middle of the bar in the Silverbeck Hotel and the proprietor would impress this fact upon new arrivals. He certainly made a good job of convincing me, but lost credibility a few years later when he reorganised his bars and moved the counter with the brass line, marked N and S a few yards to the left and further north.

The Silverbeck was one of three good hotels in Nanyuki and within my first week there I had made friends with some local settlers. 'What about joining our party for a night at Cloud Cottage next Friday?' said one of my new acquaintances. He was one of the early pioneers of what is now a highly organised outfit based at Mount Kenya Safari Club (then known as the Mawingo Hotel). He said that he would be most grateful if I would help him look after some white kneed new arrivals who would be spending the night watching game in a tree house in the forest below Mount Kenya. The following Friday was Empire Day - a national holiday, so I accepted the offer.

True to his word, he came round to the officers' mess in his 'pick-up' truck at the appointed time and took me to Mawingo Hotel for lunch and to meet the rest of the party. At about three o'clock we set off in two vehicles. We drove about two miles into the forest where we left the vehicles and walked the last half mile to Cloud Cottage. Before we started the march our leader briefed the half dozen or so fee paying members of the group about the abundance of game in the area. He told them that within the next eighteen hours they would certainly see elephant, rhinoceros and buffalo and, more than likely, lots of smaller game as well. 'Of all these animals, the buffalo is the most dangerous and that is why we we have good footholds in the trees from here to Cloud Cottage,' he said. He pointed to the first of these trees which had hefty wooden supports set in its trunk from ground level to twenty feet up in its branches. Suitably impressed and feeling they were getting their money's worth, the tourists moved from tree to tree until we arrived at Cloud Cottage. As a boy, I had an ambition to build myself a 'den' in the trees, but it had never progressed further than having a few shaky planks placed perilously in the fork of an ash tree in the garden. Cloud Cottage fulfilled all my dreams. It was a sturdy log cabin, with a verandah built thirty feet up in a forest giant complete with all the conveniences for an overnight stay.

African servants had gone ahead and were already getting 'steam up'. They greeted us with tea and sandwiches when we had climbed up the ladder which they had let down through a hole in the verandah. Our leader pointed out the salt lick in the open ground to our front, and explained that it was there that the animals would come after dark. We had a few hours to spare before last light so, after we had stowed our kit, the leader and I went to have a closer look at the salt lick. I was at the time a new boy in the art of reading the tracks of big game, but it was not hard to recognise the spoor of buffalo, rhino and elephant when they were pointed out to me in the mud around the salt lick.

Mount Kenya forest is as impenetrable as the jungle of Malaya and those animals that favour the dark regions, in particular the black rhino, have their own runs through the thick tangle of undergrowth. I was being shown one of these, which resembled a smaller version of the London underground system, when one of the Africans gave a shout to warn us that a rhino and its calf were coming down the tunnel. A quick sprint across no-man's-land to the safety of the ladder saved us from what could have been a nasty confrontation.

Nothing much happened before 8pm, and then we were treated to an unforgettable spectacle of African wild life. All the large animals were there and an almost continuous procession of elephants passed below us. A high powered lamp illuminated the area but the animals, if anything, seemed to appreciate the assistance we gave them to lick their delicious salt. Later on in the evening a full moon broke through the clouds above Mount Kenya and we sat well into the night watching animals and listening to cicadas and bull frogs.

At first light the following morning servants were getting breakfast ready and cleaning the place before we started the return journey to the forest edge. There had been rain during the night and the air was fresh: eggs and bacon had never tasted so good. Just in case the tourists had forgotten our leader's words of caution he reminded them of the procedure to be adopted if an angry buffalo happened to be about, and then we started off.

There was no sign of the vehicles when we arrived at the place where we had left them, so we continued to walk. At last we found them - stuck in mud from the deluge during the night. Even with the assistance of the tourists it was difficult to extricate them. At last it was done and we all climbed aboard for the journey back to The Mawingo Hotel.

When we had off-loaded the tourists the leader took me back to my bungalow in the officers' mess compound. After thanking him for a splendid time I went indoors for a shower before getting dressed for a working half day. I knew that I was a little late for morning parade, but it was a Saturday and there was not much going on.

I was putting on my puttees when the orderly officer stuck his head around the door and said, 'Buck up, there's a good chap, the adjutant wants to see you.' If someone had said that to me in my last unit I would have feared the worst, but on this occasion the impending storm did not reveal itself until I arrived at the adjutant's office and knocked on his door. 'You have been absent without leave. I want an explanation,' he said. At first I thought he meant that I was late for morning parade and I tried to explain to him that I had been stuck in the mud above Mawingo Hotel. 'What were you doing up there?' he snorted, as if he thought I had been visiting a brothel. I told him that I had been doing nothing more illicit than watching big game licking salt, and furthermore, on a public holiday - Empire Day.

The adjutant had a book on his desk. He opened it, inspected its pages and said, 'I do not see any application by you to go into the forest for an overnight stay.' This was another of those occasions when I just stood still and said nothing; rather like the business of the second in command and the sergeants' mess clock. 'Seven extra orderly officer duties and obey the rules in future,' said this new breed of seagull.

Eighteen months after joining the 3rd Battalion The King's African Rifles I was appointed adjutant, but only after the incumbent had been murdered by one of our African soldiers when we were serving in Malaya. If ever there was a case of stepping into a dead man's shoes, this was it.

From the day I became adjutant I was determined not to become a tyrant. It was my fond and pious belief that I was the pathfinder of a new and enlightened breed of SEAGULL until only recently, when I attended a comrades dinner. One of my hosts for the evening was a retired non-commissioned officer who chatted with me about old times. He seemed to know me well, but as hard as I tried I could not remember anything about him. 'Which company were you with?', I said. A look of astonishment came over his face as he replied, 'Why yours of course, 'HQ' Company of The Borderers'. He went on to say, 'Surely you remember the day when you came around the lines on inspection and put me on a charge for having a dirty bed space. I'll never forget that day for as long as I live', he said. 'We were more frightened of you than the adjutant'. This shattering exposure of my psyche has shown me how I must appear to others. Thank goodness I do not have much authority over people nowadays, but I treat the cat and the dog well - at least, I think I do.

CHAPTER ELEVEN

On a Wing and a Prayer

It was the pigeon loft under which I lived for a week in a deserted Italian house in Asmara in Eritrea in 1950 that gave me the idea of using an alternative means of communication to my wireless sets.

As signals officer of my unit I was always being chased by the commanding officer for the shortcomings of the radios. There was very little that I could do about it. I did not really understand how they worked and my efforts to repair them when they went wrong usually made them worse.

We had been garrisoning a scruffy little village on the outskirts of Asmara for a week after a Muslim fanatic had thrown a bomb into a Coptic Christian funeral procession. The effect was like putting a thunderflash into a wasps' nest and the battalion had been hard pressed to find enough men to keep the two communities from slaughtering each other.

When we eventually moved back to barracks I thought about the pigeons in the loft of the house we had used and I spoke to my signals sergeant about catching some of the birds and training them as message carriers. He was interested in the idea and, as we had reached rock bottom in communications efficiency, he thought we should give it a try. When we decided to go ahead with the project there was no shortage of helpers from the signals platoon. Within a few days a loft of generous proportions was constructed half way up a water tower behind the signals stores.

When everything was ready a few of us went back one evening to the deserted house armed with a pair of crook-sticks (for lifting telephone cables over trees etc.), a mosquito net, a ladder and a wicker basket. We lifted the mosquito net over the loft with the

 aid of the crook-sticks and then I climbed up the ladder inside the net. I gently explored the loft with my hand until I found a bird. As soon as I closed my fingers around it there was pandemonium and I was quite unprepared for the rush to escape. Pigeons can work up a fair head of steam in a small space and I was pounded on all sides by birds whose

only thought was to get away from me and the confines of the mosquito net. More for self protection than trying to catch pigeons, I found that my hands were full all the time. All that I had to do was pass them down to a soldier beneath who put them straight into the basket. Within a very short time we had as many birds as we wanted, had loaded them into a jeep and were heading back to camp. We put them directly into the loft where an ample supply of food was available to make them feel at home.

I had managed to get an old Army pamphlet on pigeon management and from it I learnt that new birds must be kept in the loft for seven days and fed every day just before dusk. On the eighth day the birds should be let out just before their feeding time, so that they could have some exercise and then return for their food. Thereafter they would stay quite happily in the loft and would return from considerable distances.

For the next seven days the 15 or so pigeons ate a considerable amount of food and some of the more mature birds put on so much weight that I wondered if the exit from the loft was going to be large enough to let them out. On the evening of the eighth day the entire signals platoon turned out to see what would happen. I climbed up the ladder on the water tower, opened the door of the loft and stood back. There was a pause before the first bird came forward to have a look around. He then spread his wings and flew up into the evening sky. This was the signal for the others to take off as well.

We never saw them again.

Not all was lost. When I looked inside the loft I could see a few birds huddled together in a corner. I left the door open and a few minutes later watched them vainly trying to flap their wings. They were too young to fly, so they went back inside and ate the food I had put down for them. After a few weeks passed they plucked up courage to jump off the water tower and it was a delight to watch them as they exercised in their new found freedom.

For the first couple of days they were content to stay near the loft and then they became adventurous and went off to explore one of the fine legacies which the Italians had left to their former colony - the aerial ropeway. This engineering marvel, which ran near the camp perimeter, had been designed to carry coal in large buckets from the seaport of Massawa up and over the large

67

spectacular mountain ranges to Asmara, eighty miles away and eight thousand feet above sea level. It had not been used commercially for a long time, but once a week a button was pressed and the whole one hundred and sixty miles of ropeway creaked into action and ran for about half an hour. My pigeons used to sit on the wire and because it was so well oiled they could always be recognised by their little black backsides.

The birds became fairly tame as they were fed on the sort of food not readily available to less priveleged birds in that part of Africa. The cook sergeant kept me well supplied with bread, dried peas and lentils and upon this diet they soon developed into fine plump birds.

When I considered that they were old enough to do some serious work I took them for flights in multiples of half mile distances. Before long they were finding their way back to camp from twenty miles away.

The commanding officer who up till now had had doubts about my signalling skills, started to show an interest in this new activity. I explained

Tell that bird to stand to attention when I speak to it!

the reason for the large packing case half way up the water tower and the system of string and pulley that ran from a lever in the signals office to a spring loaded door on the front of the loft. The routine went like this - 1. Pigeon lands on platform in front of closed door. 2. Platform depressed and rings a bell in the signals office. 3. Signals clerk pulls lever and opens door of loft. 4. Pigeon hops inside. 5. Signals clerk relaxes lever and closes door. 6. Signals clerk climbs ladder, catches pigeon and recovers message. It was all very impressive and the CO was pleased with what promised to be a new era in our communications system. From the look on his face I believe he had a vision of pigeons winging their way around the peaks of the Eritrean mountains on a sort of aerial milk run.

This fantasy could never get off the ground for two good reasons. Firstly, pigeons will only fly in one direction; you have to take them to a distant point and then they will fly

back home. Secondly, hawks. Eritrea abounds with all manner of birds of prey whose favourite food is pigeon. The chances of a pigeon travelling on His Majesty's service over the sort of terrain found near Asmara without being seen by a hungry carnivore were fairly slim, and in the early days of my pigeon post I lost a few birds. A grave impediment to their mobility was the message, in a plastic bag, strapped around one leg with an elastic band. When attacked by a hawk the poor bird must have felt like a Spitfire with its wheels down trying to take evasive action from a Messerschmitt.

There was also the problem of transporting the birds. They never took kindly to being pushed into cardboard boxes and being bounced around on the back of a mule or on the back seat of a jeep. I suspect that some of my signallers felt sorry for them and on occasions would release the pigeons prematurely.

One day the CO told me that he and the brigadier were going to visit one of our detachments, about forty miles away, and this would be a good opportunity for the brigadier to see the pigeon post in action. My most trustworthy bird was a snowy white female, (marred only by a black ring on her bottom). She was placed in one of the specially prepared cardboard boxes and handed over to the intelligence sergeant who was detailed to accompany the party.

When they arrived at the detachment, the intelligence sergeant set about preparing a message stating they had arrived and would be starting the return trip in about one and a half hours time. The CO casually told the brigadier about the contents of the cardboard box and the old boy was fascinated as he watched the procedure with the plastic bag and the elastic band. 'How remarkable!' he exclaimed. 'I have not seen this done since I was a subaltern just after the Great War. Does it work?' 'Oh yes, Sir,' replied the sergeant, 'she'll be back in Asmara in about 20 minutes.' He then released the bird.

The pigeon flew to about one hundred feet and made a number

of large circular passes over the camp. 'Just getting her bearings,' said the sergeant, 'she'll be off the next time.' He was right, she did go off - but in the opposite direction to home base. 'Humphh,' said the brigadier, 'she will end up in Addis Ababa if she takes that route.' With a motion to the CO that he wanted to start work on more serious matters, he stomped off.

About twenty minutes later as the brigadier, the detachment commander, the commanding officer and the intelligence sergeant were striding around the perimeter of the camp a solitary white bird flew in from the south and settled on a thorn tree next to the cook house. 'Isn't that your pigeon?' said the brigadier. He was correct in his assumption unless, by a remarkable coincidence, there was another pigeon in Africa with a plastic bag tied around its leg. 'Uh - yes, Sir, I believe it is,' said the CO, who was now becoming somewhat embarrased by my pigeon and who wished that it would fly away in any direction. The brigadier then took over. Stooping down, he picked up a handful of gravel and hurled it at the bird. Pigeons are sensitive creatures and they value their long association with man. This unfriendly act by a  senior officer who should have known better could have destroyed the trust I had carefully built up over the last few months. As the brigadier was a good shot and was bending down to collect another handful of gravel, the bird did not wait for another salvo and flew off once again in the direction of Addis Ababa.

The inspection of the detachment came to an end during the late afternoon and the party started their return trip to Asmara. Meanwhile I was waiting outside the signals office scanning the sky for the sight of my pigeon. I realised that something must have gone wrong because, for once, our radio communications were working reasonably well. I had been given a running commentary by one of the signallers who had been watching the antics of the brigadier and the reluctant pigeon. I had also been given the time they left the outpost and I knew, within half an hour or so, when they would arrive in camp. I also had a pretty good idea what the CO would say to me if I was not in possession of the pigeon post message.

From where I was in my observation post I could see the main gate and my heart sank as I saw the CO's jeep approaching. The provost sergeant and a few regimental policemen tumbled out of the guard room and saluted as the jeep passed them and headed in the direction of the officers' mess. 'Well, that's it,' I thought, 'it's only a matter of time before my pigeons get the order of the stock pot.' With this glum thought in mind I decided to slink off to my quarters and bury my head. But just then a flash of white appeared over the roof of the signals office and as I looked up I saw my beautiful white bird banking in fast flight around the water tower. The signals clerk was alerted by my shouts of joy and a few seconds later we heard the bell ring as the pigeon landed on the platform. It was all working like magic. The ringing stopped as the clerk pulled the lever and the bird went inside the loft. The distant door was closed as I sprinted across to the water tower and climbed the ladder two rungs at a time. I opened the door carefully and gently removed the plastic bag from the pigeon's leg. I gave her a handful of corn and then quickly returned to the ground. I dashed into the signals office to get a date/time stamp on the message and to log it into the book.

I felt that I could face the commanding officer and the brigadier with confidence and I made my way to the officers' mess. It turned out better than I hoped, for on my way to the mess I met the CO and the brigadier on their way to see me. The CO was looking sick as he had had enough of me, my pigeons and the brigadier. 'Did your bird turn up?' asked the brigadier. My answer was to hold up the small piece of paper. He chuckled, slapped me on the back and told me how much he appreciated initiative. I glanced across to the commanding officer who was staring at the piece of paper in disbelief. Eventually, but only after he had submitted the piece of paper to intense scrutiny, a grin spread over his face as he handed it back to me.

From that moment, and for some considerable time onwards, I held the position of 'most favoured subaltern'. It seemed that I could do no wrong and, to add coals to an already healthy fire, the brigadier asked me to address the joint operations planning committee at his headquarters on the subject of 'communications in a hostile environment.'

All this happened over forty years ago but I still remember with pleasure my days as a regimental signals officer and the pigeons which brought such fun to our communications system.

When I retired from the Army in 1980 I built a dovecote and erected it in the garden. The half dozen or so snowy white pigeons that lived in it brought a special tranquility to our household. My wife, who knows the story about my pigeon post, understood why I was so fond of them.

CHAPTER TWELVE

Dits and Dahs

I have experienced few complete failures in my life, but one of them was trying to teach national servicemen of The South Wales Borderers how to use Morse code.

The signals training pamphlet stated that messages transmitted on carrier wave, using Morse code, would travel further than normal voice communication. Certain wireless sets we used had this facility, but even though my signal sergeant and I spent hours trying to train our signallers to transmit messages with a key in a series of dots and dashes, we never achieved any real success.

At the end of my three year tour of duty with The South Wales Borderers I joined the 3rd Battalion The King's African Rifles in Kenya. When I met my new commanding officer he was interested to hear I had been the signals officers of my previous unit. He was short of an officer to fill that specialist appointment and, as we were under orders for active service in Malaya, I dropped into his lap like a ripe plum. Warrant Officer Platoon Commander Kathuka, of the Kamba tribe, had been doing the job for the last 12 months and he was summoned to the CO's office to meet his new boss. We got on well from the start.

When Kathuka and I walked across the playing fields towards the signals lines I was able to learn something about him. He had been with the KAR since the end of the war, he spoke very good English and was, by African standards, well educated. He had the natural dignity of a member of his tribe and he was proud to be a warrant officer in The King's African Rifles. He was also proud to have commanded the signals platoon for 12 months and, if the truth be known, he must have been somewhat disappointed about handing over to me - a 'new boy' as far as the KAR was concerned, who couldn't speak a word of Kiswahili.

When we were about 200 yards away from the huts where the signals cadre was receiving instruction I could hear a lot of noise. Kathuka opened the door and I thought some sort of black magic ritual was taking place. 'What on earth is going on?' I asked. 'We do this first thing every morning,' replied Kathuka, 'Morse code and PT, Sir.' He went on to explain that the first 40 minute period of the day was a mixture of learning the Morse alphabet and some strenuous physical training.

The askaris were coming to the end of one bout and were bathed in perspiration. They had a few minutes rest before the instructor rapped the table with his stick and said, 'Watu wote tayeri?' (is everyone ready?) 'Tayeri, Effendi,' (Ready, Sir,) was the response. 'Sekia!' (listen!) said the instructor, with his stick raised like a choirmaster. 'ABLE', (the first letter in the old phonetic alphabet) said the instructor. Back came the answer from the askaris - 'DIT DAH' (the Morse symbol). 'BAKER' was delivered from the front, 'DAH DIT DIT DIT', came the chant, with askaris already prancing on the spot in time with the dits and dahs. CHARLIE, DOG, EASY and FOX were signals for askaris to mount chairs and tables or to girate on the floor. African rhythm is infectious and before long I found myself caught in the sensation of movement and sound. Not all the letters of the alphabet followed each other in sequence. The instructor produced, either by luck or sense of rhythm, a series of letters which continually altered the flow and tempo of the chant.

Everyone thoroughly enjoyed themselves and what impressed me most of all was that these askaris, after only four weeks training could read and send 15 words a minute. This may not seem much to a layman, but I can assure you it is more than adequate for a regimental signaller.

CHAPTER THIRTEEN

Shauri Ya Mungu
(It's God's Will)

There used to be a certain type of British officer who, despite any bother caused by the natives, would make the early morning flight of sand grouse his first priority of the day.

My commanding officer for most of the three years I spent with the 3rd (Kenya) battalion of The King's African Rifles from 1951 to 1954 was such a person. We were to see action together in the jungles of Malaya during the communist uprising, and in the forests of Kenya during the Mau Mau campaign. Being his signals officer, and later his adjutant, I was always close to him wherever he went.

When I joined the battalion, the colonel was in his element. Bird life abounded on the slopes of Mount Kenya and everything from a guinea fowl to an elephant could be found further afield in the Northern Frontier district. One week-end shooting safari with the colonel would provide enough feathered and hoofed meat to stock up most of the larders in the Nanyuki area.

Six months after arriving in Kenya, for what I expected to be a leisurely three year tour of duty in a pleasant part of Africa, I found myself taking the advance party of the battalion to Malaya. We were the path finders for the remainder of the battalion who arrived about three months later. By that time we had completed the course at the Jungle Warfare School at Kota Tinggi in South Johore and had become adept at moving about in the hostile green environment which makes up most of Malaya.

Our first operational area was in the Triang district of central Pahang. There was a road of sorts that ran north and south of our company positions, but it was the railway which provided us with the easiest means of getting about.

Bandits abounded in the Triang area, and so did jungle fowl and wild pig. It wasn't the CO's job to go about shooting bandits, there were plenty of askaris to do that, so as soon as he had made sure that the operational side of things was tied up, he unpacked his shot gun and set about preparing for his favourite sport. I used to go with him sometimes to shoot wild pig or whatever the Indian, Chinese or Malay beaters would drive towards us. On one such occasion I found myself standing in an overgrown area of rubber, but with a reasonable view for about 75 yards ahead of me, when I heard the far distant yelps of the beaters' dogs hot on the scent of something. As I stood there wondering if I was going to be the lucky one, I looked about me to see if I had any support. There was no sign of anyone and I began to think about that tiger that had taken a goat from a kampong not four miles away only a few days ago. I did not have long to think about it as a large male pig, pursued by a pack of mongrels, headed straight for me. A Malayan wild pig is a formidable animal. There is none of the farmyard porker about this beast, he is all bone and gristle with two very sharp curved tusks which can do a lot of damage. I remember raising my rifle and taking a bead on the animal's head as it shortened the distance between us. I waited until it was only a few yards away, and then I fired. It was a good shot and the boar never knew what hit him. It dropped dead at my feet.

There was a shortage of game about that day and it turned out that I was the only one of the party to kill anything. We left the beaters to arrange for the animal to be carried back to our host's bungalow while we went on ahead to have lunch. Despite the fact that he had not had a kill, the colonel was delighted with my success and congratulated me warmly on my marksmanship. Our host's curry, and the cold Tiger beer with which we washed it down, set the seal on a very pleasant day and we were asked if we would like to take part in another shoot the following Sunday. 'Splendid idea', said the colonel, 'bandits and such-like permitting'.

Our armed escort of half a dozen askaris had been looked after in the servants' quarters, and when they could see we were ready to depart they took up their positions with the jeep and ferret scout car. Just as we were about to leave, Jack Watson, who had laid on the shoot and lunch, said, 'Oh, by the way Bob, what part of the pig, would you like?'. I was not too sure about the anatomy of the pig, and not wishing to deprive the beaters and their families of a good meal, I replied, 'I'll take the head if that's alright'. I must have had some idea about preserving the thing as a trophy but later on that day, when the head was delivered to battalion headquarters, I realised that such a plan would not be feasible without the help of a taxidermist. The boar's head then became a problem and it looked as if there were two choices open. We could eat it or we would have to dig a hole and bury it.

Whatever I decided had to be done quickly, so I called for the African cook from the officers' mess.

Corporal Macheru was an unsophisticated fellow who looked upon food as a substance which made the body function properly. Any process other than boiling meat or burning it in the embers of a fire was, he considered, a frivolous waste of time. He had been in The King's African Rifles for ten years though, and he was quite used to the strange culinary practices of British officers. He listened to my instructions about how I wanted the boar's head prepared for the evening meal the following day. I completed my orders by telling him to put the head in a galvanised bath of salt water to keep it fresh.

On the Monday morning Corporal Macheru, having told the quartermaster's ration storeman he did not require any meat that day, set about the practicalities of roasting the boar's head. It soon became obvious to him that unless extensive modifications were made to his oven there would be no possibility of getting it inside. He told me that if I was still intent upon eating the head, we would have to think of some other way of cooking it. I began to wish I had asked for a leg or a shoulder, but the boar was large everywhere. Even so, we could have cut some slices off the other joints, but with the head - it was all or nothing. When he told me he had burned our boats as far as any more meat from the cookhouse was concerned I realised we had a problem. 'Well, what do you suggest, Corporal Macheru?' I said. The cook rubbed his big black nose and said he might be able to do something with a Soyer stove. I nodded acceptance to his idea and told him to make sure the finished product not only tasted good, but looked good.

A few words of explanation are required at this stage about the Soyer stove. It was invented by a Frenchman named Soyer at the time of the Crimean War. The French have always given a high priority to cuisine, even in times of war, and this utensil was geared to the requirements of the French army in the terrible winter of 1854-55. While their British brothers in arms were attempting to brew up tea and soup in their billy cans the 'frogs' were living in comparative luxury, thanks to Monsieur Soyer and his general purpose stove. The advantage of the Soyer stove was its ability to operate in any sort of weather. The fire basket was integral to the machine, so the kindling wood did not get wet and the large chimney ensured good all round circulation of heat. They were easily transportable and, if the truth be known, they were most probably the greatest single factor in gaining victory over the Russians in 1857.

Corporal Macheru received the cook sergeant's permission to borrow one of the stoves and when he set it up outside his own kitchen he found that just like Cinderella's slipper the boar's head, wrapped in a couple of towels, fitted perfectly.

Towards evening I went to see Corporal Macheru to find how he was getting along with the preparation of the boar's head. The cooking process had come to an end and he had returned it to the galvanised bath, I was unable to see it as it was still wrapped in towels and covered in ice which he had extracted from all of the six paraffin operated refrigerators in the camp. Corporal Macheru, with a big grin, assured me that all was well.

The Indian station master at Triang was not on speaking terms with us as we had requisitioned his ticket office and waiting room for the officers' mess. Battalion headquarter's officers lived in a variety of tents and bashas and it was our custom to assemble in the mess before dinner, which was usually served at 8pm. I had been detained in the signals office deciphering a secret message, and this made me rather late. I joined the others in the ante room (late ticket office) in time to have one drink only before we went into the dining room.

The colonel was a stickler for mess etiquette and, even in those dark days of the Emergency, he insisted upon officers being dressed properly in the evening. This meant wearing long trousers with shirt and tie and sleeves rolled down. Mess staff wore white drill with red 'stove pipe' hats with black tassels.

Sergeant Onyala, the mess sergeant, reported to the commanding officer, in Kiswahili, that dinner was ready, - 'Chakula tayeri effendi.' The colonel led the way into the dining room (late waiting room) and as he moved through the doorway, I saw him leap sideways with a cry of, 'What the devil is that?' I thought he had seen a cobra, but when I pushed my way forward I became aware of the reason for his convulsion. I had an advantage over the other officers because I knew that the gruesome thing on the serving table was a boar's head. It was hardly recognisable as the dangerous end of the animal I had shot the day before, but its tusks provided a clue to its identity. One of the ears was cocked up while the other hung low like that of a spaniel. A solitary eye gazed with an opaque stare across the room, unbalanced by the empty socket of its twin on the other side of the skull. The snout had parted company from the upper jaw and was elevated at an acute angle like a blunt nosed missile prepared for take off. To complete the incongruous spectacle Corporal Macheru, with a  rare flash of African aestheticism, had stuffed a paw-paw between its yellow teeth.

After the initial shock of such a revolting sight, the officers saw the funny side of Corporal Macheru's effort and they bent themselves double with mirth. Their humour was short lived however when the colonel asked me what we were having for supper. The glum look on my face and my attempt to place a slice of cheek on my plate brought home to them the truth of the situation. When it was found that there was no meat available, I was subjected to some rather nasty remarks. Triang was not the sort of place where one could go out for a meal, so after a fruitless search of all the cupboards in the kitchen, the quartermaster sent for a box of compo rations.

I was pretty unpopular with everyone from the CO downwards and I expected to get the sack, but somehow I weathered the crisis; most probably because nobody else wanted the job of food member.

I have steered well clear of boars' heads since that awful experience in Malaya forty years ago, but on many occasions I have admired the way the experts make such a good job of the glazed pig's head centre piece on the buffet table at officers' and sergeants' mess parties. I can't remember anyone ever asking for a slice though!

The railway line which ran north and south through our operational area provided the best means for contact with our rifle companies. We had our own locomotive and a couple of 'flats' filled with stones which were pushed in front of the engine in case bandits decided to blow up the line. The coaches were 2 x four wheeled bogies covered in armour plate which afforded complete protection to the occupants from rifle and machine gun fire. When the commanding officer of the outgoing unit left Triang I remember him saying to our colonel, 'Best of luck and remember, don't eat kippers before you travel on the armoured train.' I should have heeded that piece of advice because a few weeks later I accompanied the colonel on one of his visits. The daytime temperature in Malaya is always in the top '90's,' but inside the armoured train the heat was unbearable. Once it got going the small amount of draught which came through the vents eased the position somewhat, but then bounce and vibration took over. The springs of the bogey were not designed to put up with

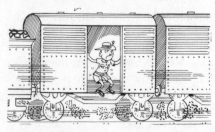

the weight of armour plate and once the thing started to go up and down the occupants became captives of a giant trampoline. It was not long before I staggered to the doorway and parted company with my kippers.

We had travelled for about five miles when the train slowed down and stopped. I stuck my head out of the door and asked the Indian engine driver what had gone wrong. He did not speak any Malay but he jabbered back to me in his own language. Musabi, the commanding officer's orderly who could speak some Hindi, told us in Kiswahili, that the driver had seen a large pig go into the lallang (tall grass) beside the railway track, and that he thought the bwana mkubwa (big master) might want to take a pot at it.

'Hold this,' said the colonel as he handed me his M2 carbine and picked up his shot gun. He leaped out of the train and jumped into the lallang. I was able to follow his progress by the nodding heads of grass as he ploughed deeper into the cover in search of the pig. Just ahead of the train was a cutting and I can remember thinking that it would be a perfect place for terrorists to set an ambush. I therefore took up position where I could cover the colonel if we came under fire.

A shot rang out from the direction taken by the CO, followed by another and then I could see the nodding heads of grass getting closer as the colonel retraced his steps. 'Only managed to get a brief look at him,' said the colonel, 'and then he was off like a bat out of hell.' Musabi hauled his master aboard, and then with a nod to the driver, we continued our journey.

A few weeks later one of our patrols attacked a bandit camp and killed most of the occupants. As usual there was a mass of documents, diaries, books and posters to collect and back load to Police headquarters in Mentakab. A few days later, after they had been examined and translated, the Special Branch officer asked me, 'Were you on the armoured train the day the colonel tried to shoot a pig?' I told him I was and then he said, 'Read this'. He handed me the translation of a report written by a communist sentry who had been in position overlooking the Triang - Kemayan railway line. It read, 'On 'such and such' a day I was on duty at post No.4 when I saw the armoured train approaching from the north. It stopped before entering the cutting and a British officer got out and went into the lallang after a pig. He fired about twenty shots and missed with every one.' The Special Branch officer asked me how many shots the colonel had fired, and I replied that there had certainly been no more than two. 'Would you like to give him this translation then,' he asked. 'Not on your life,' I replied, 'do your own dirty work!' The air was blue when the colonel read the report. Astonishment that he had been seen by a bandit sentry was overtaken by anger when he read the bit about 'missing with twenty shots'. The contents of the report became common knowledge within a very short time and some of the senior officers teased the CO about his marksmanship. 'I know that these pigs are pretty thick skinned,' said the second in command, 'but really Colonel, I would have thought you could have hit him in a vital spot with one of them.' 'God dammit, how many more times have I got to tell you, I let fly with both barrels and by the time I had reloaded the beast was about half a mile away.' I just happened to come into the mess and was made to recount every detail of the event, with special emphasis on the number of shots I had heard. For once I held the commanding officer's reputation in the palm of my hand, but he had no need to worry and I put the record straight.

After three months of chasing bandits in the Triang district two rifle companies and a tactical headquarters moved across to

Kuantan on the east coast of Malaya to take part in an operation with 1/10th Gurkhas. I was part of the Tac HQ team and had settled myself in the Government Rest House in Kuantan by the time the CO came to pay his first visit. He spent a few days with us visiting the various people and organisations responsible for administration, law and order. He also took the opportunity to meet some of the local rubber planters in the Club. I had already made the acquaintance of a fellow called Richard Buckingham who made a living from harvesting latex from a certain type of tree that produced the basic ingredient for chewing gum. Every few months he would load the stuff into his boat and take it to Singapore where he would sell it. He obviously did very well as he and his wife lived in one of the largest houses in Kuantan. One of his side lines was trading in exotic birds, and he had a large aviary in his garden which housed a number of brilliantly plumed specimens including a peacock called Charlie.

Soon after arriving in Malaya the colonel told me it was his ambition to capture a rare type of jungle fowl only to be found in central Pahang. If he was fortunate enough to get one he intended to send it to UK by sea and then have it delivered to the Tropical Bird House at London Zoo. This was a pleasant day dream for the colonel but it was not until he met Mr Buckingham in Kuantan that he realised here was a man who could be of great use to him. Over a few stiff whiskies in the Kuantan Club the colonel asked Richard Buckingham if - firstly, he could get him a cock bird of this rare breed, and secondly, if he could transport it to Singapore for onward transmission to London. Richard Buckingham sucked pensively at his meerschaum and blew clouds of blue smoke at the first request, but gave an assurance about taking the bird to Singapore once it was 'in the bag'.

The following day the colonel returned to Triang feeling that his journey had been worthwhile. On the operational side affairs were very satisfactory. A patrol of 1/10th Gurkhas had run into the headquarters of a large bandit organisation and had killed a number of terrorists. The Gurkhas and two companies of our battalion were in hot pursuit, and the chance of further success was good.

A few days after his return from Kuantan, Jack Watson, the planter who had laid on the pig shoot, came to Triang to see the colonel. 'Look what I've got for you old boy,' he said. From the back of his truck he pulled out a large wicker cage and through the bars the colonel could see the bird of his dreams. 'It's yours if you want it,' said Jack, 'give me a bottle of whisky and you can have the cage as well.' 'Done', said the colonel.

The adjutant of 1/10th Gurkhas handed me a signal which read 'Tell Smith to inform Buckingham that Jungle Cock will arrive by road on Monday'. This caused a bit of consternation in the Gurkhas' headquarters as they thought 'Jungle Cock' was the code name for some important visitor.

The quartermaster's convoy of vehicles moved off from Triang at 0700hrs. Aboard a jeep halfway down the line, was Musabi with his master's bird. He had been given strict instructions to safeguard it at all costs and to deliver it to the Buckingham household when he arrived in Kuantan. After travelling for about two hours through the jungle, the convoy commander called a halt and gave the order 'brew up'. Mess tins and burners were produced and within a short time the sweet smell of hexamine (small blocks of solid fuel) spread along the track. Musabi, having slaked his thirst, looked inside the cage and saw the bird cleaning its tail feathers. Thinking that it might also be thirsty, he opened the cage door slightly to insert a can of water. This was just the opportunity the jungle cock had been waiting for and before Musabi could slam the door the bird had made its dash for freedom. With a flurry of feathers and a loud squawk the bird took off and made for the safety of a large tree, It settled on a branch about thirty yards away and thirty feet above the road.

Musabi gazed at the bird and wondered what he could do to re-capture it. He knew that a fate worse than death would befall him if he turned up in Kuantan with an empty cage. The convoy commander blew his whistle, which was the signal for everyone to board their trucks. The second whistle would be the signal to start engines prior to the leader moving off. Musabi ran down the line of vehicles and told the convoy commander what had happened. He was successful in impressing upon him the gravity of the situation and the order to disembark and adopt all round defence was given. The convoy commander accompanied Musabi and saw for himself the miscreant jungle cock in its secure position far above the ground. After listening to some quite useless suggestions for capturing the bird, the commander bent over and picked up a stone about the size of a tennis ball. He took aim and let fly; it was a marvellous shot. It hit the bird on the head and it dropped to the ground like a stone. Musabi rushed to pick up his valuable charge, but with horror saw that the magnificent scarlet comb was missing. The bird was as bald as a coot.

Within a few seconds the bird's eyes opened and, thankful for small mercies, Musabi popped it back into the cage. But where was the missing piece of flesh? The convoy commander, satisfied that he had completed what he had set out to do, blew his whistle again. Musabi then reminded him that it was he who had deprived the colonel's bird of its comb and that he, along with himself, was not going to see much daylight once the bwana mkubwa found out what had happened. Everyone was assembled under the tree to carry out a search for the missing piece of flesh. It was quite hopeless: after another 30 minutes the convoy commander gave the order to move on.

As soon as he arrived in Kuantan, Musabi went along to the Buckingham's house. Mrs Buckingham was in the garden and as soon as she saw the bird in the cage she realised that something awful had happened. As Musabi spoke no English, the interpreting was done by Private Juma, the driver of the truck. She considered the matter for some time and then told Musabi not to worry as everything would be alright by the time the colonel arrived. Musabi must have been under the impression that the memsahib had some way of making the comb grow again as he went off to his tent in the Gurkha lines with peace of mind.

When the colonel arrived in Kuantan a few days later he went to see his bird. He found it sitting on a perch in the aviary in apparent good health, but minus its comb. 'What on earth has happened?' he exclaimed. Mrs Buckingham laid her hand on the colonel's shoulder and said, 'I'm afraid it was all my fault. When your orderly brought the bird I put it in the aviary with Charlie the peacock. There was an awful commotion and Charlie attacked your bird ripping off its comb.' She went on to say,

'Musabi was marvellous. Despite the danger of being badly scratched by Charlie's claws, he rescued the jungle cock but, alas, the comb was torn off. We tried to graft it on again, but it didn't work.' Musabi had been standing alongside his master while Mrs Buckingham was making the explanation. He did not understand what was being said, but when he saw Mrs Buckingham give him a wink he felt that things were going well. He knew he was out of danger when the colonel said, 'Asante sana Musabi, shauri ya Mungu tu,' (Thank you Musabi, it was God's will).

I do not know if the colonel ever knew the real story about his bird. After the disappointment of seeing his jungle cock turn into a skin-head he did not pursue his project. Musabi continued to give faithful service to his beloved master who was devoted to him.

The bird seemed to be quite content without its comb and was released to the wild. It might have had to suffer a loss of status in the pecking order of its flock but that was surely better than spending the rest of its life in a cage in London Zoo.

CHAPTER FOURTEEN

Mau Mau Memories

British officers who served with the 3rd Battalion The King's African Rifles in Malaya in the early '50's were proud to belong to such a fine unit. Not only did we achieve more success in a single period of 18 months than any other infantry battalion but we, like the Gurkhas, were all 'regular'. Other British Army units were on a continuous cycle of national service. This is not to imply that NS men were inferior to regulars but it took a long time to train them and then, when they reached peak efficiency, it was time for them to return to Blighty for demob. All this was to change for us though when in June 1953 we set sail from Singapore on Her Majesty's Transport 'DILWARA' for our home port of Mombasa.

While we were in Malaya the first breath of Harold Macmillan's 'wind of change' began to blow in Kenya. This pleasant and prosperous country, slowly at first and then with increasing fervour, produced a movement of 'freedom fighters' from its Kikuyu community no less courageous and dedicated to their cause than the communists we had been fighting in Malaya.

The Mau Mau emergency was at its height when we arrived at our newly built barracks in Nanyuki, but before we could start operating our askaris had to take leave. They had saved about eight weeks and that, plus a day for every 20 miles marching for those who lived far from the rail or bus routes, meant we were out of action for a considerable time.

I, as the adjutant, was soon back on duty though and I was horrified to read the directives about our role in the emergency. The first thing to happen was a severe pruning of African warrant officers, non commissioned officers and askaris who were earmarked for newly raised KAR battalions where they would provide valuable expertise in fighting terrorists. Others were selected for the KAR Training Centre at Nakuru to instruct in jungle warfare. Then followed the departure of so many of our white officers, warrant officers and NCOs who, in many cases, had extended their service for operations in Malaya. Our once proud battalion was soon diluted to the same level of expertise as other KAR units who were fighting Mau Mau 'freedom fighters'.

I use the term 'freedom fighters' after many years reflection upon the ideals of these brave men. At the time we called them bandits, terrorists and many other uncomplimentary names. On big operations thousands of so called 'loyal' Kikuyu would be transported into an area where they would provide a cordon. Armed with bows and poisoned arrows, with every tenth man carrying a shotgun, they provided an effective back stop. Security forces from the KAR, British infantry units, Kenya Regiment and Police would act as beaters and any Mau Mau caught lying up in banana or maize plantations would be flushed out like pheasants and shot if they did not surrender. We were all conditioned into believing that Mau Mau were sub human. Our soldiers were issued with a book containing horrifying photographs of Mau Mau atrocities. Forty years on my worst memory is the sight of heaps of dead Mau Mau who chose to die rather than break the oath they had taken to bring freedom to their country.

Unlike the 'freedom fighters' of the '60s, '70s and '80s who were equipped with AK 47 automatic rifles and rocket launchers, Mau Mau, except for some who had been able to get hold of stolen weapons from the police or white farmers, made their own weapons. These usually consisted of a piece of African hardwood fashioned into the shape of a rifle upon which sat a piece of metal tube. The chamber was cut to take a .303 round and the firing pin was a nail on a piece of rubber which was pulled backwards and released by the firer. It was an extremely hazardous operation and many Mau Mau were killed when they fired their 'guns'. Nevertheless, they were important status symbols and were used with considerable success to impress the mainly law abiding natives when Mau Mau demanded food and clothing. As always in these campaigns it is the poor villager who suffers most. On one side he has the 'freedom fighter' exhorting him to support the campaign on the pain of death if he refuses, and on the other side, the security forces destroying his crops, burning his house and confiscating his cattle if he doesn't give them information. I have seen the result of such intimidation in Malaya and Kenya. Chinese and Kikuyu are adept with parangs and pangas and they can alter the contours of the human body if the party line is not followed.

Even in 1954 people in Great Britain were only fed information approved by the 'establishment', but a news reporter managed to get hold of a story about a certain infantry battalion commander who offered a cash prize to anyone in his unit who could provide evidence of a Mau Mau 'kill'. This was a turning point in the accountability of security forces, not only to their superior headquarters, but to the public at large. A high powered parliamentary team led by Mr Fenner Brockway came to Kenya to put specific questions about giving cash gratuities for 'kills' to every commanding officer, second in command, adjutant, regimental sergeant major and company commander of every combat unit.

In addition to those people required to answer questions, anyone else could volunteer to give evidence. Nobody from the 3rd Battalion The King's African Rifles opted to do this but as the parliamentary team's terms of reference were far reaching I was mindful of the large wooden barometer which was attached to the side of the fish market in Kuantan, Malaya. Whenever we or any other unit of the security forces in the area made a 'kill', a policeman would take a can of red paint and a brush and make another six inch mark up the pole. This was not in the same category of what Mr Brockway and his team had in mind, but even so I do not think they would have approved of that sort of thing in Kenya.

Christopher Nunn was a fine young national service subaltern who took part in the longest deep jungle patrol the battalion made during its tour in Malaya: when he and his patrol came out after six weeks they were all in poor shape. General Sir Gerald Templer, the High Commissioner, happened to be at Chris's company location when the patrol returned. He suggested to the company commander that the young British officer should have his ulcers attended to and colour put back in his cheeks at Government House, Kuala Lumpur. Within the hour Chris was aboard the helicopter on his way to KL for a two week holiday with General and Lady Templer.

A few weeks after taking up our first operational station in Kenya in 1953, Chris took a patrol into the heartland of Kikuyu country south west of Fort Hall. They based themselves at a police post and it was there just after 'stand down' one evening that a gang of Mau Mau attacked. The ferocity of their assault on a well defended position was unusual, but was most probably due to the effect of hasheesh and an increase in morale due to some high velocity weapons they had managed to obtain. Chris was shot during the initial exchange of fire. Although badly wounded he continued to organise the defence of the police post throughout the night: it was not until the first crimson streaks of dawn appeared that the enemy withdrew. Radio communications in those days were non-existent during the hours of darkness and, as the telephone line had been cut (again), we were unaware of what had happened. I remember the ambulance arriving at battalion headquarters at about 8am. In Malaya Chris would have been evacuated by helicopter, but such luxuries were unknown in Kenya. He was still conscious after an uncomfortable 20 mile journey over atrocious roads, but he died an hour later.

One of my subalterns radioed in one day that he had engaged a Mau Mau gang and was bringing a few bodies and a prisoner back to base. He arrived about two hours later and started to off-load four dead Mau Mau. One other Kikuyu was lying on the floor of the truck and there was much blood about him: I could see he was badly wounded. A couple of askaris got hold of his feet and started to drag him towards the tailboard, but I intervened and told them to leave him alone until a medical orderly arrived. I climbed inside the truck and saw that he had gunshot wounds to both legs, his partially opened shirt revealed a large hole in his stomach from which part of his intestines protruded. His eyes were like those of a wild animal and, as I approached him, he snarled like a leopard. When I spoke to him in Kiswahili and told him he would be well looked after, he levered himself onto his elbows and spat in my face. The medical orderly came with a stretcher and he was taken to the aid post, but he was dead within the hour.

Tommy Thomas and I served together in Eritrea with the 1st Battalion The South Wales Borderers. I had not seen him for three years until the tent flap opened one day and in he walked. 'I'm your new second in command,' he announced. We had a few days together before I set off for Nairobi to be a member of a general court martial trying a British KAR officer accused of torturing Mau Mau suspects. The poor chap had found his six prize polo ponies hamstrung in their stables with bamboo skewers stuck up their backsides and this, said his counsel, made him act irresponsibly. On the second day of the court martial I received a call from battalion headquarters informing me that there had been an unfortunate accident and that Tommy Thomas was badly injured. When I returned to my company a few days later I found out what had happened. It seemed that Tommy had received information about an impending Mau Mau attack on a Kikuyi guard post and had gone off to warn them. Kikuyu guard posts were rather like Saxon villages of the 5th century. The huts were built on the top of mounds of high ground and were made of mud and wattle walls with thatched roofs. A strong wooden fence, laced with sizal fronds and thorn bush, surrounded the huts and a ditch about 15 feet wide and 12 feet deep formed an outer perimeter. Within the pit thousands of 'panjis' (sharpened bamboo stakes) were driven into the ground 12 inches apart.

During daylight hours a drawbridge spanned the ditch, but when the sun dipped behind the Aberdare forest the drawbridge was raised to the vertical position. Tommy had left his vehicle at the bottom of the hill and accompanied by three or four askaris he made his way to the guard post. Operations at night are always tricky affairs, especially when trigger happy natives are likely to fire first and ask questions afterwards. Tommy shouted in English that he wanted the drawbridge lowered so that he could enter. The occupants of the guard post replied in a mixture of Kikikuyu and Kiswahili that he should come back in the morning and that if he didn't clear off he would get some poisoned arrows and buckshot coming his way. Tommy, quite unaware of what they were saying, continued to walk towards the post until he came to the ditch, and fell in.

Tommy was built like a tank and he spread-eagled himself on the panjis at the bottom of the ditch. His horrified escort managed to convince the Kikuyu guards that a 'mzungu' (white officer) had skewered himself and that assistance was required.

It was a hazardous job removing Tommy from the pit. Had the panjis been spaced further apart he would have suffered even more horrible injuries but, like an Indian fakir lying on a bed of nails, the volume of spikes in close proximity to each other saved him from worse injury. Even so, his stomach, chest and legs were punctured in many places and he suffered severely from shock. Tommy was made of stern stuff though and he withstood a journey of 40 miles over corrugated roads to the provincial hospital at Nyeri. He was taken into the theatre for a major operation.

I went to see him as soon as I could. He was by this time looking his old self again. As we were talking he started to grimace and show signs of discomfort. I asked him if I should call a nurse but he shook his head and said that the feeling he was experiencing happened every half hour. Then a look of ecstacy appeared on his face as he let off the longest, loudest fart I have ever heard. The bed clothes, which I thought had been supported on a metal frame, collapsed slowly like a deflating barrage balloon. It came to an end when Tommy asked me to pass him a can of Tusker beer from the cache under his bed. Half an hour later he started to twitch again as the process of expansion recommenced. Even though Tommy had a massive frame he could not cope with these huge inflations and deflations and eventually he blew the stitches which held his insides together. Once more he was placed on the dangerously ill list and hovered on the edge of death for a few months until he was cas-evacd to UK.

I did not see him again until we served together with the 1st Battalion The Welch Regiment in Libya in 1959. I went to the swimming club with him one day and when he stripped I saw for the first time the scars which covered his body. I asked him if he had any problems and if he could eat prunes. He assured me that everything was alright. Sadly, Tommy died in Qatar in 1980.

Soon after Tommy's accident I received a replacement for my long serving and extremely experienced British company sergeant major. The new chap had never served with Africans before and by the look of him had never worn khaki drill before. His bush hat, with an Arabic 'telata' (figure 3) and a crows neck on the upturn, looked very new and required some dust and sweat to give it character. But it's easy to make fun of a new arrival - Africa would soon sort him out. He had already been given a 160 pounder tent and an orderly and I told him to settle in for the rest of the day. 'Go and chat to the askaris,' I said. 'Some of them speak a bit of English, but just say 'Jambo, habari yako?' (Hello, what news?) to the rest.'

About ten minutes later my orderly barged into my tent and said, 'Effendi, bwana sergeant major mpya yeye anguka karibu ya zariba'. (Sir, the new sergeant major has fallen down near the perimeter fence). I hastened after Pte Kipleli and saw the prostrate form of the sergeant major. A few Samburu soldiers were kicking dust over him - water was far too valuable a commodity where they came from, but it seemed to do the trick as his eyes went round like a pair of lemons in a fruit machine. 'Good heavens sergeant major', I said, 'what's happened?' The warrant officer raised himself to the sitting position and eyed the inscrutable Samburu with a look of horror. 'It's them and that cow, Sir,' he gasped. I let him recover and then helped him to a place in the shade under a large fig tree. He could hardly bear to relate the details but I gathered he had seen some askaris doing something with a cow. The cow in question was one that the district officer had given me for the askaris to slaughter for food. It had been part of a herd confiscated from a village whose inhabitants had not been forthcoming with information about Mau Mau. I always gave cows to Somalis to slaughter as they would do it the Islamic way and then everyone would be able to enjoy the meat. Samburu tribesmen come from the northern frontier district of Kenya. When at home they live mainly on a diet of cow or camel milk mixed with blood which they extract from a vein in the neck of the beast. The Samburu in camp that day clustered around and caught every drop of blood they could from the slowly expiring cow. Just as the animal was giving its last breath, the new sergeant major turned up. 'Jambo, habari yako?' he said. 'Jambo, Effendi, habari mzuri.' (Hello, Sir, news is good), and then as if drinking a toast, they raised their mess tins and drank the warm blood. Still as white as a lily in an undertaker's parlour, the sergeant major said, 'I don't think I can get used to this, Sir.' He didn't, and soon found a more suitable home with a British battalion where the rations came up in the company quartermaster sergeant's truck.

The Mau Mau campaign was a messy affair with much loss of life on both sides. The so called 'loyal' Kikuyu lost 1800 killed but figures are not available for those who were killed in acts of tribal retribution later on. The Security Forces suffered 590 killed while the cost to Mau Mau was 12,515 of whom 1,015 were hanged.

It was Jomo Kenyatta, labelled the most evil of all Mau Mau and banished to Lodwar in the Turkhana district of Northern Kenya, who was eventually recognised as the only person who could bring peace and stability to his country. He became the first black President of independent Kenya on 12th December 1963 and was thereafter respected throughout the world for his wisdom and magnanimity. He died as the acknowledged 'grand old man of Africa' in August 1978.

CHAPTER FIFTEEN

A Stranger in Paradise

Pembrokeshire is without doubt one of the most beautiful counties in Wales, but that does not necessarily mean that it is the ideal location for an infantry battalion, especially one like the 1st Battalion The Welch Regiment which took up residence in Llanion Barracks, Pembroke Dock in October 1954.

1/Welch (for short) left UK in 1951 to go to Korea as part of the United Nations force. They covered themselves with glory and earned yet another Battle Honour to carry on their Colours. After a year on active service in the front line they were withdrawn and sent to Hong Kong for a two year tour of duty. Imagine then, seasoned warriors and others who had joined the battalion in Hong Kong, used to the good life in the best overseas posting in the world, arriving at a wind swept railway platform at Pembroke Dock on a cold October night. It certainly did nothing for retaining soldiers who had the option of extending their contract or returning to 'civvy street'.

If they thought that Pembroke Dock rail station looked grim, they had another surprise in store when they arrived in Llanion Barracks. Perched on top of a very steep hill, the barracks was a splendid place for flying kites: the wind came at it from all directions. The barracks were built in the 1840's at a time when 'functional' rather than 'aesthetic' was the key word. Red brick can look quite nice when wisteria and virginia creeper cling to it, but if its only adornments are drain pipes and cast-iron staircases, it does not present a pleasant picture. Barrack rooms were long and rectangular and contained thirty men. A locker and a bed, which carried four blankets and two sheets folded and 'boxed' from before breakfast until after tea, was the soldier's 'bedspace' where he could recharge his batteries and, on Saturday mornings, lay out his kit for the platoon commander's, company commander's or commanding officer's inspection. There was always someone who wanted to check the soles of boots (with the obligatory 13 studs - polished), coils of spare laces and mess tins brightened with 'Bluebell'.

This sort of inspection, with the odd route march thrown in for good measure, was symptomatic of the times. The fact of the matter was that we had no role and very little to do. At times like that people got under each other's feet and it made for poor morale. There was some light at the end of the tunnel though. We were told that in April 1955 (the following year) the four rifle companies of the battalion would be allocated to various training camps around the country. This meant that our soldiers would be responsible for the smooth running of camps where Territorial Army soldiers would be doing their annual fortnight training. My company, of which I was second in command, was detailed to move to the Royal Armoured Corps Ranges and Training Area, Castlemartin; about ten miles away from Pembroke Dock.

I arose quite early on my first full day at Castlemartin camp, had breakfast and then went to see the soldiers who would be forming up for muster parade. As I walked past camp headquarters the adjutant poked his head out of his window and said, 'Hello, I'm Gerald, I don't think we've met. Come inside and meet the commandant, he likes to see everyone on the first day.' Gerald was a stocky officer with thick eyebrows, heavy horn rimmed spectacles and a gruff voice. He wore highly polished ammunition boots under his barathea service dress trousers. It's funny how little things can give a chap away. Army boots, instead of the proper shoes from your regimental tailor, would have never been tolerated in my regiment. After we had looked each other over, Gerald opened the door into the commanding officer's office and introduced me. All I received was a curt nod of his head and a motion from his hand for me to sit down. My company commander, Major Dicky Randell, had also been accosted by the adjutant, so I took a chair next to him. Also present were a number of officers who were responsible for technical aspects of the gunnery range.

'Now listen here,' began the commandant, 'My name is Lieutenant Colonel Harold Witherspoon of The Royal Tank Regiment and my job is to make sure that this place is run efficiently. I have no time for shirkers, dawdlers, nincompoops and drunkards. Do I make myself clear?' There was not much we could say to a question like that, so we all nodded and looked attentive. 'You will be here until the end of September', he went on, 'and I expect you to set high standards and maintain them. Do you understand?'. We all nodded again. 'Right then, you', he said, pointing to an officer who had a black beret on his lap, denoting that he too was a member of The Royal Tank Regiment.

'Why were those empty cases not backloaded to Ordnance?'. The officer responsible for the shell cases mumbled a feeble excuse which did nothing to placate the commandant. 'I'll not have it, do you understand? You make sure that you get those things back on time in future.' The next one to get a 'broadside' was the motor transport officer. 'Why were two of our three tonners without their tool kits this morning?' he spat. The MTO went through the 'goldfish' routine, and said nothing. 'See to it in future,' snapped the colonel. Everyone so far had received a rocket and I began to feel uneasy about this chap who would be my boss for the next six months. Up until then I had not been told what my duties would be, apart from looking after and supervising soldiers.

Suddenly I found myself looking at the end of the commandant's finger as he thrust his arm in my direction. 'Why were your boilers at 100lbs pressure at 6 o'clock this morning?' he rasped. As I had no idea what he was talking about, I thought I had better play for time. 'Good heavens, Sir, 100lbs did you say!? There's something wrong there, I'll make sure the pressure is eased off,' I said. 'No you won't you b--- idiot, you'll make sure that it is at least 120lbs', cried the colonel. I thought that the storm had blown over, but more was to come. 'Tell me, how are you working your sh--s?' he enquired. Once again, I had not the faintest idea what he was talking about. Nobody had told me that among a number of jobs I would have, would be that of messing officer with responsibility for managing a large kitchen and dining hall. 'SH---S' could mean all sorts of things, and I went through a mental selection process. SHEETS - SHAFTS - CHEFS - SHIFTS. 'Did you say SHIFTS, Sir?' I replied, selecting the word that seemed most appropriate, but without having any idea of the context. The effect of what I said to Colonel Harold Witherspoon was as if he had been stung by a hornet. 'How dare you use a word like that to me?' he thundered. 'Any more language like that from you and you will be going back to your regiment with an adverse report.' I murmured an apology and wondered what he thought I had said!

'What was all that about?' said Dicky Randell when we had been dismissed, 'you seem to have succeeded in upsetting him.' 'I've never seen him before', I replied 'and it looks as if I am not going to see much more of him.' Before leaving camp headquarters I asked the adjutant if he could advise me about the business of 'boilers' and 'shifts'. It was then that I became aware of my duty concerning the feeding of the masses. 'The quartermaster does the job during the winter, he will tell you everything you want to know,' said the thoughtful Gerald.

The quartermaster was a mine of information and it puzzled me why the commandant wanted me, an unknown quantity, to take over as messing officer.

A week went by without any trouble, and then the phone rang in my office in the cookhouse, it was the adjutant. 'The commandant would like to have a word with you, can you come across?' 'Anything wrong,' I asked. 'No, he just wants to have chat, I think,' was the reply. I tripped across the sports field and went into the adjutant's office. 'The commandant will see you now,' he said, motioning me to enter. I saluted Colonel Harold and waited for him to offer me a chair. Not a chance. 'Why is your cookhouse in a filthy condition?' he barked. I was struck dumb for a few seconds and then said, 'I'm sorry Sir, I didn't know you had been there this morning.' 'I have not been there this morning,' he replied. 'I don't have to go there to see that the place is filthy.' He leaned back in his chair and let me ponder on his words for a few moments, before he continued: 'Look out of the window and tell me what you can see on the cookhouse.' I did as I was told, but nothing seemed to be wrong with the place. As cookhouses go it was a rather nice one. It did have some moss on the north facing roof, so I said, 'I'll get someone up on the roof and get that moss off, Sir.' 'not MOSS you idiot - SEAGULLS,' he bellowed. I could have kicked myself for not saying 'seagulls', but there were seagulls everywhere in Castlemartin as it was in the middle of one of the largest bird sanctuaries in the country. I still could not see the connection between seagulls and a filthy cookhouse until the colonel said, 'Seagulls are scavengers and they love filth and dirt, that's why they are sitting on the roof of the cookhouse. Now get that place cleaned up and I will be along at 11 o'clock to inspect it.'

No scrum half ever crossed the sports field faster than me as I went back to the cookhouse to make sure that everything was clean and tidy. It was of course, as I had an efficient catering staff who took pride in their work. The cook sergeant heard about the rocket I had received from the commandant and said, 'He caught you with the 'old seagull routine' did he, Sir?' When I nodded, he said, 'That's one of his pets, he's hot on seagulls but leave it to me.' The cook sergeant went into the dining room and saw one of the soldiers from my company who was doing duty as a dining room orderly. He and a few others like him were responsible for cleaning tables and hot plates and generally keeping the place clean. Private Maldwyn Clutterbuck had not endeared himself to the cook sergeant because, even though he had a rich baritone voice, he knew only one song and he sang it all day and every day. 'I'm a Stranger in Paradise' was worse than the water torture practiced by Chinese Triads and he had nearly driven everyone crazy by his non stop rendering of the tune. 'Right, you there, Private Clutterbuck, I've got somewhere better than Paradise for you, follow me.' The cook sergeant led Clutterbuck to the boiler house where there was a huge pile of coke in the yard. 'Fill that

bucket with coke and get up that bank. Whenever you see a seagull, let fly at it.' Maldwyn Clutterbuck was without doubt the most satisfied soldier in my company during that lovely summer of 1955. His daytime routine was one constant session of sun bathing until a seagull arrived, then he would fling a lump of coke at it. The cookhouse roof was kept clear of the scavenging birds, the commandant was pleased, the catering staff were able to sing among themselves while Private Clutterbuck became word perfect in his beloved song.

The standard of service and cleanliness in the officers' mess was not good enough and this was mainly due to the inefficiency of the mess sergeant, who also came from my regiment. Colonel Witherspoon did not like him and for once I agreed with him. I was not surprised therefore when I heard he had been given the sack. His replacement arrived the same day and when I saw who it was I knew we were going to have even more trouble.

Corporal 'Panther' Thomas had been the battalion sports storeman until his promotion to this new job. He had earned quite a reputation, particularly in rugby circles, as he carried the sponge bag on great occasions such as the Army Rugby Cup Final at Aldershot. 'Panther' always received a cheer when his stocky frame, propelled by legs pumping like pistons, could be seen running with his sponge bag towards some poor incapacitated forward who had been kicked in the teeth. He had earned his nick-name in Korea where, according to legend, he had strangled a couple of Chinese soldiers who had unwittingly stumbled into his trench. The lighter side of his character was his ability to bring tears to the eyes of those who heard his rendering of the ballad 'Eskimo Nell'.

'Panther' set about his task of brightening up the officers' mess ante-room as soon as he arrived. He brought with him a collection of beer mats and cheap ash trays from the local brewery, and he spread these awful objects around the mess until the place looked like some third rate restaurant. 'Panther' had rarely dressed in anything other than a track suit, so I hardly recognised him in his 'blues' uniform when I went into the mess. The commandant came in soon after me and 'Panther' asked him what he would like to drink. 'I'd like a gin and tonic if you please,' said the colonel. 'Panther' returned a few minutes later with a glass on a salver. 'There you are, Sir. I've put some ice and lemon in it. I hope it's to your liking.' Colonel Witherspoon was a man of instant likes and dislikes, and the awful beer mats and ash trays had already raised his blood pressure. He was about to tell the new mess sergeant to get rid of them, when 'Panther' said, 'Excuse me, Sir, did you beat a tenor or a side drum?' None of us knew anything about the colonel's background, but it transpired that he had joined the army as a drummer boy when he was fifteen years of age. He progressed quickly through the ranks, and during the second world war received a decoration for gallant conduct when he was blown out of three separate tanks in one day. In getting out of one of these tanks, he fell awkwardly, breaking his leg

'Panther', who had noticed the colonel's limp, thought he recognised the slight drag of the left leg, which is the common swagger of drummers. There was a long pause before Colonel Witherspoon said, 'Many years ago I used to beat a side drum. How did you know?' 'Panther' beamed and replied, 'I saw the way you walked as you came along the road, Sir, and I said to myself, 'Once a drummer boy, always a drummer boy.'' For the first time since we had known him the colonel was struck dumb; all he could do was glower at 'Panther' as he cleared some glasses away.

After a remark like that, 'Panther's days were numbered, but he accelerated his departure by falling out with the mess corporal. The mess corporal was not a member of The Welch Regiment, and therefore, according to 'Panther' not a proper soldier. He did not react quickly enough one day when 'Panther' gave him an order, so 'Panther' picked up a large kitchen knife and stuck it through his neck. At his subsequent court martial, he must have given a favourable impression to those who tried him because he was soon back on the rugby touchline, wearing a lance corporal's stripe and carrying the first fifteen's sponge bag.

Somehow or other I managed to keep out of trouble for the rest of the time I was at Castlemartin. On the day I left I was loading suitcases into my car when Gerald, the adjutant said, 'The colonel would like to have a word with you before you go.' Harold Witherspoon was gracious enough to thank me for all I had done while under his command: 'I only wish I could have the same team next year, but I will have to start with a new lot in six months time for the next training season,' he said. I had a mental picture of my successor being bombarded about his boilers and seagulls, but that is the army system, and we all know how it works.

CHAPTER SIXTEEN

Strictly Regimental

If I close my eyes and put my mind into neutral I can see Fletcher as he was 40 years ago when I first met him. I can see his tousled head with its tight light coloured curls, his broken nose, his battered ears and his lean frame; always bent slightly forward. I can see his grubby overalls and his boots, not well dubbined as one might have thought, but doused in kitchen fat. Fletcher was the officers' mess cook, not a member of the Army Catering Corps but one of those dedicated band of men from within the regiment whose tools of trade were ladles and saucepans as well as rifle and bayonet. I do not remember Fletcher for the excellence of his cooking, which was never more than ordinary, but there were certain things which happened to him, that are still pin sharp in my mind.

He came to see me one day and told me he could not find his boots. He had looked throughout the kitchen and his bunk, which adjoined the kitchen, but they had been missing for three days and he felt that they were irretrieveably lost. He informed me that he put his boots outside the door of his bunk when he went to bed. Facetiously, I asked him if he wanted them cleaned, but he replied saying he had a skin complaint which caused a bad smell and if he opened his window to clear the air, he got a stiff neck. Why anyone should want to pinch Fletcher's boots was difficult to understand. There were far better pickings in the batmen's quarters - but there it was, the boots were missing and he would have to pay for a new pair. For the next few days Fletcher could be seen paddling around the kitchen in a pair of daps which soon became embalmed in kitchen waste and resembled footwear of a low caste native sweeper.

It was not until the end of the week that the mystery was solved. Friday was the day when Fletcher emptied the stock pot. As the large stainless steel cauldron was winched over to one side and the contents deposited into swill bins, a pair of boots came into view among the debris of bones and vegetables at the bottom of the pot. With a shout of joy he recovered them and rinsed them off under the tap. He let everyone know he had found his boots and that after a week in the stock pot they were more comfortable than before. A week later he told me that the skin complaint which had troubled his feet for years had completely disappeared. He was quite oblivious to the sick looks on the officers' faces whenever he mentioned soup and he was quite upset the following week when he had to pour away an almost full stock pot.

When we went overseas two years later Fletcher, after a tour of duty in the soldiers' cookhouse, came back to the officers' mess. The national service officers were a new bunch and they had not heard about the 'stock pot' business, but some of the old hands looked upon Fletcher's return to the mess with suspicion. He settled down quite well though and cemented good relations with the locally employed civilian staff who worked in the kitchen.

We had a marvellous camp on the north east coast of Cyprus. Behind us towered mountains covered with pine trees and before us lay a beach of golden sand lapped by the warmest clear blue water in the northern hemisphere. In front of the officers' mess was a rocky promontory which, by a freak of nature, had been formed in a number of parallel ridges with water filled gullies between. The largest of these gullies was an almost perfect water polo pitch, except for one thing. Right in the middle was a finger of rock, like a stalagmite, which gave centre forwards a painful experience if they swam into it.

It was an easy matter to rectify and one morning I went along to the pool with some plastic explosive, primers, detonators, and

a length of safety fuse. I dived to the bottom and packed the explosive into as many cracks around the base of the rock that I could find. I connected up all the bits and pieces and then came ashore to where the other end of the safety fuse lay. The adjutant insisted I put up a red flag, just in case somebody happened to be near the pool.

When this was done I pressed the contact on the battery. The finger of rock took off like a rocket and quite by chance, a shoal of fish happened to swim by at the time. The force of the explosion lifted them en masse out of the water.

Fletcher and some others of the mess staff had been watching from the mess verandah and within seconds they had equipped themselves with buckets and were down and into the pool collecting the fish which I had killed. They looked like trout and were all about one pound in weight. Not only was there an ample supply for the officers' mess, but Fletcher was also able to feed the warrant officers' and sergeants' mess and still have enough over to give to the civilian staff to take home. I tell this particular part of the story at length because never before nor since have I fed so many people with a single shot. I was mindful of another person who nearly 2,000 years ago did very much the same sort of thing - not so many miles away.

I was excited at the prospect of producing a splendid feast of fresh fish for the officers and I explained to Fletcher what I wanted him to do - he made a thorough botch of it! Instead of serving the fish complete with head and tail, as one would expect trout to be served, he cut them up into pieces and covered them with a thick sauce. 'Presentation' was never one of Fletcher's strong points and I just had to accept that we were on opposite wavelengths.

A few days later the CO, who now looked upon me as a sort of wizard who could produce fish at the drop of a hat, asked me if I could get him a fish for breakfast. Wearing my flippers and mask and armed with a harpoon gun, I entered the water on the far side of the water polo pitch. Usually there were plenty of fish about, but in the aftermath of the explosion it looked as if they had gone away to find a quieter place. I had almost given up hope of catching anything when I saw some movement on the sea bed. It turned out to be a bottom feeder with ugly teeth, golf ball eyes, snake like feelers and a body covered with warts. At first I rejected the thought of shooting it, but when I could not find any other fish I went back and speared it. It was even more repulsive when I got it out of the water, but I could see there was plenty of good flesh on it. I gave it to Fletcher and told him to prepare it for the CO's breakfast the following day.

Fletcher's mind worked like a computer. He had been

programmed by me not to cut off the heads of 'trout like' fish, so as far as he was concerned anything that came out of the sea kept its head on when it went into the frying pan.

It was reported that the commanding officer nearly leapt out of his chair when the fish was put in front of him. Fletcher, with a rare flash of imagination put a piece of lemon on its neck, but it did nothing to improve the CO's appetite or temper. The colonel was convinced that this was a practical joke and when I was summoned to appear before him I was quite unprepared for his verbal assault. He made it quite clear that the dining table was 'holy ground' as far as he was concerned and that I would be sacked as messing member if there were any more pranks.

The colonel had mentioned on a few occasions that he wanted Fletcher to produce West African peanut stew. It was a particular favourite of his and he was anxious to try it out on the rest of us. I carefully recorded the CO's instructions about how to produce this exotic dish and then went in search of Fletcher. I passed on the CO's recipe and told him to be ready at 07.00 hrs the following day to go with the quartermaster's convoy to the supply depot in Famagusta, from where he could nip across the road to the large market and collect all the produce he needed for the peppery stew.

The QM's convoy returned in the late afternoon and I saw Fletcher walking towards the mess with a sack over his shoulders. I asked him if he had got all the things the commanding officer had detailed. He replied, 'Yes, Sir, everything but red chillies - so I bought some green ones instead.' The CO had stipulated that red chillies were essential to produce a good peanut stew, so I was somewhat reluctant to give Fletcher orders to go ahead before checking with the colonel. I took a few of the green pods out of the bag and inspected them closely. 'Are you sure these are chillies?' I asked, 'they look like beans to me.' 'Oh yes, Sir, they're green chillies alright. I picked 'em special,' said the cook. I selected one and bit it very carefully. There was no sensation of fire as one would expect from a chilli and when I opened the pod I could see without doubt it was a bean. 'You're an idiot, Fletcher,' I said, 'now I shall have to tell the CO the peanut stew is off.' Fletcher slunk off to his tent as I went in search of the commanding officer.

The colonel was sitting on the verandah reading a newspaper. I told him about the mistake with the chillies and he said, 'How could he possibly confuse beans with chillies? - let me have a look at them.' One of the mess servants was told to find Fletcher and tell him to report to the CO with the bag of 'beans'. A few minutes later Fletcher appeared carrying a paper bag. The commanding officer pulled a green 'thing' out and studied it carefully. He turned it over, smelt it and then announced that it was a green chilli and would be suitable for his favourite stew. 'I'm sorry, Sir', I said, 'but I must disagree. It's not a chilli, it's a bean - I've just eaten one.' The CO once again took up the green 'thing' and examined it closely. 'This is a green chilli, there's no doubt about it,' he pronounced. I knew I was on firm ground, so I picked a 'bean' out of the bag, put it in my mouth, chewed it and swallowed it. 'There you are, Sir, they're beans,' I said. It was a pretty convincing demonstration so the colonel, feeling I had proved my case, selected a nice big one, popped it into his mouth and chewed it. What the subsequent investigation revealed was that Fletcher's bag contained a mixture of beans and chillies.

Anyone who has eaten a full blooded red or green chilli will never forget the experience. The CO, who had been unfortunate

 with his choice, turned purple and tears spurted out of his eyes like a garden sprinkler. I told Fletcher to get some bread and butter, as someone had once told me that this was the antidote to chilli burn. I spread thick wedges of butter on the bread as Fletcher and the

mess sergeant stuffed it down the CO's throat. This brought on a choking fit and we then had to slap him on the back to allow him to breathe properly. At last all his tubes were clear and we managed to cool him down. The cooling process went only as far as his mouth and throat were concerned though, and when he had recovered his composure I became the victim of all his anger. It was useless to try and tell the colonel it was all an unfortunate mistake, he really believed he had been 'set up'. I was considered to be the main culprit and lost my job as messing member. West African peanut stew was never mentioned again.

Once a week an Army Kinema Corporation film came up with the ration truck. When the officers' turn came to see it, we erected a projector on the mess verandah and beamed the film to a screen on top of a pair of 6 foot tables. Occasionally, when the wind blew hard and the screen was not tethered properly, the contraption would topple over and fall into the water polo pool. One evening after supper we were all sitting on the verandah watching a 'western'. There had been a gun battle, but the action had switched to the bedroom, when all of a sudden shooting started again. It took a second or two for us to realise that this time there were real bullets flying through the air and we all dived for cover as lead thudded into the wall in the area of the projector. I am ashamed to admit it, but my head was lower than anyone else. There was only one officer who had the courage to get up and find where the shots were coming from. He sprinted around the side of the building and saw headquarter company arms storeman reloading a 9mm Browning automatic pistol before pumping another magazine of rounds through the side of Fletcher's tent, The would be assassin was brought down in a flying tackle, disarmed and marched off to the guard tent. After all the commotion had died down, we found Fletcher cowering underneath his bed none the worse for the experience.

The evidence produced at the subsequent court martial of the arms storeman explained a few things about Fletcher's character which many of us had suspected. 'Personal relationships' is a touchy subject in the Army and if you step out of line you can find yourself in serious trouble. We nevertheless felt that the unilateral action of the arms storeman was rather heavy handed.

Fletcher left the Battalion soon after the attempt on his life. Besides, The Army Catering Corps were getting into their stride and he would never have been one of 'The Professionals' - he was strictly 'Regimental'.

CHAPTER SEVENTEEN

Dhavlos by the Sea

The telephone crackled at battalion headquarters in Dhavlos and a far distant voice could be heard saying, 'Do you want to buy a horse?' It was Major Dicky Randell who commanded 'A' Company based near the village of Akrades way out on the Karpas peninsula of north east Cyprus. Dicky's thoughts were never far away from horses and many of us in The Welch Regiment wondered why he had bothered to join a foot slogging outfit when he would have been far more at home in a cavalry regiment. We all liked his company though, and we appreciated the gentle way in which he approached his problems with, what he called, 'horse sense.'

The task of my regiment in those days of the 'mid fifties' was to keep order among Greek Cypriots, who wanted union with Greece. We also acted as a buffer between them and Turkish Cypriots who on frequent occasions would get annoyed with the Greeks for upsetting their quiet lifestyle. When we were not chasing gangs of Greek Cypriot 'EOKA' 'Freedom fighters' around the pine clad mountains, or waiting in ambush positions on known bandit runs, there were plenty of opportunities for enjoying ourselves. Every company had its own football and basket/volley ball pitches, and those who were near the sea had first class swimming and sub aqua facilities. Those of us who were fortunate to be at battalion headquarters had just about everything to keep us happy, albeit in a monastic way. For this we had to thank a unit which had been in Dhavlos some time before us. Their commanding officer decided that the morale of his soldiers was far more important than any tactical factors concerning the siting of battalion headquarters.

The place was like a holiday camp. In the centre of the complex of tents and barbed wire was the Louis Hotel, a strange circular building which looked more like a lighthouse than an hotel. It used to attract the odd adventurous visitor before the state of emergency was declared, but when we were there it was requisitioned and used as battalion headquarters and senior officers' quarters. We had a full range of sports pitches and, best of all, we were camped fifty feet or so above the sea where we looked across to Turkey and the distant Toros Daglari mountain range. The swimming facilities were superb. For the sub aqua enthusiast there was deep, crystal clear water and plenty of fish, and for those of a timorous disposition, a gently sloping bay of golden sand. A rocky outcrop 500 yards out in the bay, dubbed Taff's Isle (which looked remarkably like a submarine) was a challenge for our long distance swimmers. Just below the officers' mess was a stone building which we used as a boat house. It contained a few dinghies on loan from the Cyprus Forces Sailing Club. Alongside the boathouse was another building which we had turned into stables. The loose boxes accommodated two fine desert ponies which I had recently purchased from a Royal Air Force unit in Benghazi (Libya) for £5.00 each. I actually bought three ponies, but one of them died of colic on the landing craft that carried them over.

It was difficult to get a verbal profile of the animal on the crackling line, but I managed to gather it was in good order and a bargain at £15.00. Dicky's recommendation was good enough for me and we came to an understanding that he would advance the money for the horse. I could just make out that he would deliver the beast by truck the following day to a place called Khomi Kebir, where the tarmac ended.

I set off on the six mile journey to Khomi Kebir with two Land Rovers and six armed soldiers as my escort. We reached the rendezvous ahead of the other party from Akrades, so we did what most male Cypriots do in the summer; we drank coffee and ate nuts and cheese in the cool shade of a carob tree.

We did not have to wait long before we heard the unmistakable whine of the engine of an Army 3 ton truck labouring up the hill in second gear. As it came around the corner into the main square of the village, a few comatose Cypriots blinked at the sight of a large horse whose head was sticking out above the canopy frame. I admit I was surprised as well at the size of the horse and wondered if the girth and bridle straps which I had brought were going to be long enough. I had become used to the relatively small size of Middle East horses compared with those of North West Europe. Fourteen hands was about the average height, but this monster in the back of the truck was over 16 hands high.

Dicky's batman, who doubled as a groom, was nick-named Shaky because of his nervous twitch and stutter. He was dwarfed by the horse but was hanging on to the halter. When he saw me he said, 'How are we g-g-going to g-g-get him off?' I had already made a reconnaissance of the village to find a suitable off- loading point, and I was able to guide the vehicle to a place where the tail board could be laid flat on a bank. When this had been done, and after I had tested it to make sure it would be safe for the horse to cross over, I signalled Shaky to proceed. After a few prods and pushes the animal stood on firm ground.

So far, so good. The next stage was to get the bridle and saddle on. I started to undo the buckles and at the same time I asked Shaky what the animal was like to ride. 'I d-d-don't know, Sir,' he replied, 'Well, what did Major Randell say about him?' I asked. 'He's n-n-never ridden him neither,' said Shaky, and then made the devastating remark, 'I don't think n-n-nobody's n-n-never ridden him.' Despite Shaky's double negatives the awful truth dawned upon me that I had six miles of mountain road, with a nasty drop on one side, to cover on an unbroken horse. I considered putting the animal back into the truck and returning it to Akrades, but then I thought of the loss of face I would suffer if the soldiers saw me fail to mount.

'Righto then, let's get the bridle on,' I said. I had to stand on the chassis of the Land Rover to reach the horse's head, and as I slipped the head band over his ears I was aware of the dark depth of one eye as it looked hypnotically at me. The saddle was next, with a suitably lengthened girth, and then I was ready to get aboard. I asked one of the soldiers to remove his shirt and this was draped over the animal's head so that I could, at least, get settled in the saddle before I knew how he would react. One foot in the stirrup, a hefty shove from Shaky and I was up in the saddle and, so far, in command. Now came the moment of truth, and I gave the order to remove the blindfold. The bare buff soldier reclaimed his shirt and the others, who had been holding on to the bridle as if the horse was a tethered barrage balloon, leapt out of the way. They need not have bothered as the animal stood as still as the most disciplined quadruped on Horse Guards. The calm before the storm I thought as I put some gentle pressure with my calves, but still no response. The soldiers were beginning to snigger, so the time had come to take some positive action. I reached up into a tree, snapped off a stick and gave him a tap on the rump. Still no response. A harder slap, and then he started to move, but only at a slow walk.

Shaky and his team had raised the tailboard of their vehicle and were ready to return to Akrades. They watched me as I ambled off slowly in the direction of Dhavlos. I had the prospect of a six mile ride on a horse which instead of being a ball of fire turned out to be a damp squib! I developed a rhythmical motion with my legs and my stick to keep the horse moving, and in this fashion we slowly progressed along the narrow road with the Land Rovers moving in bounds in front and behind me.

We had travelled about a mile when around the bend in the road, about 150 yards ahead appeared a Cypriot riding a donkey and leading another one behind him. The effect upon my horse was as if someone had given him an immense electric shock. From a gentle walking pace I was suddenly catapulted into a gallop as the animal hurtled down the track in the direction of the unsuspecting Cypriot and his two donkeys. I was quite unable to control the horse and it was obvious there was going to be a collision.

The impact of a 16 hands high stallion upon a Cypriot donkey, not much bigger than a Shetland pony, was a bit one sided. The old man came off at the moment of strike and rolled underneath the donkey he had been riding while his steed, which turned out to be a female, was 'mounted' by my stallion. What I had not been told about the horse was that it had been used solely for stud purposes. The sight of any donkey, horse or mule drove it into a frenzy. If it was a female it had to be 'mounted' and if it was a male, it had to be attacked.

The soldiers in the Land Rovers had watched with amazement my assault upon the unfortunate Cypriot and his donkeys and they assumed I had spotted something they had not seen. As I was trying to get my horse off the donkey I could see them racing up the track with their rifles at the ready. I prayed they would not shoot the old man, who was somewhere under the writhing mass of horse flesh, and add injury to insult! I must have been able to get through to them that it was a purely sexual matter and nothing to do with terrorism, as they put their rifles down and helped the old man to his feet. They dragged the donkey away from the stallion, whereupon it shot over the side of the road and joined the other one which was going as fast as its legs could carry it for the sea, about two miles away.

Turkish Cypriots are made of strong stuff and the recovery of this one from a state of shock was swift. Within a matter of seconds he was leaping up and down and gesticulating wildly in the direction of his runaway donkeys. The soldiers had a 'whip round' for him and managed to collect a few packets of cigarettes, which he grudgingly accepted. I did my best to apologise, but he just shook his fist at me and gave a 'five fingered curse' to the stallion.

At this stage of my ownership of Satan, for that was his name, I did not realise that an identical reaction would take place every time that he saw an animal of his own species. I was therefore only slightly prepared when we met the next donkey borne Cypriot coming towards us. He was more fortunate than the first one as we had descended to sea level, and his donkey summoned all its reserve of speed to escape from the carnal onslaught.

Except for the two sudden bursts of speed, the journey from Khomi Kebir to Dhavlos had been boring and we had taken about one and a half hours to cover six miles. I was pleased therefore to see our camp in the distance and, as we got closer, the sight of the white tunic of a mess waiter on the patio of the officers' mess reminded me that I was very much in need of a cold beer. I walked Satan through the transport park and handed him over to my batman. I gave him instructions to feed and water the horse before I climbed up the path to the bluff of high ground above the stables and the boat house where the mess was situated.

Most of the officers were standing around having their drinks before lunch, and the commanding officer asked me what I thought of the new horse. I told him what had happened and everyone had a good laugh at my expense. All of a sudden there was a commotion outside and I recognised the voice of my batman. 'Sir, you had better come quickly, that new horse of

111

yours is knocking the stables down!' I bounded out of the mess and flew down the cliff path to the stables where I found the place in a shambles. 'Whatever has happened?' I asked. One of the other batmen explained that Satan had been taken into one of the stalls where he had been given a large pan of oats and a bucket of water. 'Good as gold he was,' said the batman, 'until someone brought in one of those desert ponies, and then all hell was let loose.' I recognised the same trouble I had experienced twice myself that morning. 'We'll have to get him out of there,' I said, 'take him to the contractor's shop and tie him up beneath the big tree.' I looked at the damage he had caused and calculated it would take a few day's work and a number of large gins for the quartermaster before the stables would be restored. 'Another thing,' said my batman, 'I've never seen a horse eat so much as this one.' Even an inexperienced person could see that Satan had been kept on basic survival rations. Big hollows in his side showed that he had been underfed and I realised that he would need more than the normal rations for a horse of his size to build up his strength. What I had not appreciated was the enormous capacity he had for oats. Instead of a throat and a stomach it seemed that he had a 'black hole' down which everything disappeared.

One advantage of giving him this high octane diet was that his performance as a hack improved and I spent many enjoyable hours riding him on the beach and the countryside around Dhavlos. I could not take him too far from the camp as we were in a state of 'active service' and the danger of terrorist attack was a real one.

A feature of his character which remained constant was the effect that other horses had on him. His years as a stud stallion had become too ingrained in his personality to be changed by the 'cordon bleu' treatment I was giving him. I was never able to take him anywhere near the other horses in the stables and as a result I became a 'lone ranger' as nobody could accompany me on a ride. He continued to live under the big tree by the contractor's shop, which was ideal for him during the summer months.

After six months service in Dhavlos, the time came for us to leave the Karpas peninsula and take up residence in Dhekelia Camp near Larnaca on the south east coast of Cyprus. There was no problem about taking the other two ponies with us, they were

112

quite manageable and had already become seasoned travellers. Satan was a problem though and the prospect of putting him in stables in Dhekelia, where there were plenty of ponies and a flourishing polo club, was quite out of the question. I suppose I could have sent him back to Akrades but with all his faults I had become attached to the old rogue.

The answer to this problem came two weeks before we were due to leave Dhavlos. Nikos, the locally employed officers' mess cook, came to me and said, 'I understand you want to sell your horse, Sir.' 'That's true', I replied, 'are you interested?' 'Yes I am', said Nikos, 'You see, I have some horses and I think Satan would be good for putting with them.' By 'horses' he meant 'mares' and it was obvious that he had his eye on Satan as the father of some sturdy foals and fillies. I was delighted with this splendid solution to the problem and I told Nikos he could have Satan as a gift the day we left Dhavlos. Nikos was a courteous old man and he had looked after us well during our time in the camp alongside his village. He was always pleased to prepare local dishes for us and to this day I delight my family with his way of cooking octopus with garlic and red wine.

The day before we left Dhavlos I took Satan out for our last ride. His coat was sleek and shiny and the big hollows in his side had gone. He held his head high and tossed his mane at the prospect of a good gallop on the beach. It was hard to imagine that this was the horse that had been in such poor condition only a few months before. Dicky Randell had been right and had recognised the potential of the animal.

I was busy getting my soldiers ready for the move so my batman took Satan to his new home. When all was ready and the soldiers were aboard the trucks, I gave the order to move off. As we headed east on the dust road to Khomi Kebir and beyond, I leaned out of the window to take a last look at the Louis Hotel and the rows of tents, now occupied by a Royal Artillery field battery. At the far end of the village I saw the whitewashed stone house where Nikos lived with his wife and two daughters. In the adjoining field three mares were gently swishing their tails under some trees. Standing with them, gently nuzzling the neck of a pretty little filly, was Satan. I gave him a wave and silently wished him a long and happy life.

CHAPTER EIGHTEEN
A Distasteful Task

I first saw Cyprus in the summer of 1948 when, as a junior
subaltern of The Welch Regiment, I was sent to the Middle East
to join the 1st Battalion The South Wales Borderers. My first
impression of this 'jewel' of the Mediterranean was that hell
could not be far away when day time temperatures soared into
the top '90's. I remember trying to find some relief from the heat
by spending a few hours on a tethered raft a hundred yards from
the shore at our camp a few miles east of Famagusta - only to be
burnt so badly that the medical officer read me the rules about self
inflicted wounds! Captain Jack Walliker, another officer of my
regiment serving with the Borderers, took pity on me and invited
me to join a weekend camping party in the mountains of the
Karpas peninsula (the Panhandle) near Kantara Castle. I
gratefully accepted.

We had two jeeps for eight of us and into these vehicles we
loaded four 'pup' bivouacs and enough 'compo' rations to last
three days. Cool breezes soon took over from the hot, dusty air of
the plains as we headed north into the mountains. Brilliant white
villages with their groves of olive and orange trees nestled among
rocky outcrops. When we reached the half way point to the ruins
of Kantara Castle - which had been one of the mighty bastions of
the Knights of St. John in the twelfth century, we stopped in a
small village for refreshments. In the centre of the village was a
tree ideal for providing shade for the men folk of the village who
sat chatting and playing cards beneath it. We were welcomed
with smiles and friendly gestures as we sat down alongside them.
Within a few seconds the proprietor of the adjacent coffee shop
asked us what we would like to eat and drink. He spoke good
English and Jack ordered some coffee and other things with
Greek names. That day I made my first acquaintance with
kepthetis and halvah. Deep fried wafer thin pasta envelopes of
spiced meat and tender bean sprouts were complemented with
the exquisite flavour of honey and roasted ground nuts. Tiny
cups full to the brim with a scalding black liquid, which almost
supported a spoon in the vertical position, anointed my palate
with the real taste of coffee. Saucers and bowls of other delectable
nibblets and small glasses of a deep red liqueur took over when

the coffee cups were cleared away. A considerable amount of collective discipline had to be exerted to ask for the bill and bid our friendly hosts farewell. The coffee shop proprietor, his family and other local inhabitants stood and waved to us as we climbed into our vehicles and headed further into the mountains.

The rest of the story about our camping week end is of no consequence. It was extremely pleasant but it has no relevance to what I am about to relate.

Early in 1949 the 1st Battalion The South Wales Borderers left Cyprus on the troop ship 'Eastern Prince'. We sailed south through the Suez Canal and the Red Sea to the Sudan where we travelled overland to Khartoum, which was to be our new station. I was not to know it would be another nine years before I would see Cyprus again and that next time this lovely island would be torn apart by political division and ethnic feuding.

In October 1957 the 1st Battalion The Welch Regiment was sent to Cyprus to take part in the campaign to subdue Greek EOKA terrorists (or freedom fighters) whose aim was to end British rule and establish union with Greece.

Our first operational area was in the north west part of the island with battalion headquarters at Xeros. We stayed there for about six months before moving to Dhavlos on the north east coast of the Karpas peninsula. This was familiar territory to me and the sight of Kantara Castle brought back memories of that camping trip.

One day the officers were called to an 'O' (orders) group where the commanding officer outlined the details of 'Operation Woodpecker'. The plan was to arrest thousands of passive but important EOKA supporters throughout the island and put them in a place where they could not make mischief. We were given envelopes which contained details of our own responsibilites. When I got back to my tent and opened the envelope I found I had to meet some Greek policemen at a certain grid reference on the other side of the mountain at 20.00hrs the following evening. It seemed that they would escort me to a village and then show me the house of a person who had to be arrested.

I set out the following evening with my escort in two Land Rovers and we duly met the two policemen. I had no idea where I was until we drove into a hillside village which seemed familiar. A carob tree stood in the centre of the square and Greek villagers sat at tables drinking coffee and playing cards. To them a visit from the security forces was a common occurrence and when they saw who it was, they looked at us with sullen expressions. My eyes took in the scene and my mind wound back to August 1948 when these same villagers had been so friendly and hospitable.

I wondered which one, if any of them, I would have to arrest and looked towards the senior policeman for a sign. He however motioned me to follow him and our posse filed out from the village square and down a narrow alley bordered by two high walls. We turned left at the end of the wall where there was an alcove blocked by a wooden gate. From the shadows of the alcove we could see a family of Greek Cypriots sitting in their arbour of vines having their evening meal. The father of the family sat at the head of the table facing us. His wife sat at the other end and their children, numbering five or six, sat between them.

'That is Constantis Theakus, (not his real name) the man we must arrest. He owns the village coffee shop,' said the policeman. It seemed a cruel irony that fate should produce a situation where I was made to arrest a person who had been so friendly to me ten years previously. Even though it was a hot and sultry night a cold chill swept over me. The accusation about him being an EOKA supporter did not seem to matter as I opened the gate and entered the courtyard.

Constantis looked up and rose to his feet as we approached. He was told that he was being placed under arrest and would be allowed a few minutes to pack some clothes. The policemen accompanied him into the house, leaving me and my escort standing near the remainder of the family. After what seemed an age Constantis came back into the courtyard carrying a suitcase. He put it on the ground and then embraced his children one by one. He then turned to his wife, dried her tears and held her close. After a few seconds he said, 'I am ready to go.' One of the policemen put handcuffs on him and we filed back the way we had come.

An hour later we were back in Dhavlos where tents had been set up within a barbed wire stockade. Police 'special branch' then took over and the following morning Constantis and others who had been brought in the night before were moved away in police vehicles. I did not see him again.

I was never in doubt that the only inconvenience Constantis suffered was a temporary deprivation of liberty and that after a month or two, he would have been back in his village serving coffee and playing cards with his friends. I sometimes wonder though what his fate would have been under some authoritarian regimes of recent years.

It is now 36 years since I was last in Cyprus. I received a jolt a few weeks ago when my wife came home with a bundle of glossy brochures she had picked up in the 'holiday' shop. 'Cyprus is the place I would like to see,' she said. 'How about you?'

CHAPTER NINETEEN

Eyes Front

Bring me the sunflower and I'll transplant
It in my garden's burnt salinity.
All day its heliocentric gold face
Will turn towards the blue of sky and sea.

Jeremy Reed

The usual routine for pre-war Saturday mornings on the North West Frontier of India was barrack inspection. All hands would be mustered on the Friday evening and the already brilliant stones outside the barrack blocks would receive yet another coat of whitewash. The grass would be cut by Indian gardeners, who wielded large metal rods like golf clubs but with a sharp cutting edge at the base. Other native workers would be busy removing sticks, stones and rubbish which had accumulated over the week. Early the next day everyone would be up at the first sound of the bugle putting finishing touches to their company areas.

Lieutenant 'Olly' Evans had recently joined the 1st Battalion The South Wales Borderers and he found himself in charge of his company one Saturday morning when his company commander was away on leave. Accompanied by the company sergeant major, he carried out a preliminary inspection of the lines and was about to congratulate the warrant officer on the immaculate state of the outside areas when an Indian gardener went past pushing a wheel barrow full of flowers. A few seconds later eager hands of soldiers, from another company in an adjacent block, removed the flowers and placed them in prepared beds while the Indian trundled off with his barrow for another load.

The transformation of the dry and dusty mound of earth next door into a colourful garden was as good a conjuring trick that Olly and the sergeant major had seen since they had been on the frontier. Both of them realised they had some catching up to do. After a few seconds thought Olly gave instructions for a party of men to proceed to the dhobi lines and each collect an armful of sunflowers. The dhobi lines was the place where the washing of soldiers' clothes was carried out by the contractor's staff. The abundance of water there made it an ideal place for sunflowers to grow.

The soldiers descended on the dhobi lines with picks and shovels but they found that digging out the massive plants was a hard job as the roots went so deep. 'Cut them off at ground level,' said the sergeant major. Machettes were unsheathed and the men scythed through the sunflowers until each one of them had a full load.

With less than 15 minutes to go before the commanding officer arrived, Olly and his sergeant major supervised the erection of sunflowers. Each one was about eight feet tall and when they had been jammed into the ground they presented a solid wall of bright yellow blooms.

The commanding officer, adjutant, regimental sergeant major, provost sergeant, stick orderly and CO's bugler came into sight right on time and the giant display of sunflowers made the colonel stop in his tracks. 'Good heavens - what a remarkable sight,' he said. 'Well done Olly, you have certainly brightened up the place - but I don't remember seeing these flowers last week.' Olly accepted the compliment with a humble shrug and said something about the blooms shooting up after they received some manure from the mule lines.

The CO went on to inspect the barrack rooms but he seemed to have a far away look in his eyes. When he had completed the inspection he went back to have another look at the sunflowers.

The colonel walked up and down the phalanx of flowers and said, 'There's something wrong with these plants.' Olly's mouth went as dry as the earth had been only half an hour before, and he squeaked, 'Oh - what's that, Sir?' The CO caught hold of the stem of one of the largest of the flowers and with a sharp tug pulled it out of the ground. He surveyed the rootless but pointed end of the plant. 'Just as I thought,' he said, holding the stem in such a way that Olly thought he was going to be transfixed to the wall. 'Sunflowers always face the sun', barked the colonel, 'and yours are pointing in all directions.'

CHAPTER TWENTY

Another Sacred Cow

Occasionally we are given brief glimpses behind the formal façade of the Royal family. One little cameo which illustrates the whimsical nature of Queen Elizabeth II was told to me many years ago by Lieutenant General Sir Charles Coleman, Colonel of The Welch Regiment from 1958 to 1965.

Soon after Sir Charles retired from the Army in 1959, he was offered the job of Lieutenant Governor of Guernsey - an honour he was delighted to accept.

Before taking up the appointment there were certain formalities which had to take place, and one of these was the formal kissing of hands at the palace. Fortunately for Sir Charles an old friend of his had taken up the appointment of Lieutenant Governor of Jersey a year before, and this friend gave him a ring with the intention of passing on a few tips about procedure at the ceremony.

'The Queen spent much of the time I was with her talking about Jersey cattle,' said the friend, 'and my knowledge of that breed of cattle - or for that matter, any breed of cattle was nil. You may or may not know that Guernsey has its own breed of cattle, so I suggest you do some homework.' Sir Charles thanked his friend and set about learning everything that had been written about Guernsey cattle.

When the day arrived for him to report to Buckingham Palace, he stepped lightly across the palace forecourt feeling quite confident about his forthcoming audience with the Queen.

The Gentlemen of the Household and the Lord Chamberlain were present and he was ushered into the audience chamber where Her Majesty was waiting. The formal kissing of hands took place and Sir Charles was confirmed in his appointment. The Queen then fixed him with a penetrating look and said, 'I suppose you've been mugging up on Guernsey cattle General?' Sir Charles who had been looking forward to a quiet and relaxed conversation about cows, admitted that he had become possibly the greatest authority on Guernsey and, for good measure, Jersey cattle in the world. The Queen chuckled over the memory of the discomfort of the Governor of Jersey, but was touched to hear how he had helped his friend.

CHAPTER TWENTY ONE

Promotion Prospects

I had been to see the adjutant about something or other, and was turning to leave when he said, 'By the way, you have to sit a promotion exam in six months time.' 'I beg your pardon,' I replied, 'What did you say about an examination?' He repeated what he said and fortified the unpalatable information by reeling off a number of subjects that I would have to study and pass if I wanted to be qualified to wear three pips in my shoulder. I had already been wearing the badges of rank of a captain for a year and I had not been aware that I would have to sit an examination to keep them. Besides, it was 1951, I was serving with the 3rd Battalion The King's African Rifles in Malaya and killing bandits was the top priority.

There was not much one could do about studying for examinations at that time. We were in a lonely place surrounded by jungle in central Pahang and the only books on military subjects were a few old pamphlets, a manual of military law and a copy of King's Regulations which the adjutant kept in his tent. I discovered that the examination, for which I and three other officers of the battalion had been entered, was the first one to be held in post war years.

Prosecuting the war in Malaya under that most energetic High Commissioner, General Sir Gerald Templer was a full time job for everyone, at least that was our excuse. It was not until we were within two weeks of the examination that the subjects we had to study began to occupy our minds. With two days to go before E-DAY the four of us boarded the commanding officer's Humber 4 x 4 staff wagon and, escorted by a pair of ferret scout cars, we set off for Kuala Lumpur. Each one of us had been able to get a copy of King's Regulations and a manual of military law. The adjutant had provided his copies, brigade headquarters had loaned two sets and a local rubber planter, recently retired from the Army, provided the remainder.

The examination, even after all these years, is a painful memory relieved only by the counter balance of a few nights in the bright lights of Malaya's capital city. Our lack of preparation was certainly responsible for much pencil sucking and early orders for cold Tiger beers in the mess. We returned to our unit in a sombre and dejected state, fully convinced that we had failed in all subjects.

A few weeks later we received identical small brown envelopes which when opened informed us that we had failed in all subjects except military law. This was a surprise because just before we were given the military law papers we were told that reference books were not allowed. They were collected from our tables and stacked on the dais occupied by the invigilating officer. In one way it made things quite easy for us as we could not possibly quote chapters and paragraphs. I remember recommending the death sentence for some of the more tricky questions. However, we congratulated ourselves on not disappearing completely down the plug hole, but learnt a few weeks later that the reason for our success was the error of the invigilating officer who incorrectly deprived us of our reference books. It seemed that everyone passed irrespective of how well or badly they had done.

I remember another occasion when I was stationed with the 1st Battalion The Welch Regiment in Luneburg in Germany in 1956. Along with Duncan Griffiths, Ian Mennell, Mike Dyer and one or two others I had been entered for the captain to major practical promotion examination to be held in Hameln.

The others went ahead of me as I was involved in the administration of an athletics meeting. It was not until the early evening that I collected my suitcase and books and boarded an Austin Champ. In those days they did not issue doors for Champs and, as we were well into Autumn, it was a cold ride.

I arrived in Hameln at about 9pm and it was not difficult to find the officers' mess where I was staying. Military Police signs covered every route.

Making sure that my driver had a meal and a bunk for the night, I was dropped off at the mess where my kit was deposited on the mat in the hall. I was still protected from the cold night air with my British warm overcoat and a huge scarf which was wrapped around my neck three times. A trio of lieutenant colonels greeted me like a long lost brother. 'Good to see you at last.' said one of them. 'What would you like to drink?' said another. 'A whisky would do very well,' I replied. 'I'll get your supper fixed,' said a third. I really could not have expected more civilised treatment than I received from those kind fellows, and I felt a surge of confidence for the morrow when we would have such splendid directing staff to ease us through our tasks.

With a large whisky in my hand I started to peel off my clothing. As I did so I became aware of two sets of eyes, both belonging to lieutenant colonels, looking at my epaulettes which carried three pips. The last of the bunch of three half colonels came from the kitchen area and said, 'Supper's on the table,' and then he too became absorbed with my  badges of rank. Their hospitality vanished in an instant and I was given a chit pad to sign for my large whisky.

What had happened was that they had mistaken me for the fourth member of the directing staff who had not yet arrived. I have always looked older than I am and even as a member of the school Combined Cadet Force, wearing a trench coat, I was often saluted by serving soldiers. It had been fun then, but in Hameln on that cold night in 1956 I became aware of the dangerous situation I was in.

The following morning we received instructions to assemble at a grid reference about three miles away. I did not notice at the time, but afterwards remembered the casual way officers lingered over the last dregs of their coffee as zero hour for departure approached.

As soon as I got up from the table and headed for my Austin Champ, everyone else fell in behind. With a one inch to the mile map on my lap I led the way out of barracks. We had not travelled more than 300 yards before we came to an 'umleitung' (diversion) sign. The German use of 'umleitung' signs has never ceased to amaze me. Not only are there 'umleitung' signs wherever you go, but there are 'umleitung' signs to divert you from 'umleitungs'. This happened in Hameln and it was not long before I was completely lost in the back streets of that ancient town - with a huge snake of military vehicles behind me.

Those officers who had lingered over their coffee were now the first to make unkind remarks about my map reading. Others, who had thought about their career prospects going out of the window, were looking at their watches and going white around the gills.

We finally extricated ourselves from the inner depths of Hameln and eventually, like the pied piper, I led the column to the assembly point. Standing there on the cold hillside were four lieutenant colonels, including the one they thought was me the night before. 'Where have you been?' said the one who had ordered me a large whisky. I gave a weak excuse about 'umleitungs', but I could see that I was extremely unpopular with students and directing staff alike. I spent a very uncomfortble day expecting to be given low marks. A few weeks later one of those small brown envelopes arrived and to my amazement I found that I had passed. All the other 1/Welch officers passed as well, and I can only assume that the directing staff had a conscience about my discomfort and decided to let me through as well.

I am one of those fellows who turns up for a written examination with the minimum amount of kit, ie. one red and one blue ball point pen, one fountain pen, one pencil, a rubber and a ruler. I have never felt that any of my successes, or otherwise, have been due to the tools I have used, but there are others who believe in fortifying themselves with a remarkable array of paraphernalia on their desk tops. Flasks of coffee, slide rules, geometry sets, travelling clocks, coloured inks and crayons, blotters and even slippers, changes of sweaters and Beacham's powders are part of the stock in trade of those who take examinations seriously.

One fellow I met in Sennerlager was a lighter traveller than me. He turned up with only a blue biro and a ruler. With about five minutes to go before the starting bell rang he ambled across and said, 'Just checking - it was GOLD, JUNO and SWORD from west to east?' I gave him a puzzled look and said, 'What are you talking about?' 'The beaches in France of course,' he replied. I gave this some thought before I asked him why he wanted to know about the beaches where the invasion force had landed on D-Day. 'So that I can answer the question if it comes up, you dummy,' he said. I went through a few moments of panic before I assured myself that I had studied the correct campaign and he had studied the wrong one.

I tried not to create a situation where this rather languid cavalry officer would feel the need to commit suicide, but with the seconds ticking by I had to break it to him that we were doing

'North Africa'. When this alarming piece of news was confirmed by others around him, I took him across to Duncan Griffiths who had made some pretty coloured maps on cardboard, rather like tiles you stick on the bathroom wall. With three minutes to go I left him with Duncan who was doing his best to show him what the large curved arrows of troop movements meant. After half an hour had passed I saw him leave the room clutching his biro and ruler. He was not in the mess when the rest of us got there for lunch. The mess sergeant told me he had seen the officer throw a suitcase into the back of his car and depart a few hours ago.

I must have taken a nose dive on that examination because I found myself with Duncan Griffiths, Ian Mennel, Norman Salmon and a few others in Tripoli, Libya a year or so later sitting another one.

We had flown from Benghazi where 1/Welch were stationed and had spent a few days of concentrated study in the comfortable officers' mess of The Royal Irish Fusiliers. The four days of the examination was a torturous experience and it was with relief that I inked in the last full stop.

Tripoli in those days was a splendid place to be stationed. There were plenty of good hotels, a casino, night clubs and a flourishing nurses' mess. Some of us had made use of our time in the city and as soon as darkness fell we called a taxi and sped off to the British Military Hospital and the nurses' mess. We enjoyed the girls hospitality for an hour or so and then most of us, along with some of the girls went on to one of the excellent restaurants on the sea front. Later that night we did a round of the night clubs and finally got back to our beds as the first rays of dawn were showing in the eastern sky.

I was woken within a short time by a servant with the unwelcome news that the bus would leave for the airport in 30 minutes time. It was easy to see the ones who had been night clubbing only a few hours before. They were the ones who could not bear to sit on the seats as the bus lurched through pot holes in the road leading to King Idris Airport.

I sat glumly in what was called the Airport Lounge, which could easily have been mistaken for an extension of the camel market, until the Cyprus Airways plane came in and we were called together by the air hostess. She was the daughter of a Nicosia based brigadier and was the only bit of glamour on an otherwise dull airline. 'I am sorry to say that we are over-booked. I need two volunteers to stay behind until next week,' she said.

My right arm shot up automatically and I shouted 'Me', just in case there was any competition. I need not have bothered as there were no other takers for the offer. 'We shall have to draw lots then,' said the air hostess and proceeded to do something with small pieces of paper in her pretty little hat. When everyone, except me, had taken one it was found that Duncan Griffiths had drawn the one with a cross on it. I could see from the look on his face that he considered this very bad news, made worse by having to spend a week with me whose nocturnal pursuits were not in line with his own.

Duncan insisted upon waiting until the others were airborne, just in case someone dropped dead at the last minute. It was only after he saw the wheels disappear into their niches in the wings that he accepted the fact that he was marooned in Tripoli. We boarded the bus once more and within an hour I was tucked up in bed catching up on sleep I had missed the night before.

At about 10am I was woken by Duncan who had been working on a plan to get back to Benghazi. He told me that it was our duty to try to get back to our unit. 'Rather like prisoners of war,' he said. I told him I did not feel like a prisoner of war and that as far as I was concerned the enforced stop-over in Tripoli was a gift from heaven. He was determined to go ahead with his plan though and when he outlined what he proposed to do I could see that questions would be asked if I was not with him when he got back to Benghazi.

Phase 1 of Duncan's plan had already been completed while I was asleep. He had telephoned someone at Wheelus Field, which was a large American Air Force base a few miles outside Tripoli, and asked if they had anything going to Benghazi. He was told that a DC-3 would be flying there that afternoon and if we reported at 2pm there was a good chance we would get a lift. I must have looked as miserable as Duncan looked a few hours before and I was furious that he had scuppered my opportunity to have seven days holiday. I packed my bags again, had lunch and then set off with Duncan in a taxi for Wheelus Field.

The DC-3 was on the runway and we were told to climb aboard. The engines started and we began to move forward, but instead of gathering speed, we slowed down and stopped. The door of the crew compartment opened and a large gum chewing American with a gold encrusted baseball cap said, 'I hear that there are LIMEYS aboard - and I don't carry LIMEYS.' Duncan and I had been looking out of the window to see why we had stopped and did not pay any attention to the first announcement, but someone must have pointed us out to the pilot because he marched down the aisle, confronted us and said, 'Are you LIMEYS?' Both of us were familiar with the expression despite the fact we had never been addressed that way before. We therefore nodded assent and without further ceremony the big aggressive American opened the door and said 'Get off'. Summoning up as much dignity as we could manage we descended to the runway. The door clanged shut behind us, the engines revved to full power and off went the DC-3 in the direction of Benghazi.

Duncan was anxious to recover a pound of flesh and he set off to report the matter to the base commander. But everyone had their heads down and he could not find anyone who would listen to his grievance. He finally bowed to the inevitable and we took a taxi back to the Royal Irish Fusiliers' barracks.

My fortunes seemed to be changing for the better and it looked as if I was going to have seven days in Tripoli after all. To give Duncan his due, he had a few more shots at trying to get back to Benghazi via local oil prospectors' aircraft, but this time he was on his own and he was unsuccessful.

A week later the two of us were waiting for the Cyprus Airways plane to come in at King Idris Airport and this time the air hostess had room for us and we were delivered safely to Benghazi.

CHAPTER TWENTY TWO

The RSM and the Rabbit

Putting my foot down to keep an appointment, I narrowly missed a car coming in the opposite direction on a winding stretch of road between Crickhowell and Brecon. My passenger sucked air through his teeth and said, 'That was a close one.' I agreed with him and thought to myself, 'I should have known better,' bringing to mind an incident that occurred many years before on the same stretch of road.

On that day I was cruising along quite pleasantly when I saw ahead of me a car lying on its side. As I approached I saw one of the doors open, like the conning tower of a submarine, and a head appear. I pulled up, got out of my car and went across to the vehicle to see if I could help. The passenger who was clambering out of the car was the regimental sergeant major of the unit with which I was serving. I placed my arms around him and with me pulling and him pushing he finally came out of the car like a whelk out of a shell. The second whelk in the same shell was the provost sergeant. With more heaving he was also lifted clear.

A small crowd had gathered, all eager to help, but there were no serious injuries. The RSM appeared to be concussed though, as he was sitting on the bank with a dazed expression on his face. 'Are you alright, RSM?' I asked. 'Yes thank you, Sir,' he replied, 'but it's my rabbit I'm worried about, it's still in the car.'

I looked across at the car and saw that petrol was starting to flow from underneath it. I hurried across the road and looked inside through the door window. Huddled in the corner of the other door under the glove compartment, level with the ground was a large white rabbit. 'Hang on to my legs,' I shouted to someone who was standing close by. 'Don't be a fool,' he said, 'the car could blow up any minute.' 'Just do what I tell you,' I replied, 'hang on to my legs.' I reached downwards through the horizontally positioned door, grabbed the rabbit and wriggled my way up again. Petrol was still pouring out of the car as the fellow who was hanging on to my legs gave a final pull that deposited me and the rabbit onto the road. A small cheer went up from the onlookers and a few of them patted me on the back. One woman who had a camera took a photograph of me and said, 'that's the bravest thing I've ever seen, I'm going to tell the

RSPCA what you've done.' I accepted all these plaudits and felt a glow of pride.

I had assumed that the rabbit was either concussed, like the RSM, or was so tame that it was thankful to be in the arms of its saviour. But when I looked at it closely I could see that its eyes were open and glazed. The glow of pride was overtaken by a feeling of sadness. 'One little boy or girl is going to shed tears when he or she is told that the rabbit has met with a fatal accident.' I thought.

I took the corpse across to the RSM and said, 'I am very sorry but the rabbit is dead.' He just stared at me for a moment, then he looked at the animal. I put it gently in his hands and he inspected it closely. 'You had me puzzled for a minute, Sir,' he said. 'It's been dead for some time. I bought it in the butcher's this afternoon. I'm having it for my supper tonight.'

I hastily asked the woman who had taken the photograph of me not to bother about going to the RSPCA. I told her I was shy about publicity.

CHAPTER TWENTY THREE
Cat and Dog in a Monsoon Climate

Soldiering in the tropics had been a solo pastime for me until 1963 when my wife, Nesta, to whom I had been married for three years, my son, Richard, aged two and my daughter, Gilly, aged nine months set off for Malaya on the last day of the year. We flew to Singapore by way of Istanbul and Bombay in a turbo propeller driven aircraft which would be considered uncomfortable by today's standards.

During the long flight, when we saw the sun rise twice, Nesta and I had plenty of time to think and talk about what our life would be like in the far east for the next two and a half years. I had already served in Malaya for 18 months during the communist uprising in the early 'fifties', so I was able to answer many of her questions. This time I was going out to be the second in command of a newly raised infantry battalion which obtained its recruits from North Borneo, or Sabah, to use its new name. The soldiers were to be trained in Malaya, and then, when they were fit for combat, were to take their place among the Malaysians and Commonwealth forces defending Sabah and Sarawak from the incursions of Indonesian armed forces.

We knew that we were going to live on the island of Penang, off the north west coast of Malaya, for the first nine months of our tour, and that I would have to travel to and from the Gurkha depot at Sungei Patani where our soldiers would be trained. The Gurkha depot was about one and a half hour's journey from Penang and involved crossing quite a large expanse of sea on a ferry to get to and from the mainland. It would therefore be impracticable for me to come home every night of the week, so I told Nesta that as soon as we arrived in Penang we would have to make enquiries about getting a dog to look after the family when I was not there.

The train journey from Singapore to the ferry, where we crossed to Penang, was luxurious compared with the cramped conditions on the long flight, soon we were settled in the opulent comfort of the Runnymeade Hotel, otherwise known as the Officers' Club.

We stayed in the club for a week while we found ourselves private accommodation in Georgetown. Within a few days we had selected a pleasant little house on the road to the airport and a few days later we moved in.

It was a typical Chinese bungalow with three bedrooms and accommodation for a 'live in' amah, who did all the housework and cooking, as well as looking after the children if Nesta and I wanted to go out on our own. A pleasant small garden provided us with bananas, and three towering coconut trees produced delectable nuts whenever we could arrange for them to be gathered by a special 'nut plucker'.

We were on our own as far as Europeans were concerned but our neighbours were Chinese, Malay and Indian middle class people. We made the acquaintance of our nearest neighbours who were Malay and, within an hour or so of moving in, Richard was playing with a little boy of the same age. I was aware of the large and ferocious dog kept by our neighbours, and it was obvious to me it was there for a purpose. When I asked them about the security situation in our area of Georgetown, they pointed to their dog and made fierce gestures which confirmed my suspicions. We were careful to lock our doors and bar all our windows before we went to bed.

I asked our newly acquired amah, Ah Kwa, if she knew where we could get the sort of dog that would not only guard the house, but be a friend and a pet. She said she would ask her father when she next went home. As a second string to our bow, a long term resident in Georgetown told me about two aged English spinster sisters who lived nearby in a rambling old house which they shared with their animals. They were self appointed, self financed and the nearest thing to the RSPCA to be found in Penang. I had their telephone number, so I gave them a ring. I was given a grilling by one of the old girls and I must have passed because she told me she would call me when the right sort of dog came their way.

I was having a shower one evening when I heard Nesta answer a ring on the door bell. I heard her talking to someone and then came an urgent call, 'Bob - come quickly!' I was out of the shower in a second, wrapping a towel around my middle as I skidded through the living room to see what was wrong. 'I think there's a snake in there,' said Nesta as she pointed to a sack on the door step. An old Chinese man, who had propped his bicycle against the porch, was undoing some knotted string from the mouth of the sack. I tried to speak to him but he understood neither English nor Malay. The sack was moving and it was clear there was some sort of living creature inside. 'Tell him to take it away,' said Nesta, who was by now convinced that a king cobra was going to crawl out. The old man finally succeeded in opening the sack and he pulled out a black dog. Relief that it was only a dog was overtaken by a feeling of revulsion for the way the poor animal had been treated. It had been lashed to a narrow metal carrier behind the saddle of the bicycle.

The animal was cringing on the doorstep and, although I had great sympathy for it, the dog did not conform to my requirements. The amah who had gone to a shop on the corner of the main road, returned as I was telling the old man to take it away. She spoke to him in his own language and he told Ah Kwa he had heard I wanted a guard dog. There was much arm waving by the amah and the old man before he picked up the animal and threw it back into the sack. A pathetic moan came from the dog as he started to lash it once again to the bicycle. 'Stop him,' said Nesta. 'We can't allow him to treat the poor animal like that.'

With my towel in danger of dropping to the ground I ran into the driveway and signalled the Chinaman to stop. 'How much does he want for the dog Ah Kwa?' I said. 'He say fifty dollars,' replied the amah. 'Tell him I will give him twenty dollars', I said. Another arm waving session between Ah Kwa and the old man ensued before Ah Kwa said, 'he will take twenty dollars.' I gave the old man two crisp ten dollar bills which Nesta handed me. He stuffed the money into his pocket, mounted his bone-shaker and rode away.

I unfastened the neck of the sack and once again the emaciated animal struggled to get out and sit up. The effort was too much, and it slumped onto its side. I returned to the bedroom to put on a pair of shorts. In the meantime Nesta gave the dog a bowl of water and some pieces of meat. It gently lapped the water but turned away from the food. It was hard to estimate the age of the dog as it was in such poor condition. It was jet black all over and stood about the height of a medium sized Labrador. Its eyes followed me everywhere I went and as I carried it to a comfy bed which Nesta made for it in the corner of the porch, its tongue came out and gently licked my hand. We made it as comfortable as we could and stayed with it until it went to sleep.

The following morning Nesta and I rose early and found the dog still lying listlessly in the position where I had placed it. We decided to take it to the Veterinary Hospital in Georgetown as soon as possible, so after we had finished breakfast we put the dog in the car and headed for the hospital. When we arrived we were able to take the animal straight in to see one of the Indian doctors who was on duty. He did not have to give the animal a thorough examination for it was obvious to him it was in an advanced stage of distemper. 'I am sorry, there is no hope of saving the dog, would you like me to put it to sleep?' he said. Although Nesta and I had known the the animal for less than one day we were sad when I nodded assent.

Our young son Richard, who had been kept under strict control by Ah Kwa and not allowed to touch the dog, burst into tears when we told him that the new addition to the family was dead. 'Just wait a few more days,' I told him, 'and then we will be getting another one which will be a real beauty.'

My words turned out to be prophetic as two days later I received a phone call from one of the Misses Jones. 'I think I've got the dog you have been looking for', she said, and she gave me a quick profile of the animal. 'He's just an ordinary 'pye' dog, black all over with a curly tail, about two years old - he's quite a character!' 'When can we see him?' I asked. 'Come around and have a cup of tea at about 5pm,' said Miss Jones. I thanked her and confirmed we would call on her and her sister that evening.

Richard was very excited at the good news and I had to dampen his enthusiasm in case the dog turned out to be unsuitable. He never took kindly to having an afternoon siesta and he was more trouble that day than usual.

At the appointed hour we arrived at the home of the Misses Jones and let ourselves into the garden through a small broken down gate. Inside was a wilderness - a complete contrast to the gardens of their neighbours which were kept in immaculate condition by native 'kebuns' (gardeners). All sorts of animals were wandering about. There were geese and ducks, peacocks and hornbills. Goats grazed alongside a young calf and an odd assortment of dogs and cats made up the menagerie. Just in front of the house was a dilapidated garden seat suspended on chains below a patched awning. Lying up against a cushion at one end of the seat was a black dog with a curly tail. Even though there were other Chinese 'pyes' at ground level Nesta and I knew instinctively that this one was ours. The other dogs in the garden came running towards us and jumped around us, but the one on the garden seat just sat and looked at us imperiously. He  was quite obviously the leader of the pack.

The Misses Jones came down the steps from their patio and walked over towards us. 'This is Bobby,' said Miss Alice, pointing to the dog on the garden seat. 'As you can see, he likes comfort.' 'We felt he was the one,' said Nesta, 'is he friendly?' The answer to the question was a suggestion by Miss Annie that I should extend the back of my hand for him to smell. Bobby inspected the proferred hand with a cold nose and then, with a yawn and a stretch, raised himself from the cushion and descended to ground level.

Richard had been watching these acts of introduction and, as his father was still in possession of his left hand, he felt confident enough to make his own overture. The rapport between dog and child was immediate and within a few seconds they were playing happily together. Seeing our pleasure at the antics of Bobby and our small son Miss Alice said, 'If you would like to have him we can go inside and complete the details.' There were more animals inside the house. Some were in cages like birds with broken wings, while others like kittens and puppies crawled over the floor. 'How do you manage to look after all these animals?' I asked. 'With great difficulty and lots of love,' said Miss Alice. 'If we can find good homes for them we are very pleased to hand them on but unfortunately many of our dear friends which cannot be given away or returned to the wild have to be put to sleep.' The Misses Jones went on to tell us that they made a run every morning in their car following a regular route so that the indigenous folk of Georgetown could give them their unwanted animals. These two remarkable old ladies had spent many years in Penang devoting their lives to the animals. Their great concern was about who would take over from them when they became too old to carry on.

Over a cup of tea Miss Annie told us that Bobby had come from a good Chinese home and had been innoculated against rabies and distemper. She lifted the flap of his right ear and I was able to see the serial numbers which recorded the fact. We entered our names in a book they kept and I asked how much we owed. 'Anything you can spare will be welcome,' said Miss Alice. The Malayan equivalent of ten pounds was a reasonable sum in those days, so I handed over the cash in exchange for the fine black dog which we felt sure would guard us well for the next two and a half years.

Bobby jumped into the back seat of our Humber 'Hawk' followed by Richard holding the lead. As we made our way home it became obvious that Bobby was a seasoned traveller and loved being in a car. He stuck his head out of the window like an old time engine driver and barked loudly at anyone who approached.

Ah Kwa was brushing the patio when we arrived home and she looked suspiciously at Bobby when he bounded out of the car. She need not have worried as Bobby had not yet taken up residence and established his area of authority. Just to be on the safe side Ah Kwa gave him some meat scraps which he devoured eagerly. Our small daughter Gilly, then aged nine months, had not been allowed free access to Bobby as had her two and a half year old brother Richard. It was necessary therefore to make quite sure that Bobby's so far impeccable behaviour would extend to Gilly. When they were introduced the magic chemistry of friendship was bonded at once. In the ensuing weeks and months Bobby was subjected to a demanding variety of violations of privacy such as tail twisting, eye poking and hair pulling. He took everything in his stride and in return would give Gilly a big lick across the face which would usually send her tumbling backwards.

It was not long before Bobby knew who was family and who was not. The first person to fall foul of him was a wizened little Malay who, by virtue of his trade as a coconut plucker, looked more like a monkey than a man. He was able to use his extraordinary ability to climb trees to good advantage when he came face to face with Bobby in the driveway one day. By the time I arrived to see what all the noise was about the Malay was about twenty feet above the ground and still climbing.

The coconut plucker, among other visitors and tradesmen who came to our house, soon got the idea that it was safer to rattle the large metal gates and wait for someone to come and attend to him than actually set foot in the garden. The distinctive noise made by Bobby when the gates were rattled was sufficient to let Nesta and me, or Ah Kwa, know that we had to look sharp. At that stage of Bobby's tour with us we did not usually put him on a running lead as we hated to deprive him of his liberty. Anyway, we could manage him quite well as there was a large fence around the house and we felt sure he could not get out. We were wrong of course as we had not considered the 'sex' factor. The first time he received the call to 'go forth and multiply' I saw him clear the tall wire fence with a few inches to spare. Over the next four or five days we saw nothing of him until one evening when he dragged himself into the garden through the gate we had left open for him. He was in an appalling state and it was obvious he had been engaged in a number of fights. The fur and flesh above his right eye had been ripped open and congealed blood covered one side of his face. He just managed to give Nesta one of his big slobbering licks before he sank down to the ground in front of us, completely exhausted. The kids were crawling all over him but the energy he had expended over the previous few days had used up his store of adrenalin and he was quite impervious to them.

Nesta had gone inside to get the first aid box. Within a minute or two she returned with a selection of powders and linaments. A liberal sprinkling of penicillin powder was applied to the raw flesh and an adhesive plaster kept the flap of flesh and fur in position above the eye. It was Nesta's intention to take Bobby to the vet the following morning, but after two hours sleep followed by the clearance of a full bowl of meat, he sailed over the fence and went off for another two days of canine lust.

As far as the females of his species were concerned, Bobby loved them all irrespective of height, width, length or colour, but for those of his own sex it was a different matter. Providing there was not a female around, Bobby would co-exist with black and white dogs, but the sight of a brown dog at any time would send him into a paroxysm of rage.

One such animal lived with a Chinese family a few hundred yards down the road from where we lived. The master of the household was in the habit of taking his dog for a walk in the cool of the evening - until we arrived. Bobby had made a hole under the fence for such exigencies as launching himself at brown dogs, and this he did one evening as the aged Chinaman and his dog were passing our house.

Bobby's attack was noisy and violent as he hurled himself at the brown dog. His upper mandibles clamped hard on the victim's cheek while his lower set were fixed firm behind the ear. The brown dog was held in an impenetrable vice and the kicks, shouts and exhortations to the Gods by his master made no impression upon Bobby.

Nesta, alerted by the noise, rushed outside and tried to draw Bobby away. Her efforts were to no avail so she yelled to Ah Kwa to fetch a bucket of water. Ah Kwa looked over the garden gate, summed up the situation and then waddled slowly back to the house. A few minutes later she reappeared with a large bucket. 'Quickly, quickly Ah Kwa,' said Nesta, which made not the slightest difference to the amah's speed of movement. Bobby had not relaxed his grip upon the brown dog and Nesta shrieked, 'Throw the water over him!' Ah Kwa spread her legs, took aim and swung the bucket. She completely missed Bobby and the poor Chinaman took the full force of water in his chest which knocked him to the ground. Once again Nesta yelled at Ah Kwa to get a bucket of water but the  owner of the brown dog abrogated her order by seizing the bucket which he used to beat Bobby around the head until he let go. Nesta does not speak any of the Chinese dialects but she did not need Ah Kwa to interpret the words of the owner of the brown dog. It was quite obvious to her that the long dead ancestors of the old man had been asked to wreak vengeance on the Smith family and the 'black devil' dog which lived with them.

Another of Bobby's aversions was the motorbike. The sound of a 750cc Kawasaki would set his muscles twitching and he had to be restrained when even a small two stroke machine passed by.

The road in front of our house went up a hill to the transmitting station of Radio Malaya. It was about a 1 in 10 incline and offered a reasonable challenge to a high powered machine to stretch its engine. One such machine, driven by a young Indian with his hair streaming behind him, raced up the hill one evening as Nesta and I were going for a stroll. Bobby was a good sport and he let the Indian get twenty yards ahead of him before he set off in pursuit. Over short distances Bobby had a good turn of speed and he quickly caught up with the motor cycle. He locked on to the Indian's ankle and held tight. With his balance impaired the Indian lost control of his machine as he zig-zagged across the road. He finally hit a concrete bollard and flew straight over the handle bars, with Bobby still attached to his ankle. We watched all this with horror and we were about to go to the Indian's assistance when we saw him get out of the ditch, into which he had fallen, pick up a large stick and start to beat Bobby.

Nesta and I, in unison, spun on our heels and walked nonchalantly away in the opposite direction - away from the Indian, his motor cycle, Bobby and any claim for damages.

Some of the most beautiful beaches in the Far East are to be found in Penang. We often drove to our favourite place - Lone Pine Beach, on the north coast of the island a few miles west of Georgetown. There we would sunbathe and swim in the warm waters of the Straits of Malacca to our hearts' content. Bobby loved to come with us and so did Ah Kwa, providing she could stay in the shade, as no self respecting Chinese woman could have a sun tan. While we were swimming, Bobby would be absorbed with a particular kind of crab which is found on most Malayan beaches. They measure about three inches across the top of their shells and they stand on stalk-like legs. They always seem to be on the move and when danger threatens they scurry to the nearest burrow in the sand. They move like greased lightning and, as there are always scores of crabs about with numerous burrows, they produce a bewildering pattern of movement as they criss-cross each others' tracks. Bobby could never be single minded enough to select one crab and ignore the others. The result was that he never caught anything as he weaved and twisted through the scampering crustaceans. They seemed to know just how far to keep in front of his nose before disappearing down a hole. The digging process would then start and before long the area of beach we had selected would be turned into something like a battlefield.

You can never tell by the expression on a crab's face what it is thinking, but after long periods of observing them on Lone Pine beach I am sure they enjoyed the sport just as much as Bobby.

At this stage of our tour in Malaya we adopted a kitten. I pulled into a garage one day for some petrol and as I was paying the bill I saw a cat with a litter of kittens in the corner of the shop. Richard had been pestering me for some time to get a cat so I asked the man behind the counter if I could have one of the kittens. The towkay (boss) was called and he was only too delighted to give me one. In fact he tried his best to give me all six of the litter, but I selected a pleasant little 'tabby' and put it in the car.

Bobby and cats mixed as easily as oil and water. A one time domesticated cat which had reverted to the wild had taken up residence with its litter at the back of the garage, but it had been forced to move by Bobby's unwelcome attention.

Poor little defenceless 'Friday', as we called her, carried the obnoxious 'cat' smell and this set Bobby's nose a'twitching. We had to be on constant guard for the first few days in case Bobby followed his natural instincts and had her for a snack.

During the cool evenings when the cicadas were singing in the coconut palms we would watch Bobby and Friday as they developed their relationship. It was all one-sided at first. Bobby appeared disdainful towards the small furry animals which had the patronage of his master and mistress, but he could not remain completely detached when the tip of his tail was such an object of attention. Friday would stalk it through the jungle of chairs and table legs before pouncing.

There is a certain time of year in Malaya, just before the monsoon starts, when a large type of flying beetle makes sitting out of doors in the evening a dangerous business. These beetles are attracted by lights and they come flying towards them at great speed. If you happen to be sitting in their flight path you can receive an extremely painful blow if they hit you. Friday would amuse herself for hours during the beetle season as she leapt and spun in her attempts to catch these noisy and troublesome pests. As she grew from a kitten into a young, lean and very good looking cat she became more expert in catching all sorts of flying and crawling things. She would deposit a wide variety of birds, lizards and beetles at the side of our bed for inspection.

Every household in Malaya has its chi-chas. These are small lizards about four or five inches long from nose to tail with sucker pads on their feet. They spend the daylight hours behind pictures and cupboards, but at night time they come out and scamper around the walls and ceilings in search of flies. They are

 delightful creatures and I have yet to meet anyone who does not have affection for them. In fact, among the native population, a house without chi-chas is an unlucky house.

We had the usual number of chi-chas in our house in Penang, but they were different from those in some of our friends' houses. Many of ours were minus their tails as they had ventured too far down the walls and had been caught by Friday. Chi-chas have existed on this planet longer than man and this is most probably due to their ability to jettison their tails when they are caught. They would waddle around in an ungainly way for a few days while they were growing a new one, and then the whole business would start again.

Bobby would watch Friday's nocturnal activities with interest and eventually he accepted her as a fully paid up member of the family union. When she was tired of catching beetles and depriving chi-chas of their tails she would curl up inside Bobby's legs and go to sleep.

By September 1964 sufficient numbers of our soldiers from Sabah had been trained at the Gurkha depot at Sungei Patani to allow the 2nd Battalion Malaysia Rangers to embark on the second stage of its evolution. This was to be a move into barracks of our own in the tin mining town of Ipoh in the state of Perak. This meant that we had to pack up our belongings and hand back our pleasant little house at Bukit Glugor to our Chinese landlord. We had to say 'farewell' to our neighbours and both Richard and Gilly were quite tearful about leaving their Malay playmates. Parting from Ah Kwa was an awful wrench for all of us. Not only was she an excellent amah, but she had become a good friend. The children adored her while Nesta and I were grateful to her for teaching us so much about the Malaysian way of life. She would have loved to come to Ipoh with us, but her father said she was too young to go so far away from home.

When everything was packed and we were ready to go, an

Army truck arrived to take our kit to Ipoh. My Sabahan orderly, Ibrahim, was detailed to ride in the front of the vehicle while Bobby was tied by his lead to one of the packing cases in the back of the truck. I was quite certain that with Bobby guarding our kit there would be no danger of prying hands coming over the tailboard. We had a special rotan (cane) basket made for Friday and she travelled with us in the car.

Ipoh is about 100 miles from Penang and the journey in our Humber 'Hawk' took about three hours, which included the crossing by ferry to the mainland. I, as second in command of the battalion, had already spent a few days in Ipoh supervising the take over from the 8th Hussars, the outgoing unit. I had checked all the items on charge in our new quarter and had satisfied myself that everything was in order for my family. It was therefore a pleasant experience to introduce them to the new home we were to live in for the next 14 months.

Our bungalow in Gopeng Lane was much larger than the one in Penang. It comprised a sitting room, a dining room, a spacious study, three bedrooms and two bathrooms. Adjoining the dining room was the kitchen and beyond were the amah's quarters. Surrounding the house was about half an acre of ground consisting of grass lawns and flower beds. The backdrop to the house was jungle and towering limestone gunong (rocky outcrops) which stretched up to the sky and onwards to the Cameron Highlands. The scene was breathtakingly beautiful.

Ah Ying, our new amah, and her husband, Lee with their two children Pen and Tan skidded into line on the front patio when they heard the Humber coming down the drive. They had occupied the servants quarters for about two years so Ah Ying and Lee were thoroughly conversant with our requirements. Within a few minutes of arriving, tea and cucumber sandwiches were served on the lawn.

About an hour later, after we had off-loaded the car and freshened ourselves, the whine of an Army truck could be heard as it approached the house.

There was Ibrahim in the front wearing a grin like an oriental Cheshire cat. In the back was Bobby doing his best to strangle himself in his effort to see what was going on 'up front'. He was delighted to see us and to be released from his tether.

All the old problems about relationships had to be sorted out again, so we took good care to keep hold of his collar when we introduced him to Ah Ying and the rest of her family. They all made a big fuss of him and he basked in the attention they gave him. A few choice tit bits of food from their quarters ensured an entry to his affection. Friday had been taken out of her basket as soon as we arrived and had already made her own inspection.

Richard, now three years of age, and Gilly, 15 months, were old and mobile enough to enjoy the experience of living in a new house with a new amah and the novelty of two ready made playmates. None of them were more than three years old and, even though they could not speak the others' language, it hardly seemed to matter as they exchanged toys and played happily with each other.

We thought it wise to tether Bobby when we arose the following morning so he could take his time to get to know those who called. The first person to arrive was Raslan the Malay kebun (gardener). Malays practice the faith of Islam and consider dogs unclean. Although they keep them in their kampongs (villages), they are never touched or allowed inside the house. Raslan knew he would be working for another British officer when he came down the drive-way that morning but he was not aware that his master had a dog and that it was attached to a running lead which ran from one end of the patio to the other. He had collected his bucket and spade from the amah's quarters and was heading for one of the flower beds when Bobby spotted him. It was fortunate for Raslan that the route he was taking was about six feet beyond the limit of the lead, Bobby came to a sudden halt as the tether tightened like a bow string, while Raslan nearly died of fright. He felt it was necessary to go around the corner and sit on his bucket for a few minutes until he had composed himself enough to get on with his work.

Raslan did not last long as he was a born malingerer. The only reason that he turned up so early on his first day was because he wished to make a good impression, thereafter his performance as a kebun went rapidly downhill. Bobby soon understood that he was a member of the household staff and we were able to let him run free when Raslan was working in the garden. The kebun, for his part, was careful to ingratiate himself with Bobby by throwing him the odd scrap of food.

During the afternoons throughout the year the heat is

unbearable and it was customary for Europeans to take a siesta. The franchise did not extend to the lower strata of the native population who were expected to work until the shadows lengthened in the late afternoon. Raslan must have felt he was a few rungs up from the bottom level of society as he would often creep down to the far end of the garden, where there were some bushes, curl himslef into a ball and go to sleep. Bobby, without any prompting from me, would keep an eye on Raslan and if he saw him heading for the bushes, would allow him to prepare for his unlawful siesta and then jump on him. This would make him get back to work in double time but, even with Bobby's supervision, the garden began to suffer - so Raslan had to go.

The people next door were a friendly couple. The man was Chinese and his wife English. At the entrance to their drive was a tree and from its branches hung various strips of cotton material. One day Nesta asked our neighbour the reason for the pieces of cloth on the trees. She explained they were part of the secret world of susperstition which governed the lives of most Chinese. From then on we noticed that their amah would spend some time each day tying on bits of cloth to the tree and removing others. She would light candles and joss sticks at the base of the trunk, spray incense and distribute special fake money for the spirits of her ancestors. At the end of her devotions she would place small bowls of food alongside the candles which contained such strange things as chickens' gizzards, ducks' feet, pigs' intestines and fish heads - Chinese believe in looking after their dead.

Soon after we were told about the amah's ritual we discovered that the plan for her ancestors' welfare had been aborted. Richard and Gilly, along with Bobby, had also planned a daily routine. This involved watching the movements of the amah from next door as she busied herself beneath the hantu (ghost) tree. When she had finished preparing things and had returned to the house the trio would creep, under cover of the hedge, to the tree and devour the food. As the children were fond of nuts and Bobby was particularly fond of pig and chicken guts there was a fair distribution of mid morning rations. Eventually the penny dropped and the amah decided her ancestors would be better served if she put the bowls of food in a fork of the tree.

Bobby was in the prime of his life when we lived in Ipoh and seemed to fear nothing. One evening though, as we were going for a stroll, a large black snake slithered through the grass in front of us. Bobby's reaction was immediate, he jumped sideways and took refuge behind Nesta. I did not pursue the matter and upbraid him for being a coward, he knew his limitations and cobras were not in his class.

Friday would often bring in snakes she had caught. None of them were very large and she knew her capabilities as well. As far as we were concerned all snakes in Malaya were treated with respect and whoever found one of Friday's play-things raised the alarm immediately.

Nesta was particularly concerned about snakes while we lived in the far East, and for good reason. The previous occupants of our house in Ipoh had left the door from the verandah to the bedroom open one night and had not noticed that one of their children had put a wooden plank from the ground to the verandah. This plank allowed a cobra to enter the bedroom and they came face to face with it when they went to bed. Needless to say we kept that particular door shut all the time we were in Ipoh.

My office in Ramillies Lines, the home of the 2nd Battalion Malaysia Rangers in Ipoh, was about a mile away from where we lived and Nesta used to drive me to work every morning at 7am. Our route took us along Tiger Lane, which should really have been called Cobra Lane, on account of the dead snakes which littered the carriageway every morning. Snakes like warmth and are attracted to the heat retaining properties of tarmacadam. The continuous depletion of their numbers seemed to make no difference to the new crop of squashed snakes we saw every day. It gave one an eerie feeling to know these highly poisonous reptiles, although we rarely saw them alive, lived close to our house.

The transition from daylight to darkness in Malaya is sudden. Each day we arranged a playtime period for the children and the animals to take place during the last half hour of daylight. We had a lovely garden with plenty of room for all of us to scamper around. Bobby was the most energetic member of the family and he used this playtime period to burn up excess energy. Cats do not normally feel the need to exercise but every evening as the sun dipped below the green horizon she would come and join us. She would rub her sides around our legs with her tail held high and she would arch her back and raise a paw menacingly when

Bobby approached - but with good humour, although Bobby was never quite sure! When we were ready to go indoors to bathe the children, Friday would suddenly bolt across the lawn with Bobby in hot pursuit. She had an amazing turn of speed and, like a good rugby scrum half, could spin on her axis and change direction without loss of speed. She always tied Bobby in knots and he never managed to get within three feet of her. The chase always ended by Friday climbing a tree where, from the topmost branches, she would look down at Bobby - giving a good impression of a dog who had not eaten for a week. It was then Friday's turn to feel unsure!

Friday must have found a boyfriend soon after we arrived in Ipoh as we became aware of the increasing size of her girth. She gave birth to the first of five kittens one evening just as the children were getting ready for their story before going to bed. This was the only occasion I can remember when I was let off my evening duty - the arrival of Friday's babies was far more fun.

Up until that time Bobby and Friday got on well with each other, but those tiny bundles of fur put a new edge to their relationship. Gone was the romp in the garden and so was their close companionship on the patio in the cool of the evening. Friday's duty lay with her babies and she was a good mother.

One day I saw Bobby come flying out of the garage with Friday on his shoulders. He had unwittingly gone too near the basket which Friday was using as a nest for her kittens. Thereafter he

made sure he kept away from the garage but as the weeks went by, and the kittens became adventurous, he could not always avoid them. He used to look appealingly at us when Friday had boxed his ears. Fortunately our new kebun was able to find homes for all of them when they

Friday and her kittens

were six weeks old. We were sorry to see them go, but Bobby was delighted to resume his normal relationship with Friday.

The area in which we lived mustered about eight or nine houses, some of them were occupied by British officers and their families, but we were the only ones who kept a dog.

145

During the 12 months we lived in Ipoh almost every other house in the 'patch' was burgled. I am quite sure that our good fortune was due to Bobby's visual and audible presence. He really was the terror of the neighbourhood as far as the local population were concerned.  The NAAFI boy was forbidden by the manager of the Army's general store to take his van down our drive after Bobby had bitten lumps of rubber off one of the tyres in his attempt to get at the driver. Nesta and I were pleased with his performance as a guard dog, although we were always concerned about the danger of causing injury to someone.

In early 1965 I felt confident enough with my ability to speak Malay that I applied to take the national language examination. I flew to Singapore and took the test in Nee Soon barracks. There were no problems and I qualified for the £150 grant for passing the test. I promised Nesta and the children that if I was successful we would all go on leave to the east coast of Malaya. It is not difficult to imagine the delight my good news caused when I came in on the evening flight of Malayan Airways.

We arranged with our neighbours for Bobby and Friday to be given their food each day and for Bobby to be tied up whenever Chandra, our new kebun, came to attend to the garden. For the rest of the day and night he was allowed to run free and we only hoped he would not feel the urge to go off with one of his girl friends while we were away.

We had a marvellous time on the east coast and I was able to introduce Nesta and the children to some old friends of mine whom I had not seen for 12 years years since I had been stationed in Kuantan with The King's African Rifles. All too soon it was time to return and when we arrived home we received a great welcome from all those who had now become dependent upon us - Chinese, Indian and Malay (car wash boy), as well as Bobby and Friday. Chandra greeted us in the fashion of his race, with palms pressed together as in prayer. 'Everything is in order, Sahib,' he said. I could see that this was true as I cast my eyes over the well tended flower beds and freshly cut grass. Bobby, who was prancing about with excitement suddenly transferred his attention to Chandra and leapt playfully into his arms. 'He is my friend now,' said the kebun. 'He's a very good dog and he looked after your house while you were away.' Bobby knew he was getting a good report and he positively beamed with pride.

We very nearly lost Bobby one day when the dog catchers came around. Stray dogs are a menace in Malaya and they cause great concern to the public health authorities. Teams of catchers travelling in transit vans are employed to round up stray animals. They can always be recognised by their bright yellow jackets, the ·22 rifles they carry and the long claw like implements they put around a cornered dog's head at a range of about ten feet. As they are only concerned with dogs who are not wearing collars, and Bobby always wore a stout rivet studded collar with his name and address clearly marked on it, we were never worried about him when we saw the catchers in our area.

Nesta had driven me into work one morning and had returned home to have her breakfast. As she was sitting at the dining table she heard Bobby barking in the garden. Ah Ying appeared and said, 'Come quickly, Mem (short for memsahib), the dog catchers are here.' She went on to exclaim, 'Bobby is not on his lead.' Cornflakes flew everywhere as Nesta sped from the dining room, through the kitchen to the back garden, where she saw Bobby jumping up against the fence - minus his collar. Somehow he had wrenched it off and thus had put himself into the category of 'fair game' for the dog catchers. One of them was actually walking towards the fence with a loaded gun and was about to take aim when Nesta put herself in the line of fire. The dog catcher lowered his rifle while Nesta put her arms around Bobby's head to shield and control him. Ah Ying had no such idea of standing in between Bobby and a trigger happy dog catcher, but she was most impressed with Nesta's dedication to Bobbys' welfare. We made sure that Bobby's collar was tightened to another hole from then onwards.

I have already mentioned that Ah Ying and Lee had two children who were about the same age as our youngsters. All four of them played happily together in the garden but Ah Ying made it clear to her children that our quarters were out of bounds. This rule was strictly observed until the 16th August 1965, Richard's fourth birthday. It was easy to round up a dozen extremely willing three and four year olds from the battalion officers' families to attend the party. We asked Ah Ying if her children would like to come as well. This was an opportunity for us to repay Ah Ying's and Lee's hospitality to our children a few weeks before, at Ah Ying's mother's house, when they took part in the Moon festival. It was just about the most exciting thing that had happened to our kids. When they came home they told us all about the strange food they had eaten and the evening lantern procession in which they had taken part. They returned with some rice cakes for us to eat and their beautifully painted bamboo lanterns sat on their bedside tables for the rest of the time we lived in Malaya.

The day of the party arrived and during the early afternoon the local soft drink manufacturers, Frazer and Neave, delivered the swings, slides and roundabouts which were common features at all childrens' parties. While they were being set up in the garden, Ah Ying and Lee were busy preparing the table on the patio to bear the mass of sandwiches, cakes, jelly and trifle they had been making since daybreak.

At about 4pm the first of our young visitors arrived and soon the garden became a noisy playground as the kids made the most of the soft drink firm's fun machines.

When all was going well Ah Ying went off to her quarters and a few minutes later returned with her two children bearing their birthday gifts. They approached Richard very formally and with a curtsy from Pen and a bow from Tan the presents were handed over. Like all well brought up Chinese children they were immaculately dressed. Pen had her jet black hair tied in plaits, with ribbons to match her crisp white dress with tiered skirt. Eye shadow, rouge, powder and lipstick are used by Chinese mothers on their children from an early age, and Ah Ying had made Pen into a most beautiful painted doll. Tan, although not 'made up', had been well prepared to attend this most important function. By this time our children had picked up a few words of Malay so Richard was able to say 'Terima kasi' ('thank you') to Pen and Tan for their gifts.

Bobby had been lying on the mat between the living room and

the patio, waking up occasionally when he was trodden on or hit by a flying squeaker. Suddenly he raised himself and, to his amazement saw, inside the living room, the amah's children playing happily with the other party goers. Bobby must have been aware of Ah Ying's rules about where and where not her children could go in the house, so he went across to Pen and nosed her towards the door. Then, with ever so gentle nips on her bottom, he proceeded to propel her towards her mother who was attending to the food on the patio. Nesta saw what was in Bobby's mind so she quickly caught hold of him, took him outside and tied him to his lead in the garage. After the party when we were all cleaning up, we had a laugh about Bobby's action. Ah Ying said that our children, when they visited her mother's home for the Moon festival, had prompted the same action from their dog and he had to be tied up as well.

To give Bobby a change of scene and some exercise I would occasionally take him with me when I went into the jungle to see our soldiers training. I was making an early start one day and when Bobby saw me in jungle kit he pranced around me and made it quite clear he wanted to come. When I opened the door of the Land Rover he was in like a shot!

Ibrahim, my orderly, and I set off to follow the course of the Sungei Kenas which flows into the Sungei Perak at Kuala Kangsar. It was an easy route and there were well worn paths on each side of the river. The jungle area had been designated a 'big game reserve' and we were quite happy to have Bobby with us to give us warning if he scented an animal of the same species as Friday, but much larger. Even after the passing of 30 years I can remember the first time I walked the Sungei Kenas. It is one of the most beautiful regions in Malaya and the lower reaches of the river became a favourite place of ours for swimming and picnics.

After about an hour and a half we came across our soldiers in their jungle camp. I was impressed by the way they had built their bashas (temporary huts) and by the way they had sited shallow trenches nearby; to afford them interlocking fields of fire in an emergency. Our young men from Sabah (North Borneo) were quite at home in the jungle, but it was necessary that their natural skills be tuned to the Army way of doing things.

Bobby came with me to visit one group of soldiers who had made their camp about half a mile further on. When we arrived we found they were having a rest and preparing their midday meal. Hexamine burners were bringing mess tins of rice to the boil and the soldiers were opening those marvellous little tins of food from what the Army calls 'individual ration packs'. Sabahan soldiers, even though they liked this highly nutritious food, used to supplement their rations with dried fish which they would bring with them. Even though the smell was obnoxious, it became quite tasty when cooked. This particular platoon had a large bag of the stuff and Bobby, who had been nosing around, found it. At home in Ipoh he would have turned up his nose if Ah Ying had put dried fish in his bowl but there, deep in the jungle on the banks of the Sungei Kenas, he ripped the bag open and ate the lot. He was busy searching for his next course when the platoon sergeant discovered what had happened and planted a size eight jungle boot under his tail. The gentle, courteous manners of Malaysian people is one of the pleasant features of serving in that part of the world. Those hungry soldiers did their best to convince me they did not want any dried fish anyway, but their efforts to appease my embarrassment was of no avail.

In October 1965 the 2nd Battalion Malaysia Rangers was fully trained and ready to take its place alongside other units of Commonwealth security forces defending the borders of Sarawak and Sabah against Indonesian aggression. Many of the British wives decided to return to the United Kingdom, but Nesta preferred to return to Penang and await my return in seven months time. Her reasoning was that life would be better in the beautiful ambience of that island than spending a cold winter in an Army quarter in UK.

A month before I was due to leave for Sabah we took a week's leave and went house hunting in Penang. We stayed at the government chalets, a delightful little compound of holiday homes reserved for the use of Malaysian civil servants and officers of the armed forces. We knew the island well and although we had been very happy in our previous home in Bukit Glugor, Nesta wanted to be closer to the sea and nearer the centre of Georgetown.

The place she set her sights on was an apartment in a block situated between Runnymeade Officers' Club and The Eastern and Oriental Hotel (shortened to The E & O). The place turned out to be ideal for her and the children. A number of British families were already living there, it was within easy reach of the shops and the view from the garden over the sea to Kedah Peak was superb. We went to see the administrator and to our delight a flat was available just at the time I was due to leave for Sabah. We signed up there and then.

The last few weeks in Ipoh passed quickly. There was much packing of boxes and disposing of rubbish. Nesta and I were mystified by the way our possessions increased by 100% every time we made a move.

It all seemed so familiar when the Army 3 ton truck arrived at our house in Ipoh to take aboard our packing cases for the return trip to Penang. Ah Ying, Lee and their children, now a year older, were standing in a tearful line to say 'good-bye'. Chandra and the car wash boy had also come to see us off and all of them received an enhanced payment for looking after us so well. Bobby was put in the back of truck where once again he was detailed to look after our possessions. With Friday in her wicker basket inside the Humber and with Richard and Gilly nearly falling out of the windows waving their 'farewells', we set off for Penang.

Nesta and I were quiet with our own thoughts as we drove north. We knew that in a few days I would be returning to Ipoh on my own prior to taking the advance party of the battalion to Sabah. We sped along the road which twisted and turned through the Kinta Valley wherein lies that world's greatest deposit of tin. We saw the turn off to the Chior big game reserve where only a few weeks before I had shown Nesta and the children the pug marks of a fully grown tiger. Kuala Kangsar appeared on the banks of the Sungei Perak and we were reminded of an unforgettable evening when we attended the Sultan of Perak's birthday party in his fairy tale pink palace. Onwards to Taiping which had painful memories for the both of us. I had been taken to the military hospital there with the dreaded swamp disease of leptospirosis which I had contracted at the Jungle Warfare School in Kota Tinggi. The road from Taiping to Butterworth was a familiar route for Nesta as she had travelled it on many occasions during the four weeks I had been in hospital.

At last we drove out of the vast acreage of rubber trees and saw the sea and the island of Penang in the distance; we felt we were on our way home.

One advantage of the new apartment was the close proximity of the beach, which was less than a hundred yards away. We had been confined in the car for about three hours so we felt the need for a swim. When we returned about 30 minutes later we just had time to make a cup of tea before the truck with our kit arrived. Ibrahim unleashed Bobby who within a few minutes had taken in all the smells of the garden and contributed a few of his own.

The next two days were spent unpacking some of our boxes and putting others aside for our return to the United Kingdom eight months later. We tried to get Ah Kwa to be our amah again, but she had found another job with a long term future and she quite sensibly declined our request to come and live with us. She made a great fuss of the children, but the interval of over a year had made them shy. It was not until she had left that the children implored us to let them see her again. Thereafter Richard and Gilly had to be restrained from hi-jacking her from her new mistress whenever we went past her house. Nesta interviewed some potential amahs and finally settled on a middle aged Burmese lady who suprisingly had the same name as my mother - Elsie.

Bobby had to be introduced to a new bunch of Malay, Chinese and Indians. The first commotion occurred during the first morning we were in our new home. The Indian postman came face to face with Bobby as he was about to put a letter through the

letter box. Fortunately the postman's bicycle was only a few feet away and he was able to get hold of it and use it as a shield to stop Bobby from tearing him to pieces. I flew to the postman's rescue and caught hold of Bobby's collar before he could do any harm. The Indian was speechless with fright and looked at me incredulously when I approached, still holding on to Bobby, and asked him to give me his left hand. He shut his eyes as I placed his hand on Bobby's head and then worked it around until I inserted his fingers into Bobby's mouth. Someone once told me that this was the way to forge friendship between man and dog. It seemed to work as the Indian was able to withdraw his hand and assure himself that he still had all his fingers. 'You will have no trouble from now on,' I said, and he quite voluntarily offered his other hand to Bobby who graciously sniffed it.

The last few days with Nesta and the kids flew past but I was happy with the thought that after seven months in Sabah I would return to Penang and spend four weeks leave there before returning to the UK. I was also happy in the knowledge that Nesta had got the flat she wanted, an amah who seemed to be excellent - certainly as far as Burmese curries were concerned, and a dog who would stand no nonsense from anyone.

A Land Rover arrived and Ibrahim put my kit aboard. I kissed Nesta and the children 'farewell', gave a last and somewhat choked instruction to Bobby about 'being in charge', and then I was on my way. I hardly noticed the familiar streets and buildings in Georgetown and my eyes did not clear until I was on the ferry heading for the mainland.

All the time we had been in Malaya we had communicated with our parents in the UK through the medium of the tape recorder. We seemed to be the only British family in the battalion who did this and I could never understand why others did not follow our example. From a very early age Richard and Gilly would trot off with a tape recorder and announce they were going to talk to Grandpa and Grandma. Richard was able to operate the buttons and both would chat quite naturally to both sets of grandparents who lived on the other side of the world.

Before I left Penang I bought two new tape recorders, one for Nesta and the children and one for me. I was eager therefore to receive my first taped message when I arrived in Sabah. After five days of watching every Fokker 'Friendship' aircraft of Malaysian Airways arrive on the airstrip adjacent to the camp in Tawau, the one carrying my tape finally came in. I was delighted to hear the news of the family but appalled to hear what Nesta had to say about Bobby. It appeared he had abrogated the postman's trust by nearly ripping off his trousers on his second visit to our flat. Nesta thought he was not going to take the matter further, but either his greed for compensation or his recovery from shock made him think again and report the affair to his superior officer. From then on bureaucracy took over and the saga of Bobby and the postman accounted for many furlongs of magnetic tape.

Nesta was summoned to appear at the Magistrates' Court in

Georgetown. When she arrived she was advised by her Chinese counsel to plead guilty. One look at the magistrate, a Malay, convinced her that this was good advice.

The magistrate listened to the evidence of the postman, who by now had developed a limp, and had to be assisted into and out of the witness box. He looked severely at Nesta and asked her how she wanted to plead. 'Guilty!' she squeaked. Another severe look from the magistrate was followed by the pronouncement that she would have to pay a fine of Malayan $200.00 - which was about £20.00 in those days, and quite a lot of money. More was to come though and the second arrow from the magistrate's bow was an order that Bobby would be put in quarantine to see if he carried the rabies virus. Despite Nesta's protestations that he had been vaccinated - and had a tattoo in his ear to prove it, he was duly impounded and taken away to the approved place for dogs who bite postmen. After 14 days he was returned to Nesta's ownership, but only after she handed over another cheque for Malayan $200.00 for his keep and another rabies jab. While all this was going on he was 'absent from duty' - which after all was the main reason for him being with us. I was none too pleased.

Indians come in all shapes and sizes but the one who adopted Nesta and the children, or the place where they lived, was called in Malay an 'orang gila' (mad-man). During daytime this weird, bearded and wild eyed fellow spent his time on the padang (open grassy area in the centre of the town, rather like a park in English terms). At night he would take up residence in the passage way leading to the front door of our flat and there sleep until morning. At dawn he would pick up his meagre possessions, clean up whatever mess he had made - very little really, and return to the padang.

Nesta nearly had a fit the first night she saw him. She was returning from a supper party and fell over the Indian who was asleep on the floor in front of the door. The orang gila, who was most probably used to being kicked during the night, did not move, but Nesta's agitation set off a chain reaction which caused Bobby to wake up the entire community. She opened the door as fast as she could, stepped over the somnolent Indian, at the same time keeping hold of Bobby's collar lest he attack him and cause another trip to the magistrates' court. She need not have worried as Bobby, instead of attacking, shrank back into the shadows and

154

spent the rest of the night barking in unison with the snores of orang gila.

The weird fellow would arrive every night at about ten o'clock and was quite unconcerned about Bobby who, even though he barked long and loud, would not approach him. Nesta was appalled at Bobby's reluctance to do his duty, but when it was obvious to her that the Indian had some sort of mental hold over the dog, she resorted to other means.

The administrator of the flats, a Chinaman, considered that his responsibilities extended only to collecting rent and attending to matters of maintenance. He was therefore not impressed or inclined to take action against the Indian. She then tried the local police station, but the jaundiced eye of the sergeant in charge, who recognised her from the postman affair, convinced her that she could not expect any sympathy from that quarter. In desperation she called at the headquarters of the resident British infantry battalion in Penang and asked the adjutant if he could help. 'Leave it to me,' he said. 'We'll have it fixed in no time.' When the orang gila arrived at the flat that night he came face to face with two burly British regimental policemen. They turned him around and very firmly led him to their Land Rover, put him in the back and drove off. Nesta saw him most days on the padang but he did not come back to our flat any more. That was the end of the story as far as the orang gila was concerned, but a big question mark had been entered against Bobby's effectiveness towards such people.

In one of Nesta's tapes she told me that Friday had brought a small snake into the house. Elsie inspected the reptile and said it was a baby cobra. It was dead so she tossed it over the sea wall. It is a fact that where there is one baby snake there are quite likely to be more close by. A search was made of the grounds, but nothing was found. Elsie had told Nesta that when she was a young girl she had been bitten by a cobra and she showed her the mark on her leg. Whether it had been caused solely by the snake or by someone's effort to extract the poison could not be established but, whatever the reason, she was badly scarred.

The amah lived about half a mile away from our flat and one

day soon after Friday had caught the snake she burst in through the kitchen door, slammed it behind her and said, 'Do not open the door mem, there's a cobra in the monsoon drain.' It seemed that as she was crossing the forecourt she looked into the six foot deep drain and saw a huge cobra. The open drain went around the block of flats and the cobra was obviously trying to find a way out. Nesta made sure that all the members of the family, including Friday and Bobby, were inside the flat and then closed all the doors and windows. She then telephoned the administrator and asked him to get rid of the reptile. Nobody likes being up front when a cobra is about and there was a marked lack of activity in the area of the flats until Nesta decided to set off on her own. The snake had disappeared and was not seen again, but everyone tip-toed through the grass with care for a few days afterwards.

After seven months active service in Sabah it was time for me to return to my family. The final chapter of a fascinating part of our lives was to end with four weeks leave in Penang.

Nesta and the two children, Richard now five years of age, and Gilly three and a half, were at the airport when I flew in. Bobby had been left in the car in the car park and his welcome was as enthusiastic as ever. By the time we arrived home we were all in tune with each other and it was hard to believe that I had been away for so long.

We had a marvellous holiday but all too soon it was time for us

Nesta with Richard, Gilly and Bobby

to pack our boxes and switch our minds to the business of returning to the UK. Two and a half years ago we had not given thought to the matter of handing on our animals but now, when the sands of time were running out, it was necessasy to take action on the problem. Elsie was quite prepared to take Friday, but her benevolence did not extend to Bobby with whom she had always had an uneasy relationship. We decided to ask the Misses Jones, from whom we had obtained Bobby, if they could find another home for him. They said they would try.

A week before we were due to fly home one of the Misses Jones rang to say she had found someone who would like to have Bobby. If we agreed, he would start the next chapter of his life with a Chinese 'dollar' millionaire who lived with his family in a huge house facing the sea on the road leading to Lone Pine beach. We were delighted with the arrangement, but I emphasised that we wanted Bobby to remain with us until our last day in Penang.

Two hours before we vacated our flat and started the long journey back to England a large white Mercedes limousine drew up in the courtyard. A uniformed Chinese chauffer announced that he had come to collect 'a dog' for his master. Nesta took out his two bowls, one for water and the other for food, his wicker basket - chewed at one end, his cushion, his rubber bone and his special toy - a squashy football. Bobby needed no prompting as I am sure he realised it was time to move on. He jumped into the back of the limousine, reclined against a cushion and, without a backward  glance, sped off to the home of his new family.

Bobby was just an oriental 'pye' dog, one of thousands of mongrels which scavenge, fight, procreate and generally make nuisances of themselves in Malaya. But to us he was a friend and a character whose personality enriched our lives to such an extent that we still talk about him thirty years later.

We often wonder if there were any more chapters in his life or if he ended his days happily in the home of the wealthy Chinese family. Of one thing we are sure, his standards would have remained high until the day he died.

CHAPTER TWENTY FOUR

Terra (in) Firma

One of the places visited by the regimental touring team was a pleasant little town near Swansea. Council officials were most helpful with the planning of the visit and allowed us to use the municipal park which consisted of ornamental gardens, tennis courts, a bowling green, cricket wicket and a rugby pitch. The mobile display wagon and the shooting range (in the back of a truck) were the first to arrive and it was not long before the children of the town were attracted to the park like wasps to a jam pot.

I was talking to some soldiers on the site when I became aware that the ground upon which I stood seemed to move when people passed by. I jumped a few inches off the ground and my return to earth set the soldiers wobbling like near missed skittles.

It was then that Mr Ieuan Thomas, the chief environmental officer of the borough greeted me. 'Hello Major Smith, everything alright then?' I assured him that things were in order and that we were looking forward to a good day. 'There is only one problem,' I said, 'the ground seems to wobble. Was there ever a coal mine here and is it possible that we could be standing on a covered over shaft?' I made another leap and the colour drained from Mr Thomas's face as he wobbled like a piece of jelly. He cast his mind over the 35 years he had worked for the council and after some deep thought said, 'No - not in my time has there been a mine here. Pottery - yes, but not a mine.'

We were joined by the borough engineer - Mr Iorweth Evans. Iorweth agreed about the pottery but said that he could not pronounce about a mine as he had not lived in the valley as long as Ieuan. 'I could find out for sure when I get back to my office,' he said. 'We've got records going back to the beginning of the last century.' Ieuan would have been happy to let old pots lie, but borough engineers are an inquisitive breed and Iorweth walked across to the pavilion and brought back a long metal rod with a loop on the end. Standing on the steps of the display vehicle he raised his arms above his head and drove the rod into the turf. No undue force was used or required to send the eight foot rod through the ground as far as its loop. The borough engineer withdrew the rod and we inspected the particles of black stuff which came out of the hole. 'Peat', said Ieuan, and then as an after-thought - 'could be charcoal though.' Iorweth picked up a few pieces and agreed with his colleague. It was my turn, so I picked up some of the black matter and found that it did not crumble like the others. 'Coal,' I said. 'This looks like good quality anthracite to me.' The two council officers gaped like a couple of goldfish but then realism took over as they remembered the many occasions the ground had been used for fairs, carnivals and rugby matches. 'You'll be alright, have no fear,' they said in unison. Despite their assurances I did not feel they were entirely convinced. The display vehicles could have been moved to a safer area, if I could find one. But everywhere I jumped the ground wobbled - and besides I was getting some funny looks as I leapt around the park like a demented frog. Taking the easy course and assuring myself that if the ground was going to collapse it would surely have done so when the band in their 50 seater coach passed by, I decided to carry on.

The mayor of the borough, a charming elderly lady, was our chief guest at the show we put on that evening. The 60 minute performance included a display of foot and arms drill, gymnastics, mock battle and a Beating Retreat by the band and drums. More than a hundred soldiers plus the regimental goat, pounded the turf during the finale. I do not know if she had been told or even felt for herself the undulating movement of the ground. If she did she said nothing and, as she had lived near the park all her life, she was most probably used to it.

She certainly did not appreciate the reason why I kept my camera at the ready throughout the performance. The band and drums, regimental mascot, mayor, councillors - and maybe me too - disappearing through the hallowed turf of the town's rugby pitch. It might just have been the picture of my life.

CHAPTER TWENTY FIVE

Remove Head-Dress

An infantry battalion is the result of much fine tuning which over the years has produced a well balanced combat unit. Rifle and support company soldiers get most of the glamour, but there are others such as storemen, drivers and mess servants who provide essential administrative support. The 'back up' boys accept their low profile but occasionally a moment occurs when a burst of energy, zeal or inspiration catapults them into the focus of attention.

Such was the case with Private Morris. If war had not been declared in 1939 it is unlikely that he would have ever worn battle dress but, like many thousands of other young men, he was called up for national service; he joined a battalion of Welsh infantry and saw service in France and Germany.

Morris was one of the links in the chain at the bottom of the pile, but he nevertheless performed a vital function by producing a hot cup of tea for his officer when it was most needed. His contribution is not actually recorded in the official record of the Battle for the Reichswald, but those who drank his hot tea swear that the turbo action produced was the essential ingredient for success.

When the war was won and Morris returned to his home in West Wales he missed the routine of Army life. By 1947, when Russians had taken the place of Germans as our No.1 enemy, Morris returned to his old battalion and became a waiter in the officers' mess.

During the first annual camp for volunteer soldiers after the war, the commanding officer was told that the Chief of the Imperial General Staff - none other than Field Marshall The Viscount Montgomery of Alamein would visit the battalion.

The day of the visit arrived and the field marshall drew up outside the guard room in his limousine. The quarter guard gave a crisp salute and the field marshall inspected them. He visited a platoon of soldiers on the 30 yards range and saw a demonstration of fire drill before being escorted to the officers' mess for lunch.

The commanding officer had been told about the spartan taste of the field marshall so the mess table carried some cold chicken legs and a green salad. Wine was not served and the officers had been forbidden to smoke in the great man's presence.

As soon as the pudding had been eaten the field marshall turned towards the commanding officer and said, 'What have you got for me to see this afternoon?' The colonel outlined the programme and the field marshall bounded to his feet eager to be off. Aides de camp moved ahead of him to collect his British warm (overcoat), cane and the famous black beret. The overcoat and cane were on the coat rack in the hall, but there was no sign of the beret.

'Where's my hat?' snapped the field marshall. The colonel looked vacant, the second in command, as always in an emergency bit his finger nails and the quartermaster occupied himself with his mill board. 'Where's my hat, damn it?' thundered the victor at El Alamein. It was at this point that Private Morris, still in a state of rapture after being allowed to serve blancmange to the field marshall, burst through the throng, grabbed Montgomery by the arm and said, 'Are you sure you had it on when you came in, Sir?'

CHAPTER TWENTY SIX

The Saga of Sadie Slagheap

The little town of Abercwmavon, in one of the eastern valleys of South Wales, nestles between grim and forbidding slag heaps, lightly grassed over these days but still a hindrance to those who are trying to make the valley green once more and fill its rivers with trout. The character of the people who inhabit this valley and who live in the small town is not compatible with the environment in which they live. They are friendly, warm human beings who have been pressed into a singing, rugby playing, chapel attending community by the very slag heaps that dominate them.

Abercwmavon and district has been for generations a strong source of recruits for the infantry regiments of Wales. It was therefore quite natural for this place to be chosen by my regiment as one of the towns to be visited by the touring team during its annual recruiting drive.

I was at the time responsible for these publicity ventures, and when I made my overture to the local recreation and amenities officer I was delighted with the response I received. 'We would be honoured indeed,' said Mr Dafydd Price, 'and I know I speak for the mayor as well, to have you visit our borough.' He showed me the rugby pitch where we would be allowed to set up our displays; what greater honour could there be for us. There stood the posts standing sentinel over the thick green turf that was taking a temporary respite from the rucks and wheelings, lineouts and scrums which made men out of boys in Abercwmavon. The entrances and exits were wide enough to take our vehicles and there was even a public convenience - a tidy place indeed.

The appointed day arrived, a lovely bright Wednesday in July, and I joined the officer in charge of the touring team, along with three of his subalterns for drinks with the mayor of the borough of Bryntyrion in his parlour.

Councillor Gwilym Rees, the mayor, was a vigorous young man in his early forties. He had climbed to the senior position on the council of the borough of Bryntyrion with a burning crusade for social reform. He was also well known for his ability to bulldoze opposition on the council floor.

His sherry was good and we soon got to know each other quite well. He was interested in the affairs of the regiment and he thought that it would be a very good thing if the government brought back national service. 'Discipline is what we want in this country,' he said. We spent two hours or so in his company and were entertained to lunch in a country club - once the home of a coal baron.

The evening performance of the touring team was the big event of the day. It started with a concert given by the regimental band and corps of drums. This was followed by a demonstration of weapons and equipment and then came the mock battle, with plenty of noise - which delighted the children but was not altogether appreciated by the inmates of an old peoples' home on the perimeter of the field. The finale was the marching display, 'Beating Retreat' and the lowering of the flag. The salute at the march past was taken by the mayor, Councillor Gwilym Rees.

The crowd clapped and the mayor beamed as the musicians and soldiers, led by Taffy, the regimental goat, marched off to the strains of 'God Bless the Prince of Wales'. 'An excellent show indeed,' said the mayor who was impressed with our military hardware and colourful regalia. He and the others in his party now looked forward to the final part of our programme which was a drinks party in the marquee erected near one of the goal posts.

Councillors and their wives were escorted by a trio of subalterns and it was not long before everyone had a glass in their hands. Conversation flowed easily and we found some of our guests were old soldiers of the regiment. One old lady had seen her grandson taking part in the mock battle and was as pleased as Punch. I was keeping a general eye on things when I became aware of a strange looking woman waiting to be served with a drink. All the other ladies in the party were either wives of councillors or senior executives, or councillors in their own right. They were all well dressed and many of them were wearing chains of office. The old woman queuing up for a drink was not 'dressed' by any stretch of imagination. Her hair, some of which could be seen sticking out from the side of a dirty brown beret, was grey and ragged. She had no teeth, at least I presumed this was the case, as when she spoke her nose practically touched her chin. An old blue coat covered whatever she had on underneath while badly scuffed shoes with worn down heels completed her attire. My nerves tingled and warned me of trouble when I asked her if she was a member of the mayor's party. 'Yes,' she snapped, 'and I'm thirsty. I want a glass of whisky.'

The mayor was in great form. He had enjoyed the day so far and he could see there were ample reserves of whisky on the table. He came over to me and said, 'It's been a great honour to − − −.' He stopped in mid sentence with his mouth open. A glance along his line of sight revealed that his attention was focussed on the toothless old woman staring aggressively at him over the top of her glass. When he recovered his speech he said, 'Who let her in?' Without actually admitting that I had checked her credentials, I told the mayor I thought she belonged to someone in his party. 'She's not one of us!' thundered Councillor Rees. He twisted and turned as he looked for his chief executive officer. Unable to find him, the mayor grabbed the senior police officer and said, 'What's she doing here. Can you get one of your men to remove her?'

Superintendant Emrys Lewis of the South Wales Constabularly was a police officer of considerable experience. Numerous medal ribbons on his jacket showed that he had been a loyal servant of the Crown in time of war and peace. His personal acts of bravery, often witnessed at 'throwing out time' in Abercwmavon public houses were well recorded in The Argus, but when he saw the object of the mayor's attention, the colour drained from his face. 'Good God, Sadie Slagheap,' he muttered, 'I might have known she would smell alcohol.' He turned away and said, 'I'm sorry Mr Mayor, I'm not getting involved with her.'

A strange name, I thought, and the mayor explained why. 'She goes out with an old pram picking coal from the slag and when she's got enough she sells it in the town. It's then straight down the pub where she spends it on hard drink. When she's skint, it's up the mountain again - if she can make it.'

By this time Sadie Slagheap had taken up a firm position on a small table in a corner of the marquee. She was swinging her legs and beaming at everyone through her toothless gums over a glass of whisky. The subalterns were aware that Sadie could liven up the proceedings. They had heard from other outraged members of the council how she had earned her distinctive name and they kept her topped up with a plentiful supply of high octane beverage.

Sadie's warm up period did not take long. It had been a good day on the mountain and she needed only a moderate amount of replenishment. The mayor, councillors, civic officials and their wives had looked the other way and had tried to put Sadie out of their minds, like a black cloud on an otherwise fine day. Suddenly she erupted. 'Stuck up lot of bitches aren't you?' Her remarks were directed to a group of councillors' wives whose breasts rose together like a huge Atlantic wave. 'Likes of me are not good enough for you,' went on Sadie as she developed her theme which, I was assured by the mayor was the normal routine. 'You there Gwilym Rees, with your big chain and everything. I could tell them a thing or two about you.' The mayor glared at Sadie but, whether it was his ferocious look or Sadie's decision to leave this big plum to be picked later, she switched her attack to the chief executive officer, who had finally appeared at the mayor's side.

Alec McFadden had two things in common with Sadie Slagheap. Firstly, he was a Celt, albeit from Scotland, and secondly, his great love of Scotch whisky. Despite Sadie's shortcomings, she loved her valley and the people who lived in it. Anyone who was not born in the borough of Bryntyrion was, as far as she was concerned, foreign trash. Alec McFadden was therefore anathema to Sadie and she had long been infuriated about having such a person as the top man in the borough council offices. 'I've seen you wearing that skirt of yours as if you are a woman,' she piped. 'Go back to your old Scotland we don't want you here, there's plenty of good Welsh boys who can do your job.' He was totally unprepared for the verbal assault that Sadie lashed upon him. He tried to answer back, but his mouth opened and closed like a goldfish and nothing came out.

Sadie was moving into top gear and the subalterns had lined up a reservoir of fuel to keep her going. She was knocking back the glasses as fast as they were put in front of her.

I began to wonder how it was all going to end when Major Tony Martin, the ever resourceful company commander, came to the rescue. He approached the table where Sadie was sitting, took her hand and said, 'My car is ready to take you home Mrs Slagheap.' With a firm grip he led her through the throng to the staff car waiting outside the marquee. A poker faced corporal sat at the wheel while another opened the rear door and saluted Sadie as she was helped inside. Major Martin tucked in her old blue coat and said, 'I hope you will come and see us again the next time we come to Abercwmavon.' Sadie positively cooed at the gallant major and assured him that nothing would stop her attending.

The mayor of Bryntyrion and others in his party were gazing open mouthed at Sadie Slagheap who seemed to have jumped them all in the VIP stakes. As the car moved off in that slow and dignified way favoured by hearses and royal limousines, Sadie lifted her hand in an elegant gesture of farewell. Those in uniform saluted her and even a few of the natives of Bryntyrion took off their hats.

When the mayor and other guests had gone, I called for the corporal and asked him what he had done with Sadie. 'I asked her if I should take her home, Sir, but she said she wanted to be dropped off at the pub on the corner. She got out and fell flat on her face. A couple of boys from the pub picked her up and she didn't half lay into them.'

Postscript: The borough of Bryntyrion and the town of Abercwmavon are not the real names of the place where Sadie lives. Neither is that her proper name, but it's close. Likewise, the names of the council officials and others are disguised. But if you are ever travelling through the Eastern valleys of South Wales and you see an old woman wearing a blue coat, pushing a pram up a slagheap - you'll know you are in 'Abercwmavon'.

CHAPTER TWENTY SEVEN

Sospan Fach

What is it about a little saucepan ('sospan fach' if you're Welsh) that creates such emotion among the ethnic population of the celtic homeland? There are many stories about its origin, but perhaps the words of the ancient song will help foreigners understand why Welsh people weep when they sing, what is to many, their alternative national anthem.

> The little saucepan boiling on the fire,
> The large saucepan boiling on the floor.
> The cat has scratched little Johnny.
> Young Dai the soldier,
> Young Dai the soldier -
> With his shirt hanging out.

In rugby circles the name 'Sospan' means only one place - Llanelli. This small town in West Wales is the shrine of rugby where people throughout the world come to see how the game should be played. To be a member of the 'Scarlets', as the first fifteen are called and to score a try on the holy turf of Stradey Park, is to become a saint before you are 25 years of age. The 'All Blacks' of New Zealand are a formidable side and their pre-match strategy of weird incantations and strange body movements is usually worth a few points to them, especially if they are playing on home ground. The Scots, with their bagpipes, and even the French with their cockerel, are morale boosters for their teams, but nothing compares with the secret weapon of Llanelli. Despite it being an unlawful act (I have yet to see a policeman make a determined effort to interfere), a monkey like figure will shin up one of the goal posts before the start of the match and, encouraged by the roar of the crowd, fix a 'sospan fach' on the top of one of the posts. There it will stay for the duration of the game working its magic on the brave team members below.

Many gallant rugby players, and others from Llanelli, joined the 4th Battalion The Welch Regiment during the second world war and took part in the invasion of North West Europe. When they sailed across the English Channel to land on the beaches of Normandy a 'sospan fach' was attached to the masthead of their ship, as if it was a rugby goalpost. Thereafter, to the end of the war, it travelled on the front of the commanding officer's battle wagon leading the soldiers to victory in Hamburg. The 'Sospans' was the soubriquet given to that fine battalion until 1971 when, through the process of military evolution it became the 4th (Volunteer) Battalion The Royal Regiment of Wales, with headquarters still in Llanelli.

To continue the tradition of 'sospan fach' everyone wore a small embroidered sospan on the left sleeve of their jackets. What finer sight could be seen than hundreds of small red sospans flying up and down as the soldiers of the 4th Battalion marched in column of threes through the township of Llanelli. Members of the St. John's Ambulance Brigade were always in attendance to treat those overcome with emotion.

During the mid '70's' it was announced that the Prince of Wales would visit Llanelli. Everyone was delighted and plans were made to make the visit a memorable day. The commanding officer of the 4th Battalion set a programme where drill became top priority and the quartermaster was told to make sure that soldiers' uniforms were in first class order.

With about a month to go before the great day the general from Army headquarters in Brecon said he wanted to inspect the battalion. He need not have bothered, personal and unit pride was so strong that not a toe cap had gone unpolished. The Army is rigid about such matters though and the general duly appeared one Saturday morning to satisfy himself everything was in order.

Peoples' Park in Llanelli is a splendid venue for a military parade and the general was escorted through the ranks of soldiers by the commanding officer and the honorary colonel (a retired one-time Territorial Army officer appointed to this prestigious position).

The general chatted with many soldiers, as is usual on such occasions. The honorary colonel, three steps behind, had a word for every man on parade - and he knew their names. He had joined 4th Welch as a subaltern before the second world war and was a seasoned campaigner. Imagine his surprise therefore when the general stopped in front of a soldier and said, 'What's this?', pointing at the red 'sospan' on his sleeve. 'A 'sospan', Sir', said the soldier. 'A what?', said the general who, although he had been associated for some time with Welsh soldiers, was not a Celt or even an 'adopted' Welshman. He was English through and through.

The young soldier, who was becoming alarmed by the attitude of the general towards his 'sospan', did not have chance to reply. The honorary colonel, with moustaches twitching like wireless aerials, answered for him. 'It's a SOSPAN, I say again - a SOSPAN'. The general stared at the honorary colonel and said, 'Did you say a saucepan?'. 'No, Sir, I did not. It's a SOSPAN!'. The general realised he was in deep water and that nothing would be achieved by pursuing the matter on the parade ground.

When the parade was dismissed and the honorary colonel had left, the general asked the regimental secretary, who happened to be with the 4th Battalion that day, if he had heard and seen correctly that the little red things on the soldiers' jackets were indeed saucepans. The regimental secretary, a retired officer of the Regiment renowned for his wisdom and diplomatic skill, had been a bystander on the parade and had seen steam spurting out of the vent holes in the honorary colonel's hat. He had prepared an answer.

'The story of the 'sospan' goes back to the days of the Crimean war,' said the secretary. 'All that stood between the advancing Russian troops and the British guns was a small detachment of the forerunners of this battalion. A young cook from Llanelli was the first to see them and he gave the alarm by beating his little saucepan - 'sospan fach' he called it, on a rock. This alerted everyone and the Russians were driven off with heavy casualties. 'Ever since then,' continued the secretary, 'the little saucepan, as you would call it, has been a sacred emblem of Llanelli folk and soldiers of this battalion have worn the cloth emblem on their left sleeves.'

'Good Lord!' said the general, 'I'm so glad I didn't put my foot in any further. I thought that fiery felllow was going to burst into flames without further assistance from me!'

Postscript: You may believe or disbelieve this story about the origins of 'sospan fach' - the regimental secretary has been known on many occasions to find a quick route out of a sticky situation. Sadly, volunteer soldiers are issued with khaki uniform for special occasions only nowadays, so the small red sospans are no longer part of our uniform. In 1993 the 3rd and 4th Battalions of The Royal Regiment of Wales amalgamated to form the 2nd Battalion which is based in Cardiff. In the officers' mess of 'A' Company at Morfa, Swansea, can be seen the battle scarred sospan which was carried by the old '4th Welch' during the invasion of Europe in 1944-45.

CHAPTER TWENTY EIGHT

Taking the Strain

The Regimental Chapel of The South Wales Borderers in Brecon Cathedral is the hallowed place of rest of those most sacred of emblems - Kings', Queens' and Regimental colours; the physical embodiment of honour, sacrifice and pride of a regiment. Rarely are these colours disturbed, their poles stretch parallel to the ground above the pews while the netted fragments hang in rigid line twelve feet, or so, from the floor. Occasionally a cool draught of air will touch them and cause slight movement to the silken folds. I often look at them and wonder what stories of courage they could tell; so much history compressed within a small area.

To the left of the altar hangs the huge six foot regimental colour of the 24th Regiment which survived, but only just, the battle of Chillianwallah in 1849. Its ensign and escort were mown down by the Sikh guns, but a young private soldier dashed forward and carried it to a place of safety. On the other side of the altar hang the colours which were carried from 1812 to 1825. They are much older but are in far better shape. Above the small oak casket, which contains fragments of the wreath of dried flowers, presented by Queen Victoria in 1880 in memory of those officers and men of the Regiment who died in the Zulu War, hangs the Queen's colour of the 1st/24th Regiment. Very little of the original material remains, hardly surprising when you consider it was carried for 68 years and was subjected to the full force of the River Buffalo, where it was trapped for two weeks after the disaster at Isandhlwana.

In 1989 it was decided that Brecon Cathedral needed a face lift. Contractors moved in and unsightly scaffolding soon started to crawl up the walls into the rafters where workmen began to rewire the electric fittings and whitewash the plaster. The Regimental Chapel was the last place to be done and I watched progress carefully so I could leave the colours in position until the last moment. When the time came for them to be removed I supervised the operation of carrying them to the vestry for safe keeping.

Almost a year later the long business of renovation was completed and it was time for the colours to be replaced in the chapel. The contractor told me that many of the wire stays that held the colours in position were unsafe. These wires, two to each colour - of considerable length, stretched from about 26 feet from the ground way up into the rafters. It was obvious they would have to be replaced and I made the suggestion that we use a modern material, such as nylon, with a high breaking strain. 'Good idea', said the contractor. 'Who'll get it, you or me?' I told him that I would get it and then I set about finding how much I would need. I was quite surprised when I had completed my calculations to find I needed about a quarter of a mile of the stuff.

Later that day I went to a shop in Brecon which sold fishing tackle and asked the lady behind the counter if she had some very strong nylon fishing line in stock. She asked me to wait a few moments while she went to a store room. When she returned she was carrying a box covered in dust. 'This is fifty pound breaking strain,' she said, 'Will that be strong enough for you?' I told her it would be suitable, and then she asked me how much I wanted. 'Four hundred yards, please', I replied. 'Good heavens', she gasped, 'are you going to catch a whale?' I do not know what came over me and why I did not tell her the reason for my purchase, but I replied, 'No, not a whale - a sturgeon.' There were five or six men in the shop and I was aware that they were giving close attention to everything being said. Getting quite carried away by the story I was creating, I said, 'It was seen at Caerleon last Friday and was spotted going over the weir at Crickhowell on Monday. It's expected to reach Brecon this afternoon or tomorrow.' The lady behind the counter was looking at me with her mouth open. Eventually she said, 'We get salmon here, not so many these days, but a sturgeon - we've never had one of them.' I nodded sagely and said, 'Well this one, by all accounts, is a whopper; it's estimated to be about eighty pounds.' I paid for the line, took it back to Brecon Cathedral and gave it to the contractor. 'This should keep them hanging for the next hundred years,' he said.

Two days later when I was entering payment for the nylon line in my account I found that I had left the receipt in the shop, so I went around to collect it. 'About that sturgeon,' said the lady who had served me, 'you were having me on weren't you?' I professed surprise that my word should be doubted, but she continued, 'Do you remember those men who were in the shop when you bought that line?' I nodded. 'Well,' she said, 'they were members

172

of a 'Midlands' Fishing Club. After you left they bought every inch of that fifty pound nylon line I had. They were on the river all Tuesday afternoon and Wednesday, but they didn't catch a thing. You did me a good turn though,' she said, 'that box of line had been in the store for the last 20 years and we hadn't sold any of it until you came in.'

CHAPTER TWENTY NINE

The Silent One

The path of this story has many twists and turns. It starts in Cyprus then jumps thousands of miles to a Dunlop rubber estate in Malaya. From there, five years later, it starts again in London - then the action switches to Belfast. Finally the pieces are tied together in Brecon. Officers and one regimental wife of The South Wales Borderers provide a thread for this tapestry, but essentially the story is about a tiger - Nepti, the silent one.

I first met Frank Morgan when he was a member of the camp staff for illegal Jewish immigrants in Cyprus in 1948. He used to drive the adjutant crazy because he grew his hair so long that it fell over his collar. Not being on the strength of the 1st Battalion The South Wales Borderers, even though he wore the uniform and badges of an officer of that regiment, there was not much the adjutant could do about it.

Frank was a national service officer and when the Jews were allowed to go to Palestine in February 1949, he and all the other members of camp staff were posted elsewhere.

Four years later I was in Malaya with the 3rd (Kenya) Battalion The King's African Rifles and by pure chance I found that I was staying in the same hotel as Frank in Kuala Lumpur. In the few days we were together he showed me sights in the Malayan capital that I would not otherwise have seen! When we parted he invited me to visit him on the rubber estate where he worked, not far from where 3/KAR was based.

A few months later I accepted his offer and travelled the 60 or so miles from Triang in Pahang to Bahau in Negri Sembilan, where the Ladang Geddes rubber estate was located. Frank met me at the station and took me to his bungalow, where I met another fellow who had been with him in Cyprus - John Milward of The Royal Welch Fusiliers. John had been none too popular with the adjutant of our battalion either, but as he wore the black flash of the 23rd Regiment on the back of his collar instead of the sphinx collar badge of the 24th Regiment on the front, he did not get the same treatment as Frank.

I spent two or three days with my old friends and wondered if I had made the right decision to stay in the Army as a regular officer. They seemed to have a very good lifestyle, even though rubber planters were number one targets for communist terrorists.

My commanding officer asked me to call at the camp of 7th Gurkha Rifles in Bahau and pay the respects of 3/KAR. Their camp was quite near the railway station, so I checked in at the guard post and made my way to the adjutant's tent. As I stooped to enter I felt a gentle but determined grasp on my right ankle, which brought me to a halt. I was in a strange position, bent almost double, legs wide apart and attempting to salute.

'Get off, Nepti,' shouted the adjutant as he reached for his swagger cane and came towards me. I looked backwards and to my amazement saw a tiger cub doing its best to drag me out of the tent. The adjutant gave her a crack over the rump and she ran for cover. He explained that Nepti had been found in the jungle alongside her dead mother by a patrol from No.4 Platoon of 'B' Company. The patrol brought her back to Bahau and gave the cub to the manager of the Ladang Geddes estate whose youngest

daughter, Jane, had taken a fancy to her. Jane's father and mother soon found that a six week old tiger cub was even at that age too boisterous for their young daughter, so it was sent back to 7/Gurkha. Jane's elder sister, Merilyn was at school in Malacca. When she came home from time to time she and Jane used to visit Nepti in the Gurkha lines.

Jane with Nepti and Captain Webb, 7/Gurkhas.

I duly paid respects from The King's African Rifles and then it was time to catch the train back to Triang. The last I saw of Nepti, as a cub, was a pair of yellow eyes staring at me from a fold in the adjutant's tent wall.

Just before I went to Cyprus again in 1957, to take part in the EOKA (union with Greece) campaign, I spent two weeks leave in London. One day a friend and I visited the 'big cats' house in London Zoo. To my surprise I saw a large metal plate on one of the cages which read 'NEPTI - PANTHERA TIGRIS (TIGER) Presented by 7th Gurkha Rifles, 18th August 1952.' My friend wondered what had happened when I was rendered speechless for a few seconds. She then thought I had taken leave of my senses when I told her that five years previously in Malaya my leg had been held fast in the jaws of the tiger which now confronted us. Never the one to lose an opportunity to draw a crowd, I became quite a celebrity among fellow visitors as I related my story. My friend, who knew me fairly well then - but very well now after 34 years married life said, 'Ok - that's enough, let's see if you have any more friends in the snake house.'

In 1973 the 1st Battalion The Royal Regiment of Wales was engaged on an 18 month tour of duty in Belfast. I was invited by the commanding officer, Lieutenant Colonel Robin Godwin-Austen, an old South Wales Borderer, to pay them a visit. During an enjoyable five day stay Robin held a dinner party to which I was invited. I found myself sitting next to Merilyn Hywel-Jones, the wife of Major Ian Hywel-Jones, another South Wales Borderer. During dinner our conversation ranged over many subjects and she told me that her father had managed a rubber estate in Malaya called Ladang Geddes. She spoke about two wild planters called Morgan and Milward and she told me about her sister Jane who had, for a short time, kept a tiger cub called Nepti.

Merilyn contributed a few more details about Nepti. She told me how sad it was when she and her family came home in 1953 and saw Nepti in London Zoo. By this time the tiger was almost fully grown and quite unrecognisable from the cub they knew only a year before. When Jane and her young brother were asked, in fun, by the keeper if they would like to go inside the cage, they fled in terror! Jane is now a journalist and lives in Denmark. She does not remember much about the real Nepti, but she has a small worn stuffed toy tiger, called Nepti, which she keeps at home.

Nepti with her keeper in London Zoo.

Nepti did not have much of a say in the pattern of her life. After the death of her mother, she spent some happy days with the Gurkhas and at Ladang Geddes estate, but then it was steel bars and concrete for the rest of her life. She died of a ruptured liver on the 8th April 1959 when she was eight years old.

CHAPTER THIRTY

Cross the Piste at Someone's Peril

One of the most enjoyable features of being a public relations officer with Rhine Army was covering the annual ski meeting in Bavaria. Not only did I enjoy it myself, but I was able to take my wife and two small children along with me. We used to travel by car from our home in Lubbecke, Northern Germany during the first week in January and head for Oberjoch in the Algau Alps, a journey of about 500 miles. After the first year (1967) when we battled through blizzards to get there, the following two years - though no less horrific in weather terms, were made somewhat easier by being travellers on a familiar route.

The whole village was taken over by skiers of 2nd Division of the British Army for two weeks. This was convenient for us and beneficial to the local economy, public relations were excellent without any effort on my part. My job was to take photographs and write stories about soldiers taking part in winter sports for local newspapers in the United Kingdom. In those days we had to work hard to attract young men and women to join the Army and this sort of publicity was considered useful.

One day my cameraman and I were on the slopes looking for suitable photo opportunities when I heard a shout. I looked up the hill and saw a heavily built figure on skis heading towards me. Being ski-less and unable to move out of the way, I was relieved when the person narrowly missed me. In his effort to change direction though he lost his balance and collided with a tree. Dropping my camera equipment, I floundered through the snow towards the person to see if he had hurt himself. 'Are you alright?', I asked. 'No I'm not bloody alright,' he said, 'neither would you be if you'd hit this tree.' The skier was obviously British and, by the sound of his voice, was an officer of considerable seniority. I grabbed his arm and attempted to get him on his feet, but he yelled, 'Put me down.' Within a few seconds a trio of experienced skiers skidded to a halt and took over. I soon became aware that the person, who had hit the tree was Lieutenant General Sir --- ---, the corps commander and that he had broken a leg. I could see I was not in a position to help and, anxious to protect my identity, I floundered back to my camera equipment and sped away as fast as I could. It is not often in one's

177

career that an opportunity presents itself to incapacitate a corps commander! I realised I had commited the unforgivable act of crossing the piste without skis and that this would not be dismissed lightly. It became common knowledge in Oberjoch that the public relations officer had caused the trouble and my own general (of 2nd Division) asked me why I had to pick on the corps commander when there were so many other people available. I tried to explain that I did not 'pick on the corps commander'. If anything he had picked on me as there was plenty of room on the mountain for him to go skiing.

For the next two days the corps commander was confined to the local hospital where his leg was encased in a large plaster cast. On the third day he felt well enough to walk around the town on crutches. I was coming out of one of the souvenir shops near the bottom of the ski lift when I nearly collided with him again. There was an explosion when he recognised me and I beat a hasty retreat for the second time in three days.

Things are rarely as bad as they seem at the time and the corps commander was soon able to dispense with his plaster and crutches. I used to meet him quite often at his headquarters in North Germany and he would glower at me and say something about, 'bloody pedestrians should not be allowed ----.' We both moved on, he to greater heights and me to a recruiting publicity job in Wales. We did not see each other for quite some time.

The commanding officer of the infantry training camp in Crickhowell, South Wales in the mid '70's' was a fellow who had gained a reputation for unusual ideas. He was talking to my wife at a cocktail party when the name of Lieutenant General Sir --- --- was mentioned. My wife outlined the events on the ski slope in Bavaria and this led the CO to produce a plan which involved me. The following day he checked the accuracy of the facts and then asked me if I would like to join the top table for lunch in two weeks time when the general would be visiting the camp. I was pleased to accept.

A week later I found out there was a price to pay for having lunch with my old corp commander. The CO outlined his plan. 'When the general arrives at the mess you will be standing in the hall dressed in Arctic combat clothing, carrying skis and wearing snow goggles. I will bring him over to you and will say - 'I believe you know this officer, General' - that will be the signal for you to remove the snow goggles.' I was struck dumb for a few seconds while I digested the high explosive content of what the CO planned to do. When I recovered, I replied as courteously as I could that I would rather put my head in a lion's mouth. The commanding officer pressed me hard but I stood my ground. I thought the invitation to sit at the top table would be withdrawn, but it was not and we all had a thoroughly pleasant time.

General Sir --- --- greeted me like an old friend and asked me if I had been skiing lately. I told him I had never been much of a skier and that skating on thin ice was more in my line.

CHAPTER THIRTY ONE

Standing Proud

It's good to attend a wedding now and again. It causes you to dig out your morning dress, check for moth holes and find if it's still in fashion. Your wife looks upon the celebration of nuptials as a good excuse to plunge her account at Harrod's or Harvey Nicholls into deep trouble. It makes you do lots of things out of the normal routine and, although you may grumble at the cost of a present for the bride and groom - one of whom you last saw as a pimply faced horror and the other, never before this day, you get a glow when the both of them greet you like a favourite uncle and aunt.

It was like that a few months ago when Nesta (my wife) and I were invited to the wedding of the daughter of some old friends. The ceremony was to take place in Woking, which meant an over-night stop for us in a reasonably adjacent hotel. We found one in a picturesque village and resolved to return and spend more time there one day. If it had not been for the wedding we would never have known of its existence.

With a few hours in hand we ambled slowly along the A319 in the direction of Woking. Suddenly I let out a gasp and turned my head sideways, causing the car to cross the white line in the middle of the road. I was back on track within a second but Nesta said, 'What was that about?' I did not give her a direct answer but looked for somewhere to turn around. A few minutes later I was driving into a place which bore the sign 'GORDON'S SCHOOL'. 'What are we doing here.' she asked. I drew up alongside a life size bronze statue of a British Army officer wearing a 'fez' sitting cross legged on a heavily caparisoned camel. 'That's why,' I said, 'It's General Charles Gordon, governor general of the Sudan. The last time that I saw the statue was when I was with The South Wales Borderers in Khartoum in 1949.'

An obliging house master came along and assured me that it was the same statue I had seen in the Sudan 44 years

The statue in its permanent home in Gordon's School, Woking.

previously. Three years after the country had been given its independence, he explained, the statue was brought home and presented to Gordon's School on 2nd April 1959. We sat in the car for a while, Nesta occupied with the Daily Telegraph crossword and me with memories of the Sudan so many years ago.

I was a 22 year old officer when I travelled with the 1st Battalion The South Wales Borderers from Cyprus aboard the SS 'EASTERN PRINCE' through the Suez canal and down the Red Sea to Port Sudan. Any romantic thoughts about the desert were dispelled when we saw the mud hut hovels which comprised the township and the ugly piles of (Welsh?) coal used to fuel locomotives of Sudan Railways. The heat, even at that time of the year (April) was sticky and oppressive. Further inland, in Khartoum, we would find it hotter but less oppressive without the humidity of the coast. The journey from Port Sudan to Khartoum took about 18 hours with one night aboard the train. From Atbara we followed the east bank of the River Nile south to Khartoum. Desert met the eye for a full 360 degrees, broken only by the mighty river and the metal track. It was a landscape such as I had never seen before. Every window was crowded as we approached Khartoum. Desert gave way to cultivated land irrigated by centuries old methods of drawing water from the river. Groves of date palms provided a contrast in colour to sand and gravel while crowds of natives dressed in long white 'night-shirts' raced along the track beside us.

At last we pulled into Khartoum railway station and were greeted by a guard of honour from the Sudan Defence Force with their regimental band. That moment etched itself deeply into my mind. The rigid ranks of immaculate black soldiers wearing khaki drill smocks, shorts, long black puttees over leather sandals with scarlet flower pot 'taboosh' on their heads, gave us the message that we would have to measure up to their high standard of turnout. The band, equipped with conventional instruments, played Arab music. It was a new sound for most of us; it certainly stirred my blood. In the months ahead I would spend time with these fine soldiers on the borders of Kenya and Uganda. It was the beginning of my love affair with Africa and Africans which has been a part of me from then to the present day.

A queue of Army trucks was waiting outside the station to take us to our new home in South Barracks. It was no more than a 10 minute ride before we were able to disembark and take stock of the sprawling mass of stone buildings built to the same style as those found in India before the war.

Anxious to explore Khartoum, a few of us took a taxi that evening and drove down Kitchener Avenue to The Grand Hotel. We already felt that we had entered a time warp, but we were transported even further into the 19th century when our taxi driver pointed out one of General Kitchener's gun-boats, the 'Melik', which he had used on his campaign of 1896-8, tethered to a tree alongside the Blue Nile. Further along the road we passed the governor general's palace re-built on the same site as that of an earlier governor, General Charles Gordon, who was killed there in 1885.

The 'Grand' was, at that time, one of the great hotels of the world. It stood at the junction of the two Niles, one - the White Nile, bringing water from Lake Victoria in the heart of the 'dark' continent, and the other - the Blue Nile with its source in Lake Tana in Ethiopia. We stood on the bridge crossing the confluence and watched the different coloured waters merge into one mighty torrent that flowed north towards the land of the Pharaohs and the Mediterranean. We had a meal in the Grand Hotel and watched from the verandah as the stern paddle wheel steamer from Atbara tied up at the jetty. The first course was ful sudani, the national dish of Sudan. The main ingredient of this delightful platter is ground-nuts, but the delicate use of spices which provide a subtle and mysterious flavour make its reproduction in a cold climate almost impossible.

Our voluble taxi driver was waiting to take us back to South Barracks and this time he drove down Gordon Avenue; the second broad avenue away from the Blue Nile and parallel with Kitchener Avenue. The battered old taxi had a flimsy framework that held some canvas over our heads, otherwise it was open to the elements. We were in high spirits but quite unprepared for the magnificent sight which lay before us. Half way down Gordon Avenue was a magnificent statue of a camel with its rider wearing a

The statue in Khartoum 1903-59.

182

'fez'. The driver stopped alongside the plinth and gave us a history lesson: - 'This is General Charles Gordon, ' he said. 'He became governor of Equatoria (southern Sudan) in 1873 and he was responsible for stopping the slave trade.' He went on to explain that Gordon became governor of the whole of the Sudan in the service of the Khedive of Egypt in 1877. He visited every part of his vast desert domain and was respected for his wise counsel and firm leadership. Despite his strong Christian beliefs he was not averse to dealing harshly with those found guilty of breaking the law of the land. He hanged offenders without mercy.

In 1880 Gordon's talent for sorting out problems which defeated politicians was recognised and he was sent to China where he single handedly defused a situation which would have led to war. In 1881 he was posted to Mauritius and promoted to major general. He then went to Jerusalem for a year before being re-called to the Sudan to supervise the evacuation of the Egyptians from their expensive and ill-fated attempt to rule the Sudan as a colony. To this end he was appointed Egyptian governor general of the Sudan, but this time answerable as well to the British government whom he warned of the danger that was simmering under the direction of the Islamic leader known as El Mahdi. The British government was loathe to become involved in an expensive and difficult war against desert tribesmen and, confident that Gordon could wield his special brand of magic, sent him back to Khartoum on his own.

By 1884 the Mahdi had, by a mixture of religious fervour and strict discipline cast his spell on huge areas of northern Sudan. Gordon, with his loyal supporters, was forced to prepare siege emplacements around Khartoum. As an officer of The Royal Engineers with a professional knowledge of defence works and pyrotechnics, he produced many novel and effective measures to delay the inevitable entry of the Mahdi's warriors.

After 10 months of ever increasing distress among the 34,000 soldiers, families and civilians of Khartoum, who resorted to eating every living animal, the defences were breached and the Mahdi's forces entered the town. General Gordon, by some accounts, had returned to his quarters in his palace. When he heard the sound of the enemy in the courtyard, he faced them in full dress on the outside staircase. He made no resistance when they climbed the stairs and stabbed him to death. Gordon's head was cut off and delivered to the Mahdi in Omdurman, on the far bank of the river. Two days later the thunder of guns and the sharp crack of rifles was heard and two steamers came into view. They were carrying a small contingent of British troops who had travelled up the Nile to try and rescue General Gordon. It was obvious that Khartoum had fallen from the heavy fire directed at them. With sadness and disappointment they turned and headed back down river.

The government were hard pressed to account to the British people for the abandonment and subsequent murder of their greatest hero. Queen Victoria was devastated and led the country in mourning. It was not until 11 years later in 1896 that a strong task force commanded by General Sir Herbert Kitchener (later Earl Kitchener of Khartoum) forced a passage up the Nile and re-established British presence in Khartoum. From then until 1956 the Sudan enjoyed an age of political stability and wealth from the export of its natural resources, in the main, cotton.

Even though the Sudan was known as an Anglo/Egyptian condominium there had been little Egyptian influence there since 1884. Governor generals had always been British. Since 1956, when independence was granted, the Sudan has withdrawn into its shell and a new dark age has settled upon its people. Various regimes controlled from Khartoum have brought misery and genocide to the Negro people of the south. The Arabs of the north have been forced to accept the harsh rules of Islamic fundamentalism and the once prosperous economy has stagnated through mismanagement.

But back to Gordon's statue and the remarkable events that took place before it was erected in Khartoum in 1903. It is the work of Mr Onslow Ford RA and is a replica of the original statue unveiled by the Prince of Wales in Chatham,

The 'Chatham' statue.

the home of The Royal Engineers, on 19th May 1890. The 'Khartoum' statue was originally sited in St Martin's Place, London where the statue of Nurse Edith Cavell, executed by the Germans in World War One, now stands. It was unveiled there in July 1902 by the Duke of Cambridge. Lord Kitchener and Lord Glenesh (of the Morning Post) successfully campaigned to have the statue moved to Khartoum. In October 1902 it was put aboard the SS 'CEDARDINE' and started its journey to Egypt. Within 24 hours the 'CEDARDINE' had been hit by another ship in the mouth of the River Thames and sank. Gordon and his camel rested ignominiously in the mud 40 feet below the surface. It was raised the following day and transferred to the SS 'LESBIAN' (Queen Victoria would not have been amused!). It then recommenced its journey to Alexandria.

The 'Khartoum' statue before it was moved from London.

A month later the statue began the next stage of its journey by rail and river to Khartoum. Once again the boat that was carrying it sank and Gordon and his camel found themselves, for a second time, lying at the bottom of a river. Finally it arrived in Khartoum and was erected on a low plinth. Lord Kitchener objected and gave orders for a high stone plinth to be provided for the officer whom he admired so much.

He was not to know that his own equestrian statue would one day be erected in front of 'The War Office' overlooking the River Nile only a few hundred yards away from that of General Gordon.

General Gordon would be proud to know that his statue has found a permanent home in Woking at the school which carries his name. It was founded by public subscription at the express wish of Queen Victoria in 1885, the year of his death. Since then the foundation has had the reigning Monarch as its patron. To this day it retains its tradition of being organised on public school lines with a strong military influence. On ceremonial occasions its pupils wear the unique Gordon uniform of blue tunic and trews for boys and blue tunic and kilt for girls. They make an impressive sight when they march behind their 60 strong band.

It was time for us to leave the school and drive a few miles further on to Woking for the wedding. The bride looked beautiful, the groom looked handsome and our old friends were much the same as when last we saw them. The champagne was ice cold and the food was superb, but as we drove home my thoughts were of General Charles Gordon and my days as a young officer in Khartoum.

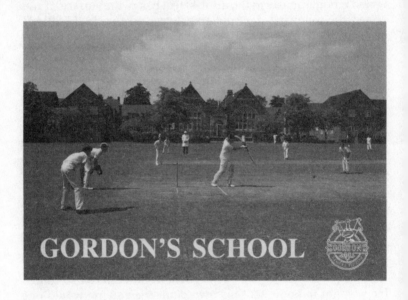

CHAPTER THIRTY TWO

Short Back and Sides

Early in this narrative I told how I stranded two army fire engines and a recovery vehicle in the mud of the River Nile in Khartoum. I was trying to impress the commanding officer with my zealousness for unit fire duties but only succeeded in causing much trouble for many people and near disaster to a unit vehicle inspection the following day. One would have thought that after such a trail of misfortunes on that August day in 1949 I would have been dismissed from the job, but not a bit of it - I was confirmed in the appointment of unit fire officer of the 1st Battalion The South Wales Borderers for another six months.

Soon after the battalion arrived in Asmara, Eritrea in January 1951 I was called by the adjutant and asked to explain why certain fire appliances were found to be in an unacceptable condition during the commanding officer's inspection of camp. I had plenty of experience of standing rigidly to attention on the unoccupied side of the adjutant's table so I just let his invective, which ended in three extra orderly officer duties, wash over me.

It was obvious that something dramatic had to be done to restore my reputation so I started to apply my mind to the best course of action. One day I was walking down the Vialle Roma, the main thoroughfare in Asmara, when the loud clanging of bells heralded the approach of a task force of the Asmara fire service. The Italians had lost the war and their colonies in East Africa but what dignity they had been able to salvage was absorbed by their fire service. The fleet of Alfa Romeo fire engines had been built with loving care in far off Italy before the war and had been kept in immaculate condition. Everything, from the big brass bells to the knobs on the water valves were polished to perfection. The fire crews looked superb, but were dressed for effect rather than practical fire fighting. Black helmet, with brass accessories, scarlet jacket, black trousers and a huge leather belt comprised their ensemble. They stood on platforms on each side of the engine adopting dramatic poses - as if they were gladiators heading for the Colosseum. Everyone - natives, Italian colonials, British expatriates and servicemen stood and admired the grand procession as it hurtled down the road and out of the far end of the town intent upon putting out whatever was on fire.

A few days later I was passing the fire station and saw that the main doors were open. I stuck my head inside to get a closer look at the fire engines. The officer in charge saw me and invited me in. He spoke excellent English and was obviously delighted that a British Army officer was showing interest in his beloved Alfa Romeos. I was treated to a fascinating exposition of his gleaming machines and was introduced to the men on duty. I was also shown around the room where the uniforms and equipment were kept and the visit ended with coffee and some excellent cream buns. We had established a good rapport and I asked the fire chief if he would consider lending me a suit of fireman's clothing and equipment for the fancy dress party that was due to take place in the officers' club the following Saturday night. He agreed and I was there and then fitted out with a helmet, tunic, a coiled length of rope, a chopper and a belt. Being rather tall, I said I would provide my own trousers.

The fancy dress party was great fun and I generated much mirth among the junior officers who congratulated me on my spectacular outfit. The commanding officer and the adjutant were not amused and thought that my choice of costume was an insolent response to my recent admonition.

When I returned the gear to the fire chief the following Monday morning I asked him if he would co-operate with me if I held a fire practice in the camp of The South Wales Borderers. He responded with enthusiasm and assured me that if there were no real fires to put out at that time, I could count on his help. Knowing that the commanding officer would be holding 'orders' at noon the following day, I booked the fire chief to stand by for a telephone call from me at 11am. I spent the rest of the day supervising my signals platoon, plus some prisoners in the guard room, collecting rubbish in the camp. It came from all directions and was deposited on a bare patch of ground between the signals store and the orderly room. When it reached the size of a bell tent I called a halt.

The following morning I went across to the adjutant's office and asked to see the commanding officer. 'What do you want to see him for?' said the adjutant narrowing his eyelids to thin slits. 'It's about holding a fire practice,' I replied. The business of the battalion's fire engines being stuck in the Nile was still fresh in his mind and he was not eager to endorse any more mad-cap schemes, but I stood my ground and asked to be allowed to speak to the commanding officer. Reluctantly the adjutant ushered me into the CO's office and listened as I told him about the friendly relationship I had forged with the chief officer of the Asmara fire service, who had been instrumental in me winning first prize in the fancy dress party. I went on to explain that I should now like to demonstrate how this rapport could be used to the unit's advantage if we ever had a serious fire in the camp. 'He's an Italian isn't he?', said the CO, 'Those buggers were shooting us only a few years ago!' This was an attitude of mind I had not considered and I had to do some nifty public relations work on behalf of the Asmara fire service before the CO was satisfied they would not settle old scores and burn the place down if we let them in. 'In fact, Sir', I said, 'I should like to hold a fire practice now just to show you what would happen in a real emergency'. I asked both the CO and adjutant if they would step outside to see what I intended doing. I led them around the side of battalion headquarters and pointed towards the great pile of rubbish I had collected. I could see from the look on their faces that they were letting themselves into a situation beyond their control, but my enthusiasm must have swayed them as the CO nodded his permission for me to carry on.

I had already briefed one of my signallers to keep a line to the Asmara fire service on hold, so I picked up the nearest telephone in the orderly room and shouted, 'Fire in The South Wales Borderers camp!'

The fire chief regarded the practice call-out as the most prestigious event to take place since he had taken command three years previously. All three fire engines were in single file on the road outside the fire station with crews aboard, pointed in the direction of our camp ready to go when they received my signal.

The fire station was only about two miles from camp and there was instant response to my call. As I was walking across to the pile of rubbish I could hear the bells ringing in the distance so I sprinted the last 50 yards in order to get the fire going. This turned out to be more difficult than I expected. A strong wind extinguished the flame from the match every time I struck one and I could see that the kindling wood was damp after an early morning shower. The sound of the bells on the Alfa Romeo's were getting louder and from my elevated position I could see the fire engines roaring down the road towards the camp. Once again I tried to set fire to the pile of rubbish but the flame would not take hold. I could see that the leading vehicle was now passing the guard room and I realised that I was going to look very stupid if I could not get the fire going by the time they arrived. I yelled to one of my signallers, 'Get me a jerry can of petrol from the battery charging shed, and be quick about it.' Within a few seconds the can arrived and I threw the contents over the pile. I pulled out my last match, struck it and put the flame into some paper at the base.

I do not remember much after that as I became enveloped in flame which burnt off every exposed hair on my body (plus many unexposed). My woollen hose tops were reduced to a couple of pieces of dried toast around my ankles and my face, so I was told, took on the look of a well boiled lobster. I have vague memories of smoke and lots of water and then I was taken to the medical centre where I was cleaned up and bandaged to such an extent that only my eyes, nostrils and mouth could be seen. I had been wandering around like a zombie during the fire practice and had not realised a mini 'Hiroshima' had taken place. I was hit by flames at the base of the bonfire but the main  force of the fire-ball had blown an assortment of blazing rubbish high into the air. Much of this was still alight when it hit the ground and the fire chief had to deploy most of his men, aided by the unit provost staff, to extinguish many small fires that were burning at the lower end of the camp.

I remained in bandages for a few days and when they were removed I was shocked to see that the flames had burnt an amazing pattern of 'tramlines' all over my face and neck. I looked like a Red Indian about to go into battle. The incongruity of my appearance was compounded by a tuft of hair on the top of my head which had been protected by my beret.

It was nearly a month before I looked presentable again. Needless to say I was not on good terms with the commanding officer. When he realised that I was not in such bad physical condition as it appeared, he told me what he thought about my ill-prepared fire practice.

The time I spent, rather like a snake, shedding one skin and growing another, was a period of extreme embarrassment. People would clutch door frames or other convenient means of support while they split their sides laughing at my misfortune. The adjutant, with typical sardonic wit, said that instead of dressing up as a fireman at the fancy dress party, I should have held the fire practice a few weeks earlier and gone as 'the Last of the Mohicans'.

CHAPTER THIRTY THREE

On a Hot Tin Roof

This the last of the trilogy of my misfortunes as a unit fire officer. The first two stories tell of how I was responsible for sinking two army fire engines and a recovery vehicle in the River Nile at Khartoum and how I blew my hair off while holding a fire practice in Asmara, Eritrea. For many years the trauma of these embarrassing events made me push the memories into the deepest recesses of my mind, but now that I am old and grey I find that I can appreciate the hilarious situations I created.

In 1959 I slipped a disc playing polo in Benghazi. I spent seven months in hospital before I was discharged and given a sedentary job in the Welsh Brigade Depot in Crickhowell, South Wales. My position on the staff roll was second-in-command headquarter company, but I was a 'factotum' with a string of other jobs - one of which was unit fire officer. Those in authority obviously had not heard of the reputation I had gained while serving in Africa.

The Army camp in Crickhowell was being modernised when I arrived in 1959. Pre-fabricated walls, flat roofs and lots of glass was a new concept as most of the barracks in the country were relics from the Victorian era. There was still evidence of war-time use of the camp in the shape of some old wooden huts, and it was there that I decided to hold my first fire practice.

To create realism the quartermaster gave me three smoke canisters, each about the size of a five litre can of paint. I set these down among a group of huts, lit the fuses and within a few seconds a dense cloud of smoke erupted. A north east wind was blowing and it carried the smoke across the playing fields to the A40 main road which runs parallel to the southern boundary of the camp. Traffic was stopped from both directions until the canisters became exhausted ten minutes later. The village constable from Crickhowell arrived on his bicycle (no panda cars in those days) just in time to start the traffic moving again. Meanwhile, the response from within the camp was negative. One platoon of soldiers marched down the road only 100 yards away from where I was positioned without turning their heads. The camp gardener was the only one to show any initiative, and it was he who drew the attention of the provost sergeant to the mass of smoke emanating from the area of the wooden huts. At last the unit provost staff came puffing along with the wheeled contraption which carried the first few lengths of hose. When all the others had been coupled together and the last one screwed on to the hydrant at the Guard Room, the order 'Water on!' was given. When the jet of water spat out of the nozzle I pressed the button on my stop-watch. I was not at all pleased with the way that the fire practice had gone and it was obvious the whole system needed to be reviewed. I was busy scribbling notes on my mill-board when soldiers appeared from all directions carrying buckets of sand and water and stirrup pumps. Water came from everywhere and as I seemed to be in the middle of the deluge, I shouted 'Ok, that will do, it's only a practice.' The provost sergeant caught hold of my shoulder, spun me around and said, 'Practice indeed, Sir, look at that roof!' It was not until I had turned half circle that I saw we had a real fire on our hands. The smoke canisters, which I had never used before, were emitting balls of fire, rather like Roman candles on Guy Fawkes night. While most of these fell harmlessly to the ground from two or three feet, a few of them went higher and some actually landed on the tarred felt roof of the hut where I had concealed myself. A considerable fire had taken hold and was blazing away merrily. The emphasis then switched to some real fire fighting which, though eventually successful, was at the expense of the hut that was a write-off. I comforted myself with the thought that those huts were due for demolition anyway and made the suggestion in the mess at lunch time that I should set fire to the remainder. The offer was not accepted and I felt I had blotted my copy book with yet another commanding officer.

A week before I was married in August 1960, I decided to hold a fire practice in the area of the quartermaster's stores which, in those days comprised a collection of large Nissen huts with corrugated iron roofs at the far (Crickhowell) end of the camp. The bugler sounded the 'Fire Call' this time and the 'fire' (not a real one) was supposed to be in the accommodation stores. The provost staff trundled the two wheeled hose truck down the road to the quartermaster's stores and on this occasion they did it in very good time. When the water started to come through I was aware of low pressure. I found the reason when I walked towards the hydrant and saw numerous punctures in the walls of the hose. This was good for the grass and plants but did nothing for putting out a fire - had there been a real one. After the bugler had blown 'Stand Down' I marked each puncture with coloured chalk. I gave an order to the provost sergeant to exchange all the faulty lengths of hose for new ones and then, the following day, went off to London to get married.

My wife and I spent our honeymoon in the West Country. One day as we were driving along the North Devon coast I switched on the radio just in time to hear the BBC Radio Wales newscaster (just across the channel) read the 'funny bit' at the end of the news. 'A fire took place last night in an Army camp in South Wales,' he said. He then went on to specify the name of the camp and the location of the fire, which was the camp cinema. He could hardly contain his mirth when he delivered the punch line .... 'The place was completely gutted and guess what? - they were playing Tennessee Williams's film 'Cat on a Hot Tin Roof'.' From that moment my honeymoon was ruined. The torrential rain did not help and after a week of being mesmerised by non-stop windscreen wipers we decided to call it a day and head for Brecon where we were going to live. A phone call to the adjutant confirmed that the camp cinema had been burnt down and, that after I had enjoyed the remainder of my honeymoon, the commanding officer had something to say to me.

The Board of Inquiry found there was insufficient hose to reach the cinema from the nearest water supply. It appeared that with the nozzle angled at 45 degrees for maximum projection, the water dropped short of the ticket office by 20 feet. I was at a loss to understand how this could have happened until the commanding officer told me I had given an order to the provost sergeant to withdraw all hoses that were punctured. I corrected him and told him I had instructed the provost sergeant to EXCHANGE not WITHDRAW the faulty hoses. The CO fixed me with beady eyes and said, 'Did you check to see that the exchange had been made?' 'No, Sir, I did not,' I replied, 'I left for London the following day to get married.' It is only recently that the Army has recognised that wives have a place in its structure. In the old days they were classed as camp followers and there are still some traditionalists who would like to keep it that way. The florid faced lieutenant colonel who was beating his desk with clenched fists was obviously in this category. 'Because you put your wedding first and fire hoses second,' he stormed, 'we now find ourselves without a cinema. I've had to lay on trucks to take soldiers into Abergavenny twice a week.' There was not much I could do or say. I only hoped that the commanding officer would release me from this unenviable duty with which I had been saddled, off and on, for quite a few years. This did not happen though and I was told that the command fire adviser intended to inspect the camp in two weeks time. 'You had better make sure everything is in order,' said the CO. I made good use of the time in hand and I was quite confident that fire precautions were 'according to the book'.

At exactly 10.00hrs on the day of the inspection, the fire adviser from HQ Western Command in Chester was ushered into my office by the company sergeant major. 'Would you like cup of tea?' I enquired. 'No thank you,' replied the fire adviser, 'I think we had better make a start. We are one minute late already.' His response to my friendly welcome made me realise that this pernickety servant of the Army Fire Service could cause trouble if he was not handled carefully.

Before the inspection started at the east (Glangrwyney) end of camp Inspector Shorthouse (a name that lends itself to some amusing permutations) told me he had parked his car just off the main road in the camp. 'I hope that I'm not breaking any rules leaving it there,' he said, pointing in the direction of the chapel. 'No, that's quite alright,' I replied without bothering to look. In those days we had no parking restrictions in the camp as car bombs were unknown.

We started in the Junior Soldiers' Wing and worked our way through every building until we were almost back to where we started. Inspector Shorthouse was appalled by everything he saw. 'Just ready to burst into flames,' was his invariable comment followed by much sucking of teeth as he made copious notes on his mill board. I remember saying to him in desperation, 'How could this place burn down, it's all concrete!' 'Heat anything hot enough and it will burn, even concrete,' was his terse reply and I saw him write some more notes, which I felt sure were comments on my frivolous attitude towards fire precautions.

We were heading towards my office after the most uncomfortable session I had suffered since my altercation with the commanding officer over the exchange of fire hoses, when Inspector Shorthouse gave a yelp and ran up the road ahead of me. It was then that I saw a car parked alongside the camp incinerator and realised it was his. Anyone with a modicum of common sense should have known that a brick built oven-like construction with a chimney stuck on the top was used for burning things. The camp gardener had just emptied a wheel barrow full of grass and leaves into it and the swirling smoke enveloped his immaculate little Ford Popular. Inspector Shorthouse disappeared into the smoke and a few seconds later the car shot out as if it had been fired by a mighty cannon. It did not appear to have suffered any damage, but for someone whose sole function in life was to prevent fires from breaking out, he was taking no chances. When I caught up with him he was squirting foam from a hand held fire extinguisher all over the engine. When that one ran out he took another one out of the car and started spraying under the chassis. When he had satisfied himself that his car was not going to burst into flames, he slumped to the ground and mopped his brow.

There have been a number of occasions in my life when my 'fairy god-mother' has come to my rescue, and this was one of them. 'You had a close shave there didn't you?' I observed. 'Wait until the commanding officer hears about this, your car could have burst into flames at any minute, didn't you see that incinerator when you parked it there?' I suggested that he should put something in his report about catering for people who could not recognise an incinerator when they saw one. On that note, when I felt I had won 'game, set and match', I bade him 'good day' and went off to the mess for lunch. The CO asked me if the fire adviser had been pleased with everything he had seen. 'Oh yes, Sir,' I replied. 'I'm sure we'll receive an excellent report.'

Inspector Shorthouse's report arrived a week later and was the linchpin for an 'outstanding' unit administrative report. The commanding officer was delighted and bought me a large gin and tonic in the mess. 'There's only one recommendation,' he observed. 'He wants a NO PARKING sign put alongside the incinerator. Why do you think he wants that?' I told him it was something to do with spontaneous combustion (heating things to such a degree that they burst into flames), and left it at that.

CHAPTER THIRTY FOUR

Flavour of the East

Until I met a Burmese army officer called Ko Ko Lay I had not tasted anything more oriental than rice puddding. It was he that I must thank for introducing me to the wonderful flavours of oriental cuisine. Our relationship lasted for 11 weeks and took place, for the most part, above the clouds in Richmond, Yorkshire.

We were both students on an Army signals course held in a collection of dreary wartime huts called Gallowgate Camp, alongside The Green Howards depot. In November and December the inhabitants of Richmond rarely see the sun. We had a slight advantage over them by being able to look down on the mantle of cloud, like a huge feather bed, which usually covered the town. The disadvantage was that we were kept in a permanent state of refrigeration.

Ko Ko Lay had spent all his life in the hot, moist climate of Burma until he was sent to the other end of the world to learn how wireless sets worked. The shock to his system of living in Yorkshire in December caused him to pile on everything he could wear. Even so he could not get warm and this, he claimed, affected his comprehension of all matters electronic. The other thing that slowed him down was British food. In his own country he was used to hot, spicy food, but nothing from the kitchen in our officers' mess excited him.

Half way through the course we had a long weekend break. Ko Ko used the vacation to visit some friends in London. When he returned he brought with him a collection of cooking utensils which included two small paraffin cookers. A few days later he asked me if I would help him make a curry. In those days (1948) there were few Asian restaurants outside London and I knew nothing about those wonderful flavours of the east which most of us now take for granted. I was only too eager to offer my services.

Ko Ko had made a plan and when the afternoon training session ended he led me across some fields to a farm he had discovered about half a mile away. Chickens were running about in the yard when we arrived and Ko Ko spotted the one he wanted; a large white cock bird surrounded by its family of hens. I knocked on the kitchen door of the farm-house which was opened by the farmer's wife. I explained to her that my Burmese friend would like to buy the white cockerel, if it was for sale. The plump lady looked at us suspiciously and asked why we wanted the bird. 'To eat,' said Ko Ko. 'You can buy a dressed one in the town,' she said. 'I don't want a dead one,' replied Ko Ko, 'I want that one over there.' The farmer's wife must have felt there was something strange about the lanky 6 foot 3 inches white man and the 5 foot 3 inches brown man so she called her husband. The farmer heard her shrill command and came to the door. Ko Ko repeated his request and thrust two half crowns towards the farmer who, recognising a good opportunity, took it and went off to deprive the assorted hens of their lord and master. When we got back to camp we went into Ko

Ko's room where he opened a holdall and produced a number of small packages which he invited me to smell. That was the starting point of my interest and love of oriental food which still gathers strength after nearly half a century. He went through the now familiar routine of pounding and mixing spices while my nostrils quivered at the new experience. The bit that I was not looking forward to happened without me or the cockerel knowing anything about it. A

Ko Ko Lay at Gallowgate Camp, Richmond.

quick twist of of Ko Ko's wrist broke the bird's neck and the carcase was given to me for entrail and feather removal.

Ko Ko's expertise with two small paraffin burners and an assortment of saucepans was something I have never forgotten. Not only did he cook the cockerel to perfection, but he also produced a number of piquant side dishes and a bowl of fluffy rice. Never have I experienced anything so delightful as my first oriental meal cooked on the floor of an Army hut on a cold winter night in Yorkshire.

A month later Ko Ko went back to Burma, which had just received its independence. It did not get off to a good start and the fortunes of the country spiralled towards anarchy. In 1962 Burma closed its doors on the world and retreated within itself - even to the present day. Ko Ko Lay is one of two Burmese I have known. The other one was our amah (servant) in Malaya (see my story 'CAT AND DOG IN A MONSOON CLIMATE'). I should love both of them to see how adept my wife and I have become in producing their glorious food.

CHAPTER THIRTY FIVE

High Pressure Means Trouble

With a few weeks to go before I retire, finally, from the Army (27th August 1993), after nearly 49 years service, I am taking stock of some of the things in the military museum I run and with which I am familiar. I look nostalgically at the Bren machine gun and the Enfield mark 4 and 5 rifles in the armoury and the old wireless sets no. 19 and 68 in 'Signals Corner'. A suit of battle dress and a pair of ammunition boots (with 13 studs in the sole - no more no less), a slidex card (low level cypher) and a can of Bluebell (metal polish). Some of you have never heard of these things; I shall not explain further. But for others of my profession and vintage, they are old friends - or enemies, as the case may be. All of them are way past their 'sell by' date, but there is one bit of kit that was going strong when I joined the Army which will still be in the front line service when I bow out. It is officially known as the Cooker Portable No.1, but to its friends - the No.1 burner.

A section of the painting 'Lull in the battle' (San Carlos - Falkland Islands 1982) by Terence Cuneo is reproduced with kind permission of the Controller RLC (ACC) Benevolent Fund.

This truly marvellous piece of equipment has been in service since 1939; many believe that without it we could never have won the war. Its CV, as issued by the Army Catering Corps is:- '-- designed to cook for 70 persons. ...can be used to cook fresh and tinned rations, producing a multi choice but basic menu. ADVANTAGES - operates on petrol. It is versatile and, when used with ancillary equipment, is an efficient cooker. DISADVANTAGES - Operating at ground level increases hygiene risks as you must 'dig in' before use. Petrol, being corrosive, eats away the inside of the tank. Annual pressure checks are essential.' When operating, the advantages far outweigh the disadvantages and, as far as hygiene is concerned, I've never known anyone worry about the 'health and safety at work' rules when the company quartermaster sergeant announces that 'all in stew' is ready.

The No.1 burner is basically a strong container which ejects petrol, under pressure, through a perforated metal ring. Initially the petrol will burn as a liquid, but as soon as the ring becomes hot the petrol changes to vapour, and that is when the burner roars into life. For best results the burner should be set at the end of a line of metal stands in a trench two feet deep. The flame travels down the tunnel heating as many as five dixies (containers) set on the top. Within a very short time the contents are bubbling away merrily.

One of the nostalgic sounds within an old soldier's memory is the 'early shift' cook getting breakfast ready. He will be going about his business as quietly as he can, trying not to wake his mates, but then comes the sound of him pumping the burner; rather like the noise of a bicycle pump. Next comes the roar as the petrol vapourises. It never annoyed me, rather, it was a comforting sound bringing the promise of strong, sweet 'sergeant major's' tea within half an hour.

Dixies on metal frames above a trench will produce hot water and fried or boiled food, but if you are in a semi permanent location you can improvise with 44 gallon drums (Royal Engineers will always provide). You can then produce a splendid variety of ovens. My wife, to whom I have been married for 33 years, thought she knew everything about me until I told her that I was the only Army officer in Kenya during the Mau Mau campaign to have a regular supply of 'fairy' cakes for tea. Under my personal direction the King's African Rifles cooks in my company constructed a huge oven of mud, stone and wattle which did everything. The power source was firewood, but when this ran out, we used a No.1 burner. The heat circulated a 44 gallon drum, which was the centre piece of the oven, before dispersing through a chimney at the top. We could fry, boil, grill, roast, bake and barbecue on this wondrous contraption and it became the prototype for a number of other, but not so efficient, ovens in the Kikuyu reserve.

But let me return to the conventional No.1 burner and a tale about another disadvantage not specifically mentioned in its CV.

In May 1953 the 3rd Battalion The King's African Rifles withdrew from Malaya where we had spent 18 months helping to deal with the communist insurrection. Some of the rifle companies travelled to Singapore by road to embark aboard the

'Dilwara' for our journey back to Kenya. Others travelled down the east coast of Malaya in landing craft.

As adjutant of the battalion, I embarked at Kuantan with a motley collection of orderly room and officers' mess staff, the drums platoon and half a dozen regimental policemen. The landing craft we travelled in was the smallest of the breed, known as a LCI (landing craft infantry). It looked like a dinky toy version of its larger cousins which carry lorries, tanks and troops. Ours was a mere 60 feet long. The captain was the fattest Chinaman I have ever seen, when he entered the wheel house there was no room for anyone else.

We slipped our moorings at about 4pm and I took a long last look at the Nan Yang Hotel on the waterfront, which had been my home for 12 months. It was the only hotel in Kuantan at that time and the top floor had been a brothel before we took it over as the officers' mess. I have no doubt that it quickly returned to its former usage. We sailed down the broad estuary of the Sungei Kuantan to the open sea and then turned south. After proceeding a few miles, the landing craft stopped and the anchor went down. Using a mixture of Malay and English I gathered from the captain that he could only travel during daylight as he did not have any maps. Many offshore islands would have caused a dangerous impediment to our passage.

Content that the captain's decision was a sensible one, I took out my fishing rod, attached a lure in the shape of a small wooden sprat and cast it into the water. After about ten minutes I felt a bite. I struck and then enjoyed another ten minutes of action with whatever was on the end of my line. Some of the crew showed interest in what I was doing but when the head of my quarry broke surface there were cries of terror. Two African soldiers came to see what had gone wrong and they also gave shouts of alarm. 'Angalia Effendi, iko nyoka mkubwa' (Watch out, Sir, that's a big snake'.) We had been told about the danger of sea snakes when we arrived in Malaya, but as we had never seen one and the swimming had been so marvellous on the beaches at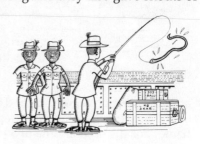

Kuantan, we never gave them a thought. The captain could be seen waddling down his ladder and he soon joined in the chorus of dissent when he saw the snake, which was now squirming around on the surface. He made it quite clear that he was not going to allow the thing to be brought aboard his ship. Chinese will eat most things including land based poisonous snakes, but sea snakes are definitely not to their taste. In this they had massive support from my Africans who considered any sort of snake, from land or sea, something to be avoided at all times. I was the odd one out, but only because I did not want to lose my sprat which had served me well over many years and which now had its head sticking out of the snake's mouth. The happy solution came eventually from the snake who, having frightened the life out of most of us, found it did not like the taste of the sprat and spat it out.

Corporal Macheru, the officers' mess cook, watched the drama and when things were sorted out he went back to the bows of the ship where the No.1 burner was in place to cook curry for the evening meal. The captain had made signs he did not want any more trouble with snakes, so I dismantled my rod and packed away my valuable sprat. As I was doing this, Corporal Macheru told me he thought something might be wrong with the burner. When I went to investigate I found that the indicator on the pressure gauge was well into the 'red'. As I stepped back to

consider the matter there was sound like a pistol being fired and a huge jet of flame shot 30 feet into the air. The instinct of self preservation is one of my strong points. I wheeled around and from a standing start cleared a 6ft table upon which sat an assortment of cooking utensils. Later, I found that a brass stud on the top of the burner blows out when pressure gets too high. It could have been lethal had I been standing over it.

The captain was back in his wheel house mopping his brow after the exertion of going up and down his ladder and the trauma of the sea snake. Suddenly the front of his ship belched into flame. For the second time in 30 minutes the captain hurled his massive frame down the ladder. He then had to clamber over a pile of baggage before he told me what he thought of me. I tried to tell him there was no danger as the petrol was burning itself out as it came down, but he was not impressed. His bad impression of me was compounded when I asked him if we could use his crew's cooking facilities for the rest of the voyage. We managed to reach Singapore two days later without any more disasters, but I am sure that the captain and his crew were glad to see the back of me.

Since then I have been wary of contraptions which operate with petrol vapour, but there was one other occasion when I had a similar experience.

It was when I visited the 4th (Volunteer) Battalion of my Regiment at camp in Scotland about 20 years ago. The commanding officer and I went to see one of the companies at their camp in the Trossachs. The midges were biting like mad, so the CO suggested we stand near the No.1 burner. Instinctively I looked at the pressure gauge and saw that the indicator was in the 'red'. 'Stand clear', I shouted. Everyone thought I had gone mad until a 'pistol shot' went off and a huge fountain of flame erupted. Two cooks went head over heels backwards over a line of dixies and the CO ran for his life. I stood still - I had seen it all before.

Retirement will be a new experience and, as yet, I do not know how I will handle it. Everything will fall into place though and like most old soldiers, I will have time to dream. Among my pleasant memories will be the start of another day heralded by the rattle of dixies and the No.1 burner roaring into life.

CHAPTER THIRTY SIX

A Ranger's Life for Me

I do not intend to write a long winded account of the time I spent with the 2nd Battalion Malaysia Rangers (1964-66). Rather, I shall describe some of the amusing and memorable things that happened during my two and a half year tour. In so doing the reader may get some idea what fun it was to raise a battalion from nothing, to train 750 young men from a remote part of the world with no previous military background, and to accompany them into their own country when a state of emergency had been declared against a potentially dangerous enemy. Sadly, there is very little opportunity these days for officers and non-commissioned-officers of the British Army to be seconded to foreign armies. I consider myself fortunate to have had two bites at the cherry - one with The King's African Rifles and the other with Malaysia Rangers.

The idea behind the raising of two battalions of Malaysia Rangers - one from Sarawak and the other from Sabah (previously British North Borneo) was a 'wedding present' from the old colonial power, Great Britain, to Malaysia on the formation of the union in 1963. The 'wedding' unfortunately got off to a bad start when tension between the Chinese of Singapore and the Malays from mainland Malaya resulted in Singapore withdrawing from the union. At about the same time President Sukarno of Indonesia laid claim to Sarawak and Sabah on the grounds that the transfer of the two states to Malaysia was a 'neo-colonialist creation'. Indonesia pursued a policy of 'confrontation' with Sarawak and Sabah which meant that there was much posturing by the aggressor but, except for a few occasions, little action. Great Britain was determined to give Malaysia a good start and backed the new alliance with military strength. Along with the resources of Malaysia's own armed forces, the combined sea, land and air power was sufficient to make President Sukarno think twice before embarking on any reckless adventures. The crisis ended in 1966 when the Indonesian dictator was deposed.

The humble beginnings of Malaysia Rangers can be traced to the communist uprising in Malaya a few years after the end of the second world war. In those days the British Army absorbed the brunt of terrorist action and, although many lessons about jungle fighting had been learned, it was acknowledged that a British soldier was not in the same class as a native when it came to tracking the enemy in jungle. The experts in this skill were undoubtedly Iban Tribesmen of Sarawak, many of whom were recruited to work with British infantry battalions in Malaya. The organisation to which they belonged was called 'Sarawak Rangers'. In 1963 this organisation, in 'suspended animation', was re-activated on conventional military lines and became the 1st Battalion, Malaysia Rangers. Sabah (previously British North Borneo) had no such tradition of military service and was proud to be the host state for the 2nd Battalion, Malaysia Rangers. Events overtook the original plan to raise only two battalions and by the end of 'confrontation' in 1966 Malaysia Rangers had expanded to three battalions. Nowadays (1995) the regiment has eight battalions.

To facilitate administration and to train the newly recruited young men, the Malaysian Ministry of Defence provided a number of clerks, drivers, mess staff etcetera as well as instructors from the Malay Regiment. Initially, the officers and most of the senior warrant officers and non-commissioned-officers came from the British Army on two and a half year tours, but as time went by they were replaced by Malaysians. The original battalions were raised in the Gurkha Depot in Sungei Patani in north west Malaya. When, after 10 months, we were able to manage our own affairs, we moved to Ipoh - the centre of the tin mining industry in the Kinta Valley of central Malaya. Companies of 100 men each were recruited at six week intervals and when the 10 week basic training course was completed the soldiers went on to more advanced training in deep jungle near the Thai border. The remnants of Chin Peng's wartime Malayan Races Liberation Army (MRLA) were still active in this area and provided a degree of realism. By October 1965 both battalions of Malaysia Rangers were fully trained and ready to take their place in the 'firing line' in their own states in Borneo.

The Case of the Rigid Banana

It is a little known fact that the fashion for those funny 'flared' trousers, wider at the bottom than they were at the knees, started in Borneo in the early 1960's. Our soldiers doing their training in Ipoh used to be the subject of a certain amount of ribaldry from soldiers of other regiments over their 'flared' trousers, but by the mid 1970's the style had become the 'in-thing' for well dressed men world-wide.

The young soldiers from Sabah were on the whole a well behaved lot; it was therefore a shock to hear that one of them had been seen fighting with a Chinaman outside a bar. The Chinaman came off second best and very nearly lost his life through a knife wound within an inch of his heart. There were about half a dozen witnesses to the crime and each one of them said that the person who had committed the assault was wearing 'flared' trousers. This vital piece of evidence, coupled with the fact that a few other 'bell-bottomed' trouser wearers were seen running away from the scene and heading in the direction of the Army camp, led the police to think that a soldier of Malaysia Rangers from Sabah was the culprit.

The British commanding officer of our battalion was none too pleased when he was acquainted with the facts but he promised the local chief of police that he would investigate the matter. Accordingly he told the adjutant to order a muster parade for 2pm that day. With everyone present the commanding officer mounted a dais and addressed the battalion. He spoke good Malay and he outlined the events of the previous evening. When he got to the punch line about the fellow with the 'flared' trousers stabbing the Chinaman he unfortunately used the wrong word for 'knife'. What he said was, 'Dia pukul orang China dengan pisang.' ('He struck the Chinaman with a banana.') The word he should have used was 'pisau' (knife). Not content with a single mistake, he reiterated the gory details a few times and on each occasion dwelt on how the 'banana' had narrowly missed the man's heart. There must have been 300 Sabahan soldiers and Malay non-commissioned-officers on parade and their faces remained expressionless. The British officers on the other hand were convulsed with mirth. Nobody had the courage to tell the commanding officer about his mistake. The culprit was never found!

Water Skiing - By Numbers

In addition to the two battalions of Malaysia Rangers there was also a small 'group' headquarters run by a British colonel assisted by a major and a clerk. Colonel Wellstead was a 'sapper' (Royal Engineer) before he received his red 'tabs'. He had an extremely loud and powerful voice and his nick-name of 'Boomer' was most appropriate.

'Boomer' Wellstead was a perfect choice for the job of Malaysia Ranger Group Colonel. He was the epitome of efficiency and everything he did was planned to the finest detail. He and his wife ran excellent parties, but while the rest of us would be content to provide our guests with just good food and wine. 'Boomer's' parties consisted of all sorts of party games which left everyone exhausted in mind and body. Ipoh, the capital of the state of Perak, has the reputation for being the hottest place in Malaya. When not engaged in jungle training it was customary to work from 7am to 1pm and then take a siesta until 4.30pm when games would be played. 'Siesta' was a word that did not exist in the colonel's vocabulary and, while others were 'getting their heads down' he was off rock climbing or hacking his way through jungle in pursuit of fauna if he could find someone to accompany him.

Ipoh Swimming Club was well attended at week-ends and was the favourite meeting place on Sunday mornings. When 'Boomer' and his family (he had three charming teenage daughters as well as a very elegant wife) arrived it was apparent that his passion for precision had brushed off on his family. When they had changed into their swim suits they would assemble at the deep end where 'Boomer' would give the command for their 'formation swimming' routine to begin. He would be the first to dive into the pool followed by his female entourage and they would engage in a remarkable display of swimming, reminiscent of the days of Esther Williams and her nymphettes in the great films of the 1940's. While the Wellstead family were in the pool it was unthinkable for anyone else to 'cool off'. Even when they had exited like five well disciplined penguins, it made the rest of us feel so inadequate that a quiet 'dip' seemed to be a pathetic comparison.

It was not long before 'Boomer' added water skiing to his list of family (and friends) activities. He kitted out his family with skis and arranged to have a motor boat available at a place called Lumut on the coast about 45 miles away. We didn't see the Wellstead family at the Ipoh Swimming Club for a few weeks as they were honing their skills with their new interest. 'Boomer' liked to do everything according to rules and was unable to find any regulations about water skiing, so he set about writing a pamphlet on the subject. He was very proud of the fact that he was the first person to create a set of rules about the sport and he kept it in his office for anyone who was interested enough to flick through the pages.

Captain John Williams of the 1st Battalion had cause to visit the colonel's office one day and saw the pamphlet on a table. 'How interesting, Sir. I didn't know that a pamphlet had been written on water skiing,' he said. The colonel smiled at the young officer and replied, ,'You are looking at the only one in existence - I wrote it!' John was not a keen water skier, in fact water skiing had not really hit the masses in 1965. It paid to keep in with the colonel though and John showed more interest in the pamphlet than he would have done if anyone else had written it. 'Do you think, Sir, I could take it home and read it?' he said. Photo copying, like water skiing, had not reached the masses at that time and 'Boomer' was reluctant to let his one and only copy of the pamphlet out of his hands, but John's interest in the document impressed him so much that he allowed him to take it away. 'Make sure you take care of it,' said 'Boomer', 'and bring it back on Monday morning.'

John put the document in his brief case and took it home. That night he put it on his bedside table so that he could read it if he woke up early on the Sunday morning. When he did open his eyes he found that his wife had gone to the kitchen to make a cup of tea and to let the dog out - (it being the servant's day off). He reached for the pamphlet but as he could not find it he turned over and went back to sleep again, but only for about 10 minutes before once again waking, this time by the licks of the exuberant Labrador puppy he had recently acquired. John, still half asleep, was roused to full wakefulness when his wife came back bearing a cup of tea and exclaimed, 'Oh! - what a mess, just look what the dog's done.' John sat up, followed her gaze and saw a mass of chewed up paper covering the bedroom floor. John and his wife didn't go to the Ipoh Swimming Club that day, just in case the Wellsteads were there. The following morning John had to confess to the colonel that his puppy had eaten the pamphlet - and 'Boomer' was furious! He was not a person to carry a grudge though and his clerk was soon at work making a new copy from the hand-written manuscript.

The Wellsteads were really a very kind and sociable family and once you got used to 'Boomer's' passion for organising everything, it was fun to be in their company. When the colonel and his family became proficient at water skiing 'Boomer' set about instructing officers of Malaysia Rangers and their wives in the sport. Some welcomed the invitation to attend a morning of water skiing at Lumut followed by a picnic on the beach. Others were not too keen - especially one officer and his wife who had a phobia about sea snakes and jelly fish which were both common in the seas around Lumut. When they eventually received their invitation they thought hard about how they could refuse without appearing cowardly. There was no way out so, with much trepidation, they set off the following Sunday for the west coast. A total of three families had been invited for this particular session and as each party arrived they were ferried to a 'waiting details' boat that was anchored about 200 yards from the shore. One officer from 1st Rangers was already being towed at speed behind the motor boat in which 'Boomer' was conducting operations. After about ten minutes of faultless skiing the officer let go of the tow and halted effortlessly beside the boat carrying the remainder of the party. 'Boomer' drew alongside and nominated the officer who had just arrived to prepare himself. He, by design or lack of aptitude, could not even manage to get his skis on the surface. When it became apparent that he was a non-starter his reluctant wife was ordered to get into the water and put her skis on. To everyone's amazement she was able to get moving on the first tow and within a few seconds was skimming over the surface at top speed in the crouch position. Everything seemed to be going very well until she parted company with the tow-rope. There was a huge splash with arms, legs and skis flailing the water. 'Boomer' was alongside her, but despite his encouragement and congratulations on a promising start he could not pursuade her to have another try. She was brought back to the 'waiting details' boat and sat quietly with her husband in the stern until it was time to go ashore for the picnic. Even then she was quiet and as soon as the couple could make their excuses they got into their car and went back to Ipoh.

Had the unfortunate lady been in possession of a copy of 'Boomer' Wellstead's water skiing pamphlet she would have known what to do when she became 'sea-borne'. The pamphlet explained - 'The crouch position should not be held for more than a few seconds once the skis are skimming over the water, and then one should stand upright. Failure to do so, as far as females are concerned, is to run the danger of receiving a high pressure enema of sea water'. 'Boomer' completed the paragraph with - 'males do not have this problem as they are equipped with a built in baffle plate'.

General Tunku Osman, Chief of the Armed Forces staff inspects 2/Rangers at Ipoh (author is on his left).

Not the Way to Treat a Headman

The completion of each company's basic training was celebrated with a Passing Out Parade. Whenever possible a senior military or civilian dignitary was invited to take the salute at the march past, meet the graduates after the parade and have lunch in the officers' mess.

A month or so before one of these parades took place, it was decided to invite two penghulus (headmen) from the tribal area in Sabah which had produced most of the recruits for the company about to pass out. Initial contact was made through the Resident's office and when the two penghulus had accepted the invitation, plans were made to bring them to Ipoh from their villages on the jungle fringe in Sabah. This was not as easy as asking a couple of mayors in UK to do the same sort of thing.

These penghulus had to be fitted out with western style clothes, travel by boat to the airstrip and then - for the first time in their lives, fly across the sea to Malaya. Looking back after the passage of 30 years it was a wonder they arrived at all.

But arrive they did. They were met at Ipoh Airport by the adjutant who ushered them into the commanding officer's staff car for the two mile drive to the barracks. The plan was to take them to the officers' mess for a cold drink before being introduced to the colonel in his office. Then would follow a tour of the camp before the parade took place at noon. Their bags were taken to their rooms and just before they set off to meet the commanding officer the penghulus said they wished to go to the lavatory. The adjutant took them outside and pointed towards the cubicles.

Only a week before, the 'house member' of the mess committee had had cause to speak to the Malay mess sergeant about the improper use of the western style lavatories by Malays, Indians and Chinese. It was not a matter of racial descrimination but a problem of hygiene brought about by the construction of the two different types of lavatory. While occidentals sit on theirs orientals squat over a hole, usually at ground level. It doesn't require much imagination to see the problems which occur when orientals squat on bogs meant for occidentals. The Malay mess sergeant had been given strict instructions to deal severely with any gardeners or other locally employed civilians who contravened these rules. He therefore acted promptly when he saw two men from his part of the world enter cubicles containing water closets. He put his boot to the door of the first cubicle and spied a person squatting on the seat. Not even giving him time to pull up his trousers he caught the penghulu by the scruff of the neck, dragged him outside and threw him down the grassy bank. He then repeated the act with the penghulu in the adjoining cubicle. The 'house member' happened to come into the mess just as the two men crawled up the grassy bank and were about to be despatched for the second time by the mess sergeant. Word of the assault was soon flashed around the camp and the adjutant anticipated the commanding officer's wishes by telling the mess sergeant to keep out of the way for the rest of the time the VIP's from Sabah were with us.

The penghulus were taken to battalion headquarters where they were introduced to the commanding officer and others. The parade was performed faultlessly and the two dignitaries took the salute as if they had done it many times before. They thoroughly enjoyed luncheon where they were able to meet the British officers and their wives. During the late afternoon they attended a football match and the evening was spent enjoying typical Sabahan entertainment of play acting and rongging (dancing with professional 'hostesses').

All of us lined up to see them off the following morning. The headmen were full of praise for the kindness and attention they had received. As they shook the commanding officer's hand one of them said, 'When you come to Sabah we should like you to visit us so that we can re-pay your hospitality'. We wondered if there was any danger of the CO being the 'fall guy' for the Malay mess sergeant's blunder.

Pearl of the Orient

The relaxed style of the Indonesian 'confrontation' campaign became apparent as soon as I landed at Tawau airport in Sabah. I flew from Ipoh in a Hercules aircraft with the advance party comprising about 50 men of the 2nd Battalion Malaysia Rangers: when we landed I was met by an officer of the Malaysian Armed Forces. 'Do you want to meet the Brigadier,' he asked. It would have been impolite to answer in the negative, so I said. 'Yes, please.' The officer shook his head and said, 'Well I'm afraid you can't - it's a holiday today.' Holidays are an ever present feature of life in Malaysia and rarely does a two week period pass without a Malay, Chinese or Indian festival taking place. Despite Malaysia being an Islamic country, all races seemed to enjoy celebrating Christmas and Easter just as much as the Christians. Another example of the relaxed style with which the Indonesians and Malays 'confronted' each other was the fact that at least half a dozen Indonesian sailing boats known as 'cumpits' were at their moorings in Tawau harbour at any one time. These small sailing boats plied their trade without hindrance over a wide area of the South China Sea.

One of my jobs as battalion second-in-command was to pursue the 'hearts and minds' campaign. A large sum of money had been voted to provide children's playgrounds and this was deemed to be an excellent opportunity to get to know the villagers. The

Tawau with Pulau Sebatik in the distance.

procedure went like this. First - a village would be selected and a reconnaissance carried out to see if the villagers wanted a playground, and if so where it should be sited. Second - the contract for the construction of the swings, roundabouts and slides to be drawn up with a local contractor in Tawau. Third - the preparation of concrete foundations in the village and finally - fourth - the delivery by me and a working party of the playground in kit form ready for assembly on the concrete slabs. The village headman would make it quite an occasion: The children would be given a day off from school and there would be speeches and toasts and, hopefully, declarations of support against the common enemy.

The day before we set off for one of the villages destined to receive a set of playground equipment, I checked to make sure it was complete and then had it loaded on a couple of army lorries. I and about a dozen soldiers, comprising the working party, made an early start as there had been almost continuous rain during the previous week. Even though it was only a round trip of some 60 miles the roads were so bad that progress could be as little as 10 miles an hour. The 'roads' through the jungle were just cleared tracks where trees had been felled by Chinese logging companies. It was quite a useful scheme for all concerned: the Chinese were able to cut down valuable hardwood trees and the Sabahan government benefitted from the revenue paid for timber as well as being able to develop tracks and bridges used by the loggers. Nowadays many of these tracks have become wide thoroughfares connecting towns and villages which in my day could only be reached by sea.

The journey was, as I expected, painfully slow. At one stage

Stuck in the mud on a logging track.

when we were crossing a log bridge, the wheels of one of the lorries slipped between two tree trunks and it took us a few hours to get moving again. As a result, our schedule was badly affected and by the time we had put the playground together and made sure that everything worked properly, it was too late to make the return journey. This was no great problem: we were operating in Borneo where the pace of life is much slower than most other places in the world. The local PWD (public works department) superintendent allowed us to occupy some atap (palm frond) thatched huts in his compound and the soldiers were quite happy to spend the night in the village, where one of them was able to see his family. I had a hut for my own use and I had brought a hammock, a mosquito net and a couple of blankets with me to be on the safe side. I could have joined the soldiers who were making a delicious curry from the contents of their emergency ration packs, but decided instead that I would go into the village for an evening meal.

When I parked my Land Rover near the padang (village green) I could see that the night shift had taken over use of the playground. Screams of adult laughter rang around the padang as grown men and women gave the swings, slides and roundabouts a thoroughly good test. They recognised me as their benefactor and greeted me again most warmly. I considered that the 'hearts and minds' of this particular village had been captured. I spent some time talking to the villagers and then became aware that I had not had much to eat since breakfast. It was only a small village and I certainly did not expect to find anything as sophisticated as a restaurant. I walked around the padang and someone was kind enough to direct me to a place where food was available. The door facing the padang was closed, so I walked around to the back of the house. I climbed a few steps, looked through a window and saw a Chinese family sitting down to their evening meal: the father of the family got to his feet and opened the door. I asked him in Malay if he could

214

serve me with food. He invited me to step inside and led me into a room normally used by the public - when they could get in. Seated at the table was a Chinese woman of middle age who listened as the towkay (owner of the establishment) spoke to her in Cantonese. She spoke to me in excellent English and introduced herself as Pearl Chung who lived a few hundred yards down the road. 'I understand you would like something to eat,' she said. I was delighted to meet such an agreeable companion and I asked her what was on offer. There was nothing like a menu in this most humble of eating establishments so I told her that anything would do as long as it came quickly. She said she had ordered a meal for herself and suggested she double the order. 'Yes, please,' I replied, 'and would you like something to drink?' She had an empty bottle of Tiger beer in front of her, and she nodded towards it.

The main course, as far as I can remember, was a pile of rice accompanied by the bits of chicken and duck that are usually thrown away in our own country. It was food nevertheless and when I had finished I was able to give my full attention to liquid refreshment.

Pearl and I sat well into the night drinking rice wine. When I knew that my driving ability would be impaired if I drank another drop, I offered to take her home. Getting her down the back steps was quite a job and an even more difficult task was to get her into the Land Rover. She directed me out of the village and along the road towards the sea. After we had gone about 200 yards she told me to turn right and follow a track between some banana trees. Eventually we came to a small atap hut with a brilliant white door. 'Here we are,' said Pearl as she stumbled out of the vehicle.

Pearl had told me she was 'attached' to someone and although our friendship was quite above board I had no wish to be confronted by a Chinaman who could be forgiven for thinking otherwise. I was about to drive away when, to my astonishment, the door was opened by a male European dressed immaculately in white drill from head to foot. 'Hello, darling,' he said grabbing Pearl around the waist and putting his other hand on the bonnet of the Land Rover. 'Who have you brought home?' Pearl introduced me and said, 'We've had a great time together.' Short of running over Pearl's boy friend I was unable to make my exit and, as he showed no intention of enquiring into what sort of 'great time' we had had together, I opened the door and got out. 'Andrew Millard,' said the man in white - 'late of the Royal Navy. Come inside old boy and have something to drink. We don't see many army chaps around here.' From the outside the house looked like most other native dwellings but once inside I found it was pleasantly decorated. A typewriter on the desk and a wide selection of books on shelves led me to believe that Andrew or Pearl did some writing. I was right in this assumption and Andrew explained that he supplemented his service pension by submitting the odd story to the Sabah newspaper printed in Jesselton (now called Kota Kinabalu). I had consumed enough rice wine that evening to last me for the rest of my time in Borneo but over the next few hours I consumed a considerable number of Tiger beers as well. Pearl seemed to have obtained her second wind and all three of us had a most entertaining time.

Andrew met Pearl in Hong Kong when he was serving with the Royal Navy. He had a shore job and spent the last three years of his service in the colony. On one of his sea trips Andrew visited an idyllic village on the east coast of Sabah (then called British North Borneo). He told Pearl about the place and when he retired they decided to live there. Andrew bought a ramshackle van and found that he could make a reasonable income using the vehicle as a taxi for employees on the logging tracks. Pearl, for her part, bought a large refrigerator and went into the ice cream business. Something went wrong with the refrigerator though and when, for the second time in six months, she caused food poisoning among the villagers, they became quite angry and literally drove the pair out of the village. They had to abandon everything that would not fit into their van and by travelling through a tortuous maze of logging tracks they eventually reached the place where I found them.

It was well into the early hours of the morning when I left them. There was not a soul about as I drove back to the PWD compound and crawled into my hammock. A few hours later when I was woken by a soldier offering me a cup of tea, the sun was already high in the sky. We were soon on the road and managed to get back to Tawau without too much trouble.

About three months later I was sitting at my desk when the phone rang. When I picked it up a voice said, 'Hello, Bob, this is Pearl. I'm staying at the Tawau Hotel for a few days. Can we meet?' Unfortunately I just happened to be off on a three day trip to Pulau Sebatik, a large island a few miles from the mainland which was our operational responsibility. I met her and Andrew once more when I paid a visit to the village to check if the playground was still there. It seemed more prudent that way!

The Silver Screen

Tawau in the mid sixties was the centre of the pornographic film industry in Borneo. I cannot speak with personal experience but I doubt if they were more sexually explicit than some of the programmes one can see these days on TV. The market for these films was the staunchly Roman Catholic Republic of the Philipines: there was also a brisk traffic in 'PLAYBOY' magazines that came in by sea and were then exported in long, thin pencil shaped boats powered by four 40 horse power outboard motors. The boats travelled so fast that nothing in the Philippine Navy could catch them. They presented a difficult target but occasionally a boat would be hit by gunfire - there were never any survivors. Those who took part in this illicit trade considered the risks worthwhile. Ten successful runs would provide crews with enough money to live comfortably for the rest of their lives.

Colour Sergeant Hamish McCleod of the Argyll and Sutherland Highlanders was the orderly sergeant of the day and was carrying out an evening inspection of 2nd Ranger's camp in Tawau. McCleod was one of the first British non-commissioned-officers to be seconded to the Sabah battalion and had proved himself to be an excellent NCO: he set a high moral standard in his personal and professional life. McCleod was accompanied on his inspection by the Malay provost sergeant and was about to tell him to 'fall out' when an unusual sound made him freeze. He moved his head from side to side until he had a fix on one of the accommodation huts. Signalling the provost sergeant to follow he tip-toed to the hut and smashed the door open with his boot. There was an exodus of bodies through every window frame and within a matter of seconds the room was empty except for one man. Corporal Lam Chop was standing stiffly to 'attention' alongside a machine that was projecting a pornographic film. The only reason why he hadn't followed the others was that he was the owner of the projector. Colour Sergeant Hamish McCleod could not believe what he saw on the screen. His strict Presbyterian upbringing in Scotland had not prepared him for the sight of human bodies writhing like a bucket of sand eels. 'Yur dirrty wee blackguard, I'll have 'yer courrt martialled for this,' he said. He gave instructions to the provost sergeant to put the corporal in the guard room while he himself switched off the machine and removed the film.

The routine for Commanding Officer's Orders (a military version of a magistrates' court) is pretty much the same wherever the British Army has left its influence. Those who are about to answer charges of misconduct before their CO are paraded outside his office, usually at noon. To create atmosphere there is much shouting of commands, stamping of feet and blowing of bugles. My office was next door to the CO's and we shared a verandah where miscreants were paraded. I looked out of my window and saw Corporal Lam Chop having his uniform and general turnout being inspected by the regimental sergeant major. Knowing him to be a good NCO I wondered what had gone wrong so I waited for an opportunity to speak to the senior warrant officer. The RSM told me about the discovery of Corporal Lam Chop's nocturnal side-line and I was dismayed to hear that he was being charged with 'Conduct to the prejudice of good order and military discipline in that he did   provide and exhibit pornographic films for the purpose of entertaining soldiers'. We had had some racial problems between Malay soldiers serving in Tawau and our own soldiers. The matter of 'flared' trousers had been the cause of a number of fights and our soldiers resented the patronising attitude of the mainland Malays. The brigade commander - a Malay himself, made things worse by taking the side of his kinsfolk. Looking at it in the bigger picture I considered that Lam Chop was doing a good job. He was keeping soldiers happy and contented within the confines of the camp thus maintaining the brigadier's blood pressure at an acceptable level. The innocuous matter of showing pornographic films was, I considered, a small price to pay.

The British commanding officer of 2nd Rangers had recently returned to UK at the end of his tour of command and had been replaced by a Malay lieutenant colonel. The newcomer was an extremely competent officer who had been commissioned at Sandhurst: all the remaining British ranks were pleased to serve under him. I therefore went to find out what he proposed doing. I was concerned when he said that he intended making an example of the NCO. I remonstrated with him but it was no use - if the charge was proved, then Lam Chop would be reduced to the ranks and suffer a term of detention. There seemed to be nothing else I could do to change his mind but as I was about to return to my office the CO's phone rang. When he replaced the handpiece he told me that the brigadier wanted to see him: 'Orders' would have to wait.

Brigade Headquarters was only a few hundred yards away and it was not long before the CO returned and entered my office. Even for a Malay, he looked flushed. He told me that the brigadier had heard about Corporal Lam Chop being caught in the act of showing pornographic films and had reacted strongly when told he was going to be disciplined. 'You will do no such thing', said the brigadier. 'You will return his projector and his film - we have booked him to give a show in the brigade officers' mess every Monday night.'

The Last Journey of Ranger Awang

During the seven months I spent on 'active service' with 2nd Rangers in Sabah we had only one fatality, and that was caused by our own, not enemy gunfire. Our operational area was the island of Sebatik (*Pulau Sebatik*) which was three miles away from Tawau where main headquarters of 2nd Rangers was based. The island was 30 miles long and ten miles wide at its widest point. The northern part of the island belonged to Malaysia and the southern part to Indonesia. The border on our side was marked by a barbed wire fence, then came a stretch of 'no-man's-land' which led to Indonesian held territory. On our side, spaced at varying distances, were huge sandbag and timber fortifications known as 'sangars'. They were in communication with each other and had interlocking fields of fire.

One of the advantages of the 'confrontation' campaign was that we were allowed to practice live firing

Log and sandbag 'basha' on the border with Inonesia.

with weapons without having the usual peace time restrictions placed upon us. This was alright as long as one did not become too blasé about the effect of high explosives. Once a week medium mortars with their base plates about two miles behind the border would bring down defensive fire (DF) into 'no-man's-land'. This was to practice drills and to make sure that immediate destruction of the enemy would occur if the signal to shoot was given. It was a rather frightening experience the first time soldiers experienced mortar bombs exploding only a hundred yards away, but the mortar-men two miles away knew what they were doing - and nothing ever went wrong!

Such a rehearsal took place one day and the occupants of one of the sangars 'took cover'. Mortar bombs rained down and the ground shook with the force of the explosions. Suddenly a soldier - Ranger Awang, slumped against one of his comrades and then slid slowly to the ground.

When the bombardment ceased it was found that Ranger Awang had been killed by a piece of mortar bomb which had gone through his head. It must have been a million to one chance as the shrapnel had entered the sangar through one of the firing slits, ricocheted off a timber support and bounced back under the parapet where Ranger Awang was sheltering. The body was taken to the mainland where the necessary formalities were carried out. A coffin with a metal liner was delivered to the medical centre and Ranger Awang was placed inside and sealed down. It was found that his parents lived in a small island called Pulau Chantek a few miles from Jesselton (now called Kota Kinabalu). They were told of their son's death and that the body would be delivered there for burial the following day.

The composition of the funeral party was myself, the regimental sergeant major, the pipe major (Malay), the Tuan Guru (Malay 'padre') and six soldiers from Ranger Awang's company. We made an early start when we boarded an aircraft which had been sent specially from Jesselton by the Malaysian Air Force. It took about an hour to fly over dense jungle before we arrived at the capital of Sabah. A Land Rover had been sent to carry the coffin and there was more transport for the rest of us. The cortege set off from the airfield and headed towards the waterfront.

One of the soldiers pointed towards a small island a few miles from the shore and told me that it was Pulau Chantek. The Land Rover pulled up alongside a jetty where a motor boat was tethered: the skipper invited me to load the coffin. It was an extremely tricky business getting it out of the Land Rover, carrying it down a rickety stairway and then into the boat which was rising and falling quite alarmingly.

When we moved off the boat sat low in the water and the waves lapped within six inches of the gunwale. There were eleven of us, plus the coffin, and this was almost beyond the capacity of the boat. As we drew near to Pulau Chantek I could see that waves were breaking on the shore and there did not appear to be a jetty. This was confirmed by the skipper who told me that he would try and get the boat as near as he could to the house where Ranger Awang's parents lived. I had not reckoned with having to wade through the surf in our smartly pressed jungle green uniforms so I ordered the soldiers to remove their footwear and roll up their trousers. We struggled in the water to get the coffin on dry land but were hampered by the under-tow of the waves. It was like a bad dream and I wondered if I would wake up and find myself comfortably ensconsed under my mosquito net in Tawau. The reality was that the Tuan Guru said that the regimental sergeant major and I would be required to go into the house and take part in certain rituals with the family before the burial could take place. I was concerned about how we would manage to get the coffin, which grew heavier each time we moved it, up a flimsy ladder to an atap house built on stilts about ten feet above the ground. But this time willing hands from Ranger Awang's family carried the coffin up the ladder and placed it in the centre of the main room. The RSM and I followed and took our place, cross legged, on the floor where we were given a cool drink and some rice cakes. I spoke in Malay to the parents of the dead boy and told them how their son had been killed: I was impressed with the dignity they showed in their sorrow. I had not attended a Malay funeral before and I was horrified when the Tuan Guru told me that it would be necessary to open the coffin. I knew that the metal liner had been welded down and I advised him that it should not be attempted. The family, however, were determined to see Awang before he was buried, so an orang besi (blacksmith) was summoned. The womenfolk went through the distressing business of saying their farewells to the accompaniment of much wailing, beating of breasts and tearing their hair. At last their devotions came to an end and the orang besi was able to close the coffin.

I had assumed that the burial would take place near the house but in fact it meant another sea trip to the other side of the island. Once more the coffin had to be carried through the surf to the boat before being transported to the burial place.

Before the interment took place it was necessary for the Tuan Guru to read from the Koran inside the grave. This gave me time to position the pipe major about 100 yards away where his 'lament' would be best heard. I also positioned the soldiers where they could fire a volley when the coffin was placed in the grave.

When the Tuan Guru emerged from the grave and the coffin was lowered the eerie sound of the pipes playing a lament startled the simple Malay folk who had never heard the sound of Scottish bag-pipes before. They accepted that this and the firing of rifles was the way that soldiers said their 'farewell'.

We had a long journey ahead of us and I had to decline the offer of Awang's family to stay over until the following day. Their son was the first soldier from their island to have died in the course of military duty. I was proud to be one of those who brought him home.

The End of the Line

Tawau was only a small town and if the state of emergency had not been declared it would have remained one of the most remote townships in Malaysia. Because it had a harbour, an airfield and was in close proximity to Indonesia it became the natural place to establish a large garrison. The influx of many hundreds of soldiers and airmen was a heaven sent gift for the tradesmen of the town, but they presented difficulties, one of which concerned the water supply. The townsfolk had no problems but when the taps were turned on in the military camps, which were at the end of the pipeline, they produced a miserable drip or nothing at all.

There was a large water tank at the top end of the camp and one day I climbed up the tower to find out just how much water there was in it. It was empty. The following day I went to see the person in charge of the water supply at the local public works department. When I told him the tank in our camp was empty he nodded and said it would have to stay that way. 'If I fill that tank it will drain the already strained system,' he said. 'Unfortunately, you are at the end of the line and you will just have to make the best of it - there's nothing else I can do.'

That evening we had the usual torrential downpour and I saw some of our soldiers standing outside their barrack rooms rubbing soap over themselves and bathing in natural conditions. That gave me an idea.

The officers' accommodation in 2nd Rangers camp was built around a sunken badminton court which looked like a swimming pool without water. When it rained the water ran into gutters below the corrugated iron roof and was carried away into the sewage system. This, without doubt, was a waste of good water so I went to see the troop commander of the Royal Engineer unit. I explained my plan of catching rain water and re-routing it into a number of 44 steel drums so situated that when the top one was full it would overflow into the next one and so on down the line. Within a few hours a truck arrived with the drums and some extra guttering and the sappers set to work. By evening all was ready and we waited for the rain to come. When it did, the steel drums were soon filled to the brim and we had more water than we wanted.

We were now able to wash in the traditional Malaysian way by standing alongside a tank of water with a saucepan like utensil to fill and pour over oneself. There is nothing more exhilarating than doing this and the cold water from the sky added additional zest to our ablutions. It was all so simple and I can't think why other occupants of the camp before we arived had not thought of it.

Rats were a problem when we took over from the outgoing unit. On our first morning in Kukusan Camp, Tawau, every officer found that his soap had gone: it was clear to see that rodents had been at work. By the time darkness fell every officer had been equipped with a rat trap. Before bed time most traps had been sprung and during the night the staccato rattle of traps going off kept us awake until we declared a truce. The rats we caught were about 15 to 16 inches long from nose to tail and were extremely vicious. Some of them tried to run off with the traps attached to their bodies and had to be killed with parangs (long knives). It took us about three days to rid ourselves of these obnoxious creatures: the quartermaster had an even greater task clearing them from the cookhouse.

Cockroaches are found everywhere in Malaya. Even in the best regulated households these disease-carrying beetles can usually be found in the kitchen. The best safeguard is to keep a cat which will make short work of them. We would have needed an army of cats in the cookhouse in Kukusan Camp to have made an impression on the cockroaches we found there when we took over from the outgoing unit. The quartermaster took immediate action when he found traces of these insects. He ordered some large cupboards to be drawn back from the wall and hundreds of thousands of these creatures, sheltering from the light, were revealed. The cooks hurled buckets of boiling water over them and when the stoves were dismantled thousands more were discovered and destroyed. The floor became ankle deep in the creatures and finally they were shovelled into sacks and taken outside to a pit where they were covered in paraffin and burnt.

If this sort of thing was a problem on the mainland it was nothing compared to the situation on Pulau Sebatik. Living in sangars was bad enough but rats brought snakes, particularly cobras, and they were considered to be the most dangerous of all hazards. When the cry 'Ular' (snake) went up there was no peace until the reptile was killed.

Company bases on Pulau Sebatik could be reached in two ways, by helicopter and by boat. Helicopters were useful for carrying senior officers on visits and to evacuate sick personnel. Their cargo capacity was limited though and only on special occasions were they used for this purpose. Our 'work horse' was the infantry assault boat designed to carry ten men equipped with paddles across small rivers. When a 40 horse power outboard motor is mounted on the stern it's performance is transformed and speeds of up to 30 miles an hour are possible. We had so much faith in them that we would quite happily set out on a 20 mile round trip from Tawau to our most distant company base at Simpang Tiga. All our soldiers were used to handling boats, but they needed to be trained in the use of outboard motors. On our first exercise in some gravel pits in Malaya one of the engines had not been attached firmly enough. When the rope was pulled and the engine roared into life it shot off the stern of the boat and was never seen again.

Some of the company bases were well concealed but our boatmen, after a three mile trip across the sea from Tawau, knew just where to enter the dense marine jungle of mangrove which ringed the island. These bases could only be reached at high tide and even then the last few hundred yards of water was so shallow that the boats had to be paddled. Mangrove had its use though. The impregnable tangle of roots was as good as barbed wire for keeping out the enemy.

When travelling by boat to Simpang Tiga on the western end of Pulau Sebatik we came under observation from the Indonesian Army base of Nunukan on an adjoining island about five miles away. Before we arrived the Indonesians had ambushed some boats travelling up the wide river and we therefore always travelled in a convoy of three boats for the last three miles. At the mouth of the river a large motor boat was permanently anchored on the Sabahan side of the border (marked by a tethered buoy). It had a permanent crew of three plus a few policemen and half a dozen Rangers. Their task was to observe, with an exceptionally powerful telescope, and report unusual movement in the Indonesian garrison. It was never a popular duty to spend three or four days on this boat which was forever straining at its anchor chain. Even the best of sailors became sea-sick. On one occasion an Indonesian gun-boat made an aggressive charge but turned back before it reached the marker buoy.

When I came to the end of my two and a half year tour of duty with the 2nd Battalion Malaysia Rangers I flew to the island of Penang on the west coast of Malaya to spend a month's holiday with my family. While I was there President Sukarno of Indonesia was deposed and the campaign came to an end. Tawau soon reverted to the sleepy little backwater town it had been before 'confrontation' started. I doubt if the Indonesian sailors in their 'cumpits' in the harbour realised that anything had changed.

CHAPTER THIRTY SEVEN

The Snowy Heights above Beirut

I was stationed with the British Army in Cyprus in 1958 during the 'Union with Greece' troubles. The 1st Battalion The Welch Regiment was on a 12 month 'emergency' tour of duty and this meant a monastic style of living in tents in some rather out-of-the-way spots on the island. Some of those who were married were sent home on courses - which was one way of seeing their families. Those of us who were single snatched a few days leave on the island when the operational situation allowed. I, personally, had no desire to go on leave, the fact that we were on 'active service' was good enough for me and besides, there was a good club alongside an American owned copper mine only a few miles up the road. I was rather surprised therefore when the adjutant asked me if I would like to go skiing in Lebanon for two weeks. He showed me the relevant paragraph in District routine orders which offered a number of vacancies to members of the British armed forces at the Lebanese Army's ski school at Les Cedres in the mountains high above Beirut. I studied the words carefully and could find no catch - so there and then my name was put forward.

I heard nothing for a few weeks and then I received an official-looking envelope from Headquarters, Middle East Land Forces. The contents informed me that I was to report to a certain officer at the Headquarters a few days

The Ski Slopes at Les Cèdres, Lebanon.

hence. I showed it to the adjutant and he told me to arrange transport and conform to my instructions. I made the journey, which took me over the Troodos mountain range and down the other side, to Episkopi on the south coast. I was in time to have a few drinks at the bar in the officers' mess and then a leisurely lunch before keeping my appointment. The fellow to whom I was ordered to report turned out to be a lieutenant colonel in a cavalry regiment. He presented a sinister appearance with his black eye patch but he greeted me warmly as I entered his office. He did not mince his words and told me that I was being sent to Lebanon to find out all that I could about the country. I was instructed to keep my eyes and ears open and write a report and forward it to him when I returned. The adjutant of my unit had said nothing about the clandestine part of my skiing trip, neither was it mentioned in the words of the District routine order. I began to feel that I was sitting in the office of this one-eyed cavalry-man under false pretences. Before I could tell him that James Bond films gave me nightmares, he stood up, shook my hand and wished me the best of luck. When I returned to my unit I tackled the adjutant about 'setting me up'. He told me that if I was 'funking out' he would erase my name from the list. Not wishing to appear a coward, but nevertheless thinking that the matter could have been dealt with a little more delicately, I prepared myself for the trip to Lebanon.

I flew the short distance from Nicosia to Beirut in an aircraft of Middle East Airlines along with two sergeants from other units of the British Army in Cyprus. I wondered if they too were on the same clandestine mission as me, but thought it better not to enquire. A young man from the British Embassy was at the airport to meet us. He introduced us to a swarthy looking soldier called Salim, the driver of the land rover who had orders to take us to Les Cedres. My joining instructions stated that ski-wear would be issued at the Lebanese Army Ski School but as I take size 12 in footwear I thought it wise to buy a pair of ski boots before leaving Beirut. Salim took over when I explained what I wanted and drove like a maniac up the long tree lined avenue from the airport to the town centre. Horn and accelerator were the two main driving essentials, with the brake used only to avoid collisions. Salim, being a soldier, could drive over traffic islands and this he did whenever we came to one. By the time we pulled up at the first shoe shop the two sergeants in the back of the truck were talking about getting a taxi back to the airport. I told them it was too late to back out. With me using my limited Arabic and French, and Salim going through the motions of stem turns, snow-ploughs and christies, the manager of the shoe shop finally got the message, and said that he had none. We went to another three shops and put on the same routine before I was forced to give up and accept the fact that Beirut was devoid of ski boots. Salim was anxious to get going as it was a three hour journey to

Les Cedres and the weather forecast was not good. He started off again at break-neck speed and jumped over three more traffic islands before emerging on the north coast road running out of Beirut towards Tripoli.

At Tripoli we turned right and headed into the mountains. If Salim's driving at sea level had scared the pants off us, it was nothing to what he had in store once we had passed through the low foothills of the huge mountain range that towered above us. Heavy rain gave way to snow as we climbed higher but the slippery roads only made Salim take corners with more of a flourish. To add to our concern steam started to cloud the windscreen. Salim drew up on a straight piece of road, lifted the bonnet and was lost to sight as steam enveloped him. He re-appeared a few seconds later grinning like a Cheshire cat saying, 'Mauyer maffeesh!' ('water finished'.) Fortunately, a stream ran along the side of the road and when the engine had cooled we were able to scoop some water out and fill the radiator. Poor maintenance, rather than a hole in the cooling system, seemed to be the cause and we were able to continue our journey without further trouble.

A full scale blizzard was blowing and darkness had descended when we arrived at Les Cedres. The land rover drew up outside a building where the two sergeants got out. Salim then took me to a building on the other side of the quadrangle which was the officers' mess. I was warmly welcomed by some Lebanese Army officers who took me upstairs and gave me some really good coffee. It was hard to imagine that I was still in the Lebanon when only a few hours ago the sun had been shining on some swimmers in the sea. Even within the warm confines of the officers' mess the blizzard could be heard and snow could be seen piling on the window frames. I took stock of my room which could be described as 'frugal but adequate' for my 10 day stay. Only two essential items seemed to be missing and those were bed sheets. I went along to the mess office and asked one of the servants if he could let me have some. He looked at me in a puzzled way and told me that he had actually made my bed for me that morning. 'Where could those sheets have gone?' was his reply. He accompanied me to my room, rolled back the blankets and said, 'There they are.' He returned to his duty and left me alone to take a closer look at the obnoxious things I was supposed to sleep between. They appeared to have been made from the same coarse material as mail bags and looked as if they had been used for that purpose for a very long time.

I unpacked my kit and went along to the bathroom. I slammed the door behind me and heard a dull thud from the landing outside. I could see at once what had happened, there was no door knob on the inside of the bathroom and the metal bar, with the outside knob, had passed through the lock. There was no way I could have opened the door, but I was not concerned as I felt sure that someone would come along and release me. The hot water gushed into the huge bath and I was able to enjoy a good soak. I must have been in the bath for half an hour without hearing a sound, and I then started to get worried. I dried myself, put on my dressing gown and inspected the door and its frame to see if there was any way I could get out. It was quite impossible. The only course open to me was to shout for assistance. I opened the heavy window frame and met the full force of the blizzard that nearly blew me back into the bath. I persevered and managed to get my head and shoulders into a position where I could see the entrance to the officers' mess. In the lee of the porch was a sentry wrapped in a great-coat. I shouted to attract his attention but he did not hear me. I tried again and this time stuck two fingers in my mouth and let out a piercing whistle. I felt that I was making progress as this time the sentry started to look about him, but only at ground level. Despite the fact that I was now covered with snow, I made one more try and levered myself as far as I could out of the window. The sound I made caused not only the sentry to look upwards, but the guard commander and a few others came out of an adjacent building to find the cause of the commotion. The extra surge of decibels was caused by my dressing gown opening thus allowing certain tender parts of my body to descend upon the top of a very hot radiator. I hastily withdrew from my position and rendered first aid to myself with copious amounts of snow.

In order not to lose contact with those on the ground I shook a very large bath towel out of he window. Within a few minutes I heard sounds in the passage-way, and then the door opened. I was still in considerable pain but I had to make light of the matter. I walked with a jaunty step back to my bedroom - but it was quite an effort!

Whilst on matters lavatorial, I was caught one day trying to remove a piece of fossilized excretia from the top of the lavatory seat in the wash room of the officers' mess. One quite sophisticated Lebanese Army officer could not understand why I was chipping the seat with the heel of a shoe and I felt somewhat embarrassed having to tell him what I was doing. He inspected the offending lump, which now had some sharp edges, and said quite cheerfully, 'There's no need for you to worry about that. There's an old Arab proverb which says - 'There's a dirty place in every man's house.'

The blizzard of the previous evening had reduced visibility to only a few yards but when I awoke on my first full day in the Lebanon the sun's rays were bringing a russet glow to the snow shrouded mountains. For the first time I was able to see the large clump of cedars a few hundred yards away that are the only trees

left from hundreds of thousands that once grew in those mountains. Nine hundred and fifty years before the birth of Christ this fine wood was used to build the temple of King Solomon in Jerusalem and, it is said, some of the trees still standing in Les Cedres were growing there when Jesus was born. Their majestic branches spreading

This cedar tree is reputed to have existed before the birth of Jesus Christ.

outwards from the trunk and parallel to the ground are more familiar in our own country these days than they are in the Levant.

I had been told the night before to report to the ski school stores at 8am to draw my kit. With a few minutes in hand I met the two British sergeants as well as the instructor/interpreter who had been detailed to help us during our stay. Arctic clothing of the same pattern used by the British Army was brought out and we were all given our appropriate sizes. Then came the skis and ski-sticks and finally the ski boots. This was the moment of truth as far as I was concerned and I began to feel uneasy when the storeman scratched his head when asked to find an extra large pair for me. He pulled out a number of boots and I felt like one of the ugly sisters in the pantomime 'Cinderella' as I tried to stuff my feet into them. It was no good, they were too small and it looked as if I was going to be left in the kitchen while everyone else went to the ball. The interpreter suggested I should go along to the one and only civilian ski shop in Les Cedres which opened at 9am. If and when I fixed myself up with footwear, I was asked to join the rest of the party at the ski lift.

I went back to the mess, had some more coffee and then, at 9am, took the short walk to the ski shop. The manager was rolling up the blinds when I arrived. He gave a sigh when I asked if he could equip me with a pair of ski boots. 'I can tell you now, Sir, that I do not have anything that will fit you.' I asked him if there was anyone else who could help me and after a few seconds' thought he replied, 'There is a man who lives in the village of Bacharre in the Kadicha Gorge not more than 15 miles from here.' He explained that it would not be difficult to find him as he lived in a cave on the right side of the road a hundred yards before you enter the village. 'His name us Haji Yusuf - he is the only man who can help you.' I thanked him and went back to the ski school to see if I could get some transport.

Salim had returned to Beirut, but another soldier was summoned and ordered to take me to Bacharre. Not only did this driver bear a remarkable resemblance to Salim but he had obviously graduated from the same driving school as his look-alike. There was a deep covering of snow on the road and driver No.2 used it to skid alarmingly around corners with drops of thousands of feet on one side. As we approached the village of Bacharre I kept my eyes open for the cave where Haji Yusuf lived. We missed it on the first run and had to turn around and try again. On the return trip it was easy to find as the opening of the cave faced towards the village. A definable track led from the road to the cave and I walked the hundred yards or so to the entrance. Haji Yusuf's boot and shoe emporium must have the best view of any shop in Lebanon. Shielded from the prevailing westerly winds it absorbed the morning sun and provided a light filled work and show place ideal for the purpose of that master cordwainer. Haji Yusuf saw me climbing the slope and stood up as I approached. Befitting a pilgrim who had visited Mecca, he wore a red stained beard and welcomed me to his cave. 'Salaam alakum,' he said. 'Alakum, salaam,' I replied - and we shook

231

hands. I told him of my difficulties in getting a pair of ski boots and I asked him if he could help. He asked me to raise my right foot to his lap and with a wooden contraption he took my measurements. He sucked loudly through his teeth, shook his head and exclaimed 'Quois kebir!' (very big!). He nevertheless nodded in an optimistic way and asked me to follow him to the back of the cave. Rows of shelves lined the solid rock wall and Haji Yusuf stopped at a place which looked as if it was a tomb for long dead beavers. He took down a pair of whiskery boots and asked me to try them on. Shaggy fur apres ski boots had yet to become the fashion in ski resorts and I suppose I can claim to be the first person to wear this avant guarde style of footwear. The important thing was that they fitted me like a glove and I asked Haji Yusuf if I could hire them for the next 10 days. He agreed, so there and then I paid him in Lebanese pounds and told him that I would return them when I passed through Bacharre on my way back to Beirut. I had spent most of the morning on my quest for ski boots and by the time I returned to Les Cedres it was nearly midday. There are only a few weeks at the beginning of the year when you can ski all day at Les Cedres. By mid March, when I was there, the snow on the piste gets slushy by noon and everyone packs up for lunch. It might be a good place to spend your honeymoon, but for someone on his own it was the most boring place I have been in in my life. Once you had walked around the clump of cedars and inspected the ski and souvenir shop - that was it. There was only one thing to do and that was to go to your room, lie on your mail bags and read whatever books you had brought with you.

Another blizzard hit us on my second night in Les Cedres, but the social climate changed for the better. A crowd of Lebanese Air Force officers arrived during the afternoon and they provided most congenial company. All of them spoke excellent English and they told me about their training at RAF St Athan in South Wales. I was born and brought up only a few miles away from the place and knew every pub in the area. We got on with each other extremely well.

I was keen to get started the following morning, but I was concerned about the effect my strange ski boots would have on the other students. I was given some idea what they might think when Gilbenk, the mess waiter, thought I had brought a dog into the mess and that it was sitting between my legs at the dining table. After breakfast I gathered my kit and walked across to the ski lift. The two British sergeants were drinking coffee at the small stand-up bar at the terminal when I arrived. Their expressions reflected what they thought about my footwear, but they were far too polite to make any disparaging remarks. One of them said, 'Glad to see you got fixed up with boots, Sir.' Our instructor arrived and soon the lift creaked into action. The two sergeants continued with basic lessons while I, graded a 'competent novice', told them I would see them at the top. I grabbed the first swinging seat that came along and winged my way up the ski slope.

I looked behind me when we were nearing the half-way point and was suprised to see how steep the ground had become. The next stage was even more precipitous so I jettisoned myself at the half-way landing stage. The blizzard of the night before had blown itself out but clouds were still thick and heavy and soon they descended over the piste. I began to feel that I should have swallowed my pride and stayed with the others. I spent a few minutes getting the feel of my skis and then I found that the skills I had learnt in Austria a few years before were coming back to me and that I could move and turn quite easily.

The previous night's fall had produced an unblemished surface and when the cloud on the piste thickened even more I became aware for the first time of the phenomenon known as 'white-out'. This happens when land and sky merge into one element. For the novice skier it is a disturbing feeling to lose control and not know where you are going. All of a sudden I felt the wind strengthen on my face and I had a feeling of moving much faster than I should in such conditions. It all came to an end when whatever slope I was descending reversed its inclination. The points of my skis dug into the snow, I parted company with them and flew about 20 feet through the air. I was immediately conscious of a very cold feeling in my feet and when I looked at them I was horrified to see that all I had on were the hairy uppers; the soles were still clamped to the skis. When the clouds began to clear I found I had left the piste, slipped into a valley and that I was on my own. Immediate 'survival' action was required if I was not to lose my toes through frost-bite, but the only implement I had resembling a tool was a cigarette lighter. The Zippo, although a little clumsy in shape, became the best known lighter in the world when it was issued to American soldiers in World War Two. I doubt if it has ever before or since been used as a hammer, but it saved my life that day when I was able to replace the nails that held the two parts of the boots together. I knew it was only a temporary measure and it took me a long time to get back to the bottom of the ski lift. I was thankful that the instructor and the two sergeants were not there to witness my embarrassment as I shuffled off to the officers' mess.

When I had changed into some decent footwear I arranged for a land rover to take me to the shoe cave in Bacharre. Haji Yusuf was where I had left him the day before and he looked sad when I handed him the boots. It was not a problem for him though and within a few minutes his sturdy foot operated sewing machine and a battery of nails put the ski boots back into working order. I returned to Les Cedres and was in time to get in some skiing before the snow turned slushy. I had no more problem with my boots and I soon became oblivious to the stares of new arrivals.

The young man from the British Embassy who met me in Beirut told me to expect a visit from the British Military Attache while I was at Les Cedres. About half way through my stay Colonel Andrew Braisby arrived. He made his presence felt as soon as he stepped from his official car. He was well known to the Commandant of the Ski School and we all had an hilarious lunch time session followed by an equally congenial evening when much good food and wine was consumed. Colonel Braisby was an officer equipped with a most ebullient personality. He had a fine war record and was a member of one of Scotland's most respected infantry regiments. He had a strange twist to his mouth, wore a monacle and possessed a booming voice. He was the centre of attention at the luncheon table and the other Lebanese officers who had not seen him before were in awe of him. He spoke perfect Arabic and French, although at one stage of the meal he was at a loss for the name of a certain animal like a wolf that frequented the area of Les Cedres. He sought the assistance of one Arabic speaking officer on his left, who was unable to help. Colonel Braisby was quiet for a few seconds then leaned back in his chair and gave an enormous howl. This was supposed to help his luncheon companion remember the name of the animal, but only succeeded in causing him to choke on his food. I learnt later that the colonel was held in high esteem among the military hierarchy in Beirut. He had the reputation of being the most unlucky officer in the British Army in terms of being shot and wounded. It seemed that many of his wounds had been inflicted in the pursuit of saving Arabs from Jews. This and the fact that some of his wounds had contorted his face - giving even more credence to his bravery, made him very popular among the Arabs. It was generally agreed that he was the ideal choice for British Military Attache to the Lebanon.

He told me a story about the last time he was wounded during World War Two, or to be exact - just after World War Two. The war in Europe officially came to an end at midnight on the 8/9th May 1945. Andrew Braisby, then a young major, was on his way to Brigade Headquarters in North Germany on the first day of peace for five years and eight months when his car broke down. The driver was still trying to find what was wrong when a dispatch rider on a motor bike came along. Andrew stood in the middle of the road, flagged him down and asked for a lift. The DR signalled Andrew to take a seat on the pillion but when he released the clutch the extra weight caused the engine to stall. To start the machine again it was necessary for the driver to put one foot on the ground and use the other to kick start the engine. After the third unsuccessful attempt the driver put everything he had into the next lunge. The extra effort caused his elbow to come into contact with the cocking handle of his sten gun that was attached to a sling around his shoulder. There was a sharp rattle of gun fire and Andrew Braisby became the first post-war casualty of the British Army when he was shot through the jaw.

By the end of 10 days in Les Cedres I was quite happy to pack my bags and return to Beirut. Colonel Braisby's staff had booked me into the Normandie Hotel on the seafront and it was a pleasant relief to sleep between crisp white sheets once more. I still have fond memories of the bazaars and fascinating streets that made up old Beirut. The broad boulevards and majestic promenade reflected the strong French influence and helped to make this city the show-piece of the Levant.

When I returned to my unit in Cyprus I gave some thought to the one-eyed colonel in Episcopi and the report he wanted me to write. I spent a long time sucking a pencil and staring at a blank piece of paper before commencing. There was not much to say. I could have made a suggestion that others with plans to ski in the Lebanon should bring their own sheets and a plentiful supply of books - but I thought that these were frivolous administrative matters with which he would not be interested. In the end I wrote a very complimentary account of the hospitality I had received and how everyone was so pro-Western. I can remember ending my report with a recommendation that more cultural, sporting and tourism ties should be forged with this haven of peace and tranquility.

A few months after I wrote my report the Muslim community in the Lebanon revolted over the Christians' pro-Western policy. The Christian president, Camille Chamoun, asked for help and a huge task force of American Marines and armour landed on the beach of Beirut and smothered the place. At the same time other Arab countries of the Eastern Mediterranean were plunged into turmoil when King Feisal 11 of Iraq and his prime minister, Nuries-Said, were assassinated. It was one of those turning points in middle east history and the shock waves that travelled through the Arab countries had far reaching consequences. As far as the 1st Battalion The Welch Regiment, with whom I was serving was concerned, it meant rapid removal from Cyprus to prop up the tottering regime of King Idris of Libya - who thought that he was next in line for the 'chop'.

I never received an acknowledgement for my report and I should be surprised if it occupies space in any government or military archive. I only hope that my highly inaccurate recommendations did not influence anyone to take precipitate action.

CHAPTER THIRTY EIGHT

The Missing Flute

I used to see Rhys Lewis regularly at regimental gatherings, but then I realised I had not heard his croaky voice and guttural laugh for some time. I enquired about his welfare and was told he was unwell. I found where he lived and paid him a visit. For an old soldier who, as he claimed, had never had cause to see a doctor in his life, the discovery that he had become a victim of diabetes was both a mental and a body blow.

A few weeks later I heard that Rhys, as a result of his disease, had had his left leg amputated, so I went to see him again at his home and was suprised to find him in a more cheerful mood than he was on the first occasion. When he heard voices in the sitting room he bounced down the stairs on his bottom. I stayed with him for about half an hour and he was in his element telling me about his service in far-off places.

After the passage of another three or four months I was told that Rhys had had his other leg amputated, so I went to see him again. His wife let me in and I could see from her drawn expression that events had taken a turn for the worse. She led the way upstairs and motioned me to enter a bedroom. Rhys was lying in a small bed with his eyes shut. He had never been a big fellow and now that he had lost his legs there was hardly anything left. 'The officer from Brecon has come to see you,' she said - and then quietly to me, 'He hasn't eaten anything for a week.' The bedclothes had been thrown back revealing a torso that was nothing but skin and bone. Slowly his eyelids fluttered and he looked towards me. The instinctive movements came flooding back to this old soldier as he saw an officer representing his regiment standing by the side of his bed. His skinny arms straightened and he drew them tight alongside his two stumps. He continued to lie at 'attention' until I said, 'At ease, Rhys.' We spoke a few words to each other but I could see the effort was too much for him. I was about to go when Rhys whispered to his wife, 'Alice, get me my flute.' Alice went downstairs and returned a few minutes later with a rectangular box which she opened and gave to her husband. 'I want you to have this flute, Major,' said Rhys. I am not an expert on musical instruments but I could see that it was a valuable article. I offered to sell it for him but he became agitated and reiterated that he wanted me to have it. He motioned me to come closer and whispered, 'You see, Major - it's not mine to sell: I've kept it ever since I joined the Corps of Drums in India in 1935.'

I promised Rhys that I would ensure it went back to the drums store. NO NAME - NO PACK DRILL. He smiled and then, with a peaceful look on his face, closed his eyes and went to sleep. He died an hour later.

(*Author's note:* Rhys and Alice Lewis are, of course, pseudonyms for the real people).

CHAPTER THIRTY NINE
Give Him Enough Rope

I sometimes wonder if things happened the way I remember them. Did I witness them, hear about them and then exaggerate the details, or just dream them into reality? One such incident I have had in mind for 45 years must have been second-hand because it happened in Wayne's Keep, Nicosia before I joined the 1st Battalion The South Wales Borderers in Cyprus in 1948. I have often chuckled over the situation where a temporary camp commandant found himself on a collision course with an irate district commander. A few weeks before I retired I was able to test the efficacy of my mind when one of the players came into my office in Brecon.

He was about to introduce himself when I exclaimed, 'Jack Medlicott!!' 'Fancy you remembering me after all these years,' he said. Jack was accompanied by his wife and I spent the next half hour showing them some of the interesting things in the regimental museum of which I was curator. They wandered around on their own for the rest of the afternoon and then, towards closing time, they came back to my office to say 'farewell'. Jack is now about 70 years old (June 1993) but except for a few wrinkles and a shock of grey hair he had not changed much from the 25 year old captain I knew in Cyprus.

We shook hands, vowed to keep in contact and then, as he was about to leave he said, 'Do you know what happened to Brigadier Anstice?' I told him that I believed the Brigadier had gone to live in Kyrenia when he retired. I paused for a moment and said, 'Wasn't there some trouble between you and him over a dog?' Jack gave a gasp and said, 'Good Lord, do you remember that business?' In answer I related the incident to him as if he was a third person.

'The Brigadier telephoned the commanding officer of the 1st Battalion The South Wales Borderers in Famagusta and asked him if he could borrow one of his officers for a few weeks to be acting camp commandant at his headquarters. The incumbent, it seemed, had been taken sick and was bedded down in the local British Military Hospital. The CO agreed and gave orders for Jack Medlicott to proceed forthwith.

Jack arrived at Wayne's Keep during the forenoon and was

directed to the brigadier's office. He was told that the camp was filthy and had to be smartened. Stray dogs, in particular, were a nuisance and he was given instructions to destroy any that were not wearing collars. A few other terse instructions were issued and he was then told to attend to his duties.

Jack ordered the provost sergeant to accompany him on his inspection of the camp and he found that the place was worse than the brigadier had described. As they approached the cookhouse a collection of dogs were scavenging at the swill bins. One of them was slower than the rest at making a getaway and the provost sergeant threw a rope around its collarless neck. Jack gave instructions for it to be taken to the 30 yards range and shot. As he was heading for the officers' mess for lunch he heard a single shot from the area of the butts.

Brigadier Anstice was standing in the ante-room with a glass of beer in his hand: he was asking if anyone had seen his dog, which always accompanied him to the mess at lunch time. When Jack was told that the brigadier's dog was a large black Labrador he began to feel that his instruction to destroy a similar animal might have been precipitate. His worst fears were realised and Jack's appointment as acting camp commandant, Wayne's Keep was terminated forthwith. He was back in 1/SWB officers' mess for tea.'

Jack listened to my account of his misfortune with amazement. 'That's just the way it was,' he said.

I am pleased that my memory, on this occasion at least, proved accurate.